SPORT FACILITY MANAGEMENT: ORGANIZING EVENTS AND MITIGATING RISKS

The Sport Management Library offers textbooks for undergraduate students. The subjects in the series reflect the content areas prescribed by the NASPE/NASSM curriculum standards for undergraduate sport management programs.

Titles in the Sport Management Library

NEW! Professor Packets now available at no charge for many of our bestselling textbooks. Visit www.fitinfotech.com for details.

SPORT FACILITY MANAGEMENT: ORGANIZING EVENTS AND MITIGATING RISKS

Robin Ammon, Jr., EdD
SLIPPERY ROCK UNIVERSITY

Richard M. Southall, EdD
STATE UNIVERSITY OF WEST GEORGIA

David A. Blair, PhD
SOUTHWESTERN UNIVERSITY

Fitness Information Technology
A Division of the International Center for Performance Excellence
262 Coliseum, WVU-PE
PO Box 6116
Morgantown, WV 26506-6116

Library of Congress Card Catalog Number: 2003108983

ISBN: 1-885693-39-7

Copyeditor: Sandra Woods
Cover Design: Jamie Merlavage
Managing Editor: Geoff Fuller
Production Editor: Jamie Merlavage
Proofreader: Jessica McDonald
Indexer: Jessica McDonald
Printed by Sheridan Books

10   9   8   7   6   5   4   3

Fitness Information Technology
A Division of the International Center for Performance Excellence
262 Coliseum, WVU-PE
PO Box 6116
Morgantown, WV 26506-6116
800.477.4348 (toll free)
304.293-6888 (phone)
304.293.6658 (fax)
Email: icpe@mail.wvu.edu
Website: www.fitinfotech.com

Acknowledgments

Sometimes during the rush of the promotion and tenure process, while we are presenting at various conferences and trying to acquire the right number of publications, some of us in higher education forget the common denominator that we all share. We are teachers and while we devote tremendous amounts of time to the issue of *research*, we forget that without our *students* most of us would not be similarly employed. This text goes out to my students past, present, and future. **RA**

Wendy Amundson, Elmer and Gladys Becker, Peter Han, Deborah LeGrande, Mark Nagel, Crystal Southall, Elizabeth Southall, Jason Southall, Thomas Southall, Douglas Wells, and the undergraduate sport management students at the State University of West Georgia. **RMS**

I would like to thank Rob for the opportunity to be involved in a project of this magnitude, for his insight, and especially for his friendship. I thank Richard for being such a great colleague and friend, and for providing wit and humor throughout this endeavor. Thanks to Geoff for his editorial expertise and collaborative approach to completing the task.

To my wife: I thank her for providing unwaivering support and encouragement in this venture. She helps me to keep in perspective that tenuous balance between work and play, and reminds me that life is to be enjoyed and that every day is a wonderful gift. **DAB**

Contents

Detailed Contents

Photos

Except where otherwise specifically noted below, all photos come from the personal archives of the authors and represent the work of the authors

Chapter 1: **Introduction**
Photo 1.1:   Examples of sports venues.
Photo 1.2:   Example of a European soccor stadium.
Photo 1.3:   Two types of baseball fields.
Photo 1.4:   Multipurpose stadium.

Chapter 2: **Planning and Producing an Event**
Photo 2.1:   A successful event requires planning.
Photo 2.2:   Different basketball games may have different goals.
Photo 2.3:   Some event tasks must be taken care of prior to tip-off.

Chapter 3: **Financing Facilities**
Photo 3.1:   Many colleges and universities have replaced out-of-date recreation facilities with new, state-of-the-art complexes.

Chapter 4: **Privatization**
Photo 4.1:   Today, many phases of facility management have been privatized. (Photo courtesy of Jay Bratschi.)
Photo 4.2:   The 1984 Olympic Games were a successful public-private partnership. (Photo courtesy of Ballpark.com.)
Photo 4.3:   Many sports stadia, such as Invesco Field at Mile High, have been constructed since 1988.
Photo 4.4:   Construction of Invesco Field at Mile High was accomplished through a limited public-private partnership.

Chapter 5: **ADA Requirements**
Photo 5.1:   Persons with disabilities must be granted equal access to an event.
Photo 5.2:   The Justice Department has identified accessible restrooms for each gender as a major priority.
Photo 5.3:   Planning for accessibility for the disabled may start in the venue parking lot.

Chapter 6: **Hiring Personnel**
Photo 6.1:   What would you include in a job description for security personnel at your venue?

Tables and Figures

Chapter One

Introduction

The World Cup, a corporate golf outing, a high school volleyball match, a Metallica concert, the French Open tennis tournament, Major League Baseball's All-Star Game, and Disney on Ice all share at least three common denominators. Do you know what they are? Actually, the answer is quite easy: They are all sport/entertainment *events*; each takes place at some type of *facility*; and each has specific *risks* associated with it.

Sport facilities are not new; arenas for sport are some of the earliest cultural artifacts. However, the first university sport-management program was not established until 1966 at Ohio University (Crossett, Bromage, & Hums, 1998). Teaching the components of sport management, including event and facility management, has been around for less than 40 years. Even though the sport facility industry has experienced substantial growth in recent years, the amount of information or published materials available are far from extensive. Knowledge pertaining to sporting events, risk, and facility management will be valuable for anyone with an interest in, or association with, the event or facility industry. Some authorities in the field maintain that if sport managers understand the varying aspects of management pertaining to events in a large facility, then they will have a relatively easy transition to events in a smaller venue (Farmer, Mulrooney, & Ammon, 1996). Therefore, understanding the management techniques of smaller sport facilities and events such as golf courses, recreation centers, and 5K races, as well as multisport entertainment facilities and large events such as the Super Bowl, is imperative for anyone interested in pursuing a career in this area. This text will limit the discussion regarding physical education and fitness facilities because these topics have previously been sufficiently addressed in the marketplace.

Examples of sports venues
a. Aquatic facility
b. Motosport track
c. Football field being converted into motocross track

Recent estimates describe sport as one of the 10 largest industries in the United States encompassing over $190 billion dollars (King, 2002). However, do not be naive enough to believe that this is just a U.S. phenomenon; sport on an international basis has also reached epic proportions. The diverse nature of sport on an international basis has produced a need for sport event and facility managers not currently met by traditional curriculums (Li, Ammon, & Kanters, 2002).

The world of sport has been strongly influenced by globalization. Sporting events today are widely viewed as a culturally universal and global phenomenon. Due to the increased internationalization of sporting events, the demand for individuals who are educated and trained to manage various international events and facilities has grown considerably in the last decade. Both corporate America and academicians believe that internationalizing the curriculum is an area that needs immediate attention (Wheeler, 1998). The same reasons can be applied to explain why sport event and facility management curriculums need to be more globally oriented (Li et al., 2002).

Globalization of Sport

Various events in sport within the past few years substantiate the global impact of sport. Rupert Murdoch, owner of Fox Sports Network, the LA Dodgers, and the British television network BSkyB, made several attempts to purchase British Premier League teams. NFL owners have allowed players, in need of further development, such as Super Bowl MVP Kurt Warner, to play in the NFL Europe Football League. Golf tournaments such as the Ryder Cup, the Solheim Cup, and the Match Play Championships not only attract the world's best golfers, but they also are played on the world's best courses. The NBA and the NHL have discussed adding foreign franchises, and both allow their athletes to play in international competitions such as the Olympic games. Major League Baseball has opened most of their seasons since 1999 in non-U.S. countries such as Mexico, Japan and Puerto Rico. In addition, MLB owners plan to allow the Montreal Expos to play 22 games of the 2003 season in San Juan, Puerto Rico. The Arena Football League continues to discuss playing in stadiums overseas. The 2002 World Cup finals witnessed a team from Brazil play a team from Germany at a stadium in Japan. When viewed independently, these may appear to be isolated events, but collectively these developments demonstrate the globalization of sport (Ammon, 2000).

> The demand for individuals who are educated and trained to manage various international events and facilities has grown considerably in the last decade.

Violence at Sport Events

Violence has occurred during sporting events throughout the past few decades. A Palestinian terrorist attack on Israeli Olympians during the 1972 Munich Summer Olympics left six dead. In addition, two died, and over 100 people were injured after a bomb went off during the 1996 Sum-

Example of a European soccer stadium

mer Olympics in Atlanta. During the summer of 2002, Major League Baseball fans witnessed two spectators jumping onto the field at Comiskey Park to attack a Kansas City Royals baseball coach. The 2002 collegiate football season witnessed violence ranging from a brawl between players at a University of Hawaii game against Cincinnati to a 67-year-old Clemson University sheriff's officer being trampled by celebrating fans attempting to tear down a goal post. Collegiate, professional, and Olympic sports are not the only sporting events where facility managers are concerned about potential violence. In January 1999, metal detectors were installed in the gymnasium of Manual High School (Denver, Colorado) before a boy's high school basketball game between Denver East and Thomas Jefferson. The installation was in response to a gun's being fired in the parking lot of the same gymnasium during an earlier game in December between Denver East and Manual (Stocker & Fitzgerald, 1998).

Some individuals may feel that the use of metal detectors was an overreaction to one isolated incident. However, the courts have held that facility managers must act on threats of violence as if the violence had actually taken place (Miller, 1993). As noted by the court in *Leger v. Stockton,* "School authorities who know of threats of violence that they believe are well founded may not refrain from taking reasonable preventative measures simply because violence has yet to occur" (p. 694). Taking the *Leger* decision (though pertinent only to school athletic events) and what we know of "foreseeability," the next few years may witness a paradigm shift in crowd management philosophy.

September 11th

The terrorist attack on September 11, 2001, had an immediate impact in many areas of our global society. Some of the more sport-oriented consequences included Major League Baseball's canceling the 15 games scheduled for that infamous day in addition to all games for the rest of that week. The NFL cancelled every game played the following weekend. All shows on Broadway were closed as well as theme parks such as Disney and Six Flags. A Madonna concert scheduled for the Staples Center in Los Angeles was also postponed ("Facilities Adapt," 2001).

Neither event and facility management nor risk management will ever be the same after that tragic September morning. The most comprehensive problem for event and facility managers after the terrorist attack was to reassure their guests about safety concerns. Many individuals who had planned to attend sport and entertainment events had second thoughts about their personal safety. This apprehension produced a residual drop in the number of tickets sold, and compiled with the slowing economy, that drop forced many event and facility managers to investigate new ways to decrease costs (Barbieri, 2001). Industry representatives were concerned about the difficult juggling act that event and facility managers were forced

Two types of baseball fields
a. "New" style baseball field (Jacobs Field) b. "Old" style baseball field (Tiger Stadium)

to undertake. On the one hand, these individuals had to effect new strategies to ensure the safety of the spectators while, on the other hand, remaining optimistic about the current safety of their facilities.

As the aftershocks of the terrorist attacks continue to vibrate throughout society, the effects on the event management industry are still unclear. Sporting events such as the Olympics

> An event risk profile is completed during the early planning stages of an event.

and soccer's World Cup provide an attractive vehicle for the celebration of global sport. Unfortunately, these events also provide an attractive target for any terrorist group wishing to make a statement. Event managers undoubtedly recognize the potential problem, but implementing a solution may not be totally within their power. Some experts estimate that the costs pertaining to security and operational changes because of 9/11 may increase event budgets by 40% (Roberts, 2001). Obviously, most events do not have such a large profit margin, and these increases would put a majority of events out of business. For example, FIFA, the governing body of international soccer, announced it was considering canceling the 2002 World Cup due to its inability to find an insurance company willing and able to provide adequate coverage. FIFA was finally able to secure the proper insurance, but other events may not be as fortunate. One alternative to this problem would be to create an *event risk profile*. This profile would need to be completed during the early planning stages of the event to determine if a viable financial plan was available for items such as insurance. If the profile was unable to identify such a plan, the event would need to be immediately cancelled (Roberts, 2001).

Some academics have pointed out that in addition to 9/11, the economy can influence the sport/entertainment industry. Attendance at concerts in 2001 was down over 10%. AMF, owners of over 500 bowling centers (a sport facility) in 11 different countries, filed for bankruptcy protection in 2001 (Fried, 2001). In addition, facilities have found out that the economy can affect their revenue streams in unplanned ways. Pro Player Stadium, the TWA Dome, the Savvis Center, Adelphia Coliseum, PSINet Stadium, Enron Field, and CMGI Field all were forced to change names when their naming-rights sponsors either went bankrupt or succumbed to financial difficulties. TV ratings have decreased, and attendance figures have flattened out or declined for many professional sports (Fried, 2001).

Positive features about the sport event and facility management business exist as well. Extreme sports had a huge impact on the 2002 Salt Lake City Winter Olympics. This has caused some sports like snowboarding to achieve almost mainstream popularity. Made-for-TV events such as the X-Games and Gravity Games are seeing a surge in TV viewership and attendance as well.

Society's view of sport has transcended from a spectator-based sport to an entertainment experience. People are now viewing sport and entertaining clients during one single experience (Mooradian, 2001). In addition, the facilities themselves are changing, with quality being emphasized over quantity. The venues are being designed to hold fewer people, but with more amenities. In the past, event and facility managers were interested in putting 50,000-80,000 spectators on bleachers in a facility that had bad toilets, bad concessions, and bad sight lines. Today, the newly constructed facilities serve 30,000-50,000 spectators sitting in individual seats (and hundreds sitting in club seats and luxury suites), with premium food, spacious restrooms, and a proximity that is closer to the action than that of many of the team's substitutes (Zoltak, 2001).

Multipurpose stadium (soccer and track)

Technology has also changed the event and facility management industry. The increase in Internet sales has affected the box office, as now there are not as many windows available to "sell" tickets (Cohen, 2001). To assist in counteracting the problem of fewer ticket windows involved in sales, one new piece of technology has been implemented at some stadiums. It is called the ATTM (automated teller and ticket machine). Customers put in their magnetic striped ID cards to redeem tickets purchased from the Internet, or a combination of tickets and cash, or to pick up tickets and use the fan loyalty program (Cohen). "Smart" fan cards are available at some stadiums such as Qualcomm Stadium in San Diego. These cards provide season ticket holders the ability to sell unused tickets over the Internet and allow for ticketless entry into the Stadium. The Louisiana Superdome provides the technology for club seat holders to order concessions via wireless devices. Finally, Choice Seat allows spectators different camera angles and the ability to research player stats and order concessions and merchandise all from the comfort of their seat at Tropicana Field in Tampa ("Into the Seats," 2002).

> The ATTM allows customers to pick up tickets purchased from the Internet, or a combination of tickets and cash, at the game.

Conclusion

A 23% increase occurred from 2001-2002 in the construction of sport stadiums and arenas, with projected costs of $7.8 billion (Cameron, 2002e). These new facilities will undoubtedly generate impressive additional television and sponsorship fees. In addition to the increased revenue streams, the increased public and media exposure accompanying the *events* at these facilities has emphasized the need for sport and recreation managers to have a clear understanding of what it takes to *manage* these facilities and events, while attempting to diminish the *risks* and accompanying liability.

Sport management curriculums have been in existence for over 35 years. These curriculums were originally developed by leaders in the sport business industry to meet a recognized need in professional sport (Mason, Higgins, & Wilkinson, 1981). These individuals, along with forward thinking academicians, have helped sport management to continue to evolve, so it now includes many diverse components that constitute modern sport. In order for event and facility management to continue to grow, however, visionaries within the field must correctly anticipate the future of sport.

Chapter Two

Planning and Producing an Event

Application Exercise

As part of your practicum experience, you and another sport management student have been hired to manage a professional wheelchair basketball game between two NWBA (National Wheelchair Basketball Association) teams to be played on your campus. You are responsible for planning and producing the event. Your staff will consist of students enrolled in your sport management program's facility and event management class.

This is the first such event ever held on your campus. You are the event manager. You have been hired to ensure that the event draws a capacity crowd and generates good press coverage and university-wide recognition for the client and your program. The planning and production of the event are up to you. If the event is a success, you will receive the praise. If the event is not a success, your reputation and the reputation of your university's sport management program will be affected. Develop a workable event management plan. Information to be included may come from interviews or observations of event managers of local high school, collegiate, or professional sport organizations. You may obtain additional information from a variety of sources, including your class notes, the Internet, this text, and your professors.

What Is Event Management?

When faced with planning and producing an event, figuring out what it is you have been hired to do—in other words, defining event management—is a necessary first step. To ensure your event's success, you need to answer several event planning and production questions.

You will find answers to these and many other sport event, risk, and facility management questions throughout this text. As you read, and during your in-class discussions, generate additional questions on your own. In any kind of management situation, things change. The answers to these questions found in this text are not the only possible answers. Don't just

Event Planning and Production Questions

What are event planning and production?	What can I learn from box office management and customer service?
Is our food service management adequate?	Do we need medical emergency and evacuation plans?
Are there some basic managerial steps in planning and producing an event?	What about beverage management?
What is risk management?	Do we need to have any contracts with anyone?
What about event operations?	What about waivers?
What is the DIM process all about?	What have I forgotten?
Do we have a handle on crowd management?	What about getting workers?
What about negligence?	

Table 2.1. Event Planning and Production Questions

think outside the box; also recognize that both the box and what's inside or outside of the box may constantly change: *Today's* answers may be *tomorrow's* questions.

What Are Sport Event Planning and Production?

Fundamentally, planning and producing a sports event, like any event planning and production, involve elements of *management* occurring within an *organization.* Planning and producing an event—both part of *event management*—occur within an organizational framework. Event management is getting things done (accomplishing goals) through people. It is a social and technical process that utilizes resources and influences human behavior to accomplish an organization's goals. Bolman and Deal (1997) describe organizations as complex, surprising, deceptive, and ambiguous. With this in mind, planning and producing a sports event will be a complex process, full of unforeseen circumstances. However, even though complexity is a given, an event manager must deal with this complexity and uncertainty and develop a plan capable of bringing a semblance of order out of this uncertainty.

> Event management is a social and technical process that utilizes resources and influences human behavior to accomplish an organization's goals.

A helpful conceptual device for the event manager is to think of every event as a triangle (see Figure 2-1). Each side of the triangle represents the important stakeholders (parties who have a stake in the event's success) who must be satisfied for the event to be considered a success: participants, sponsors, and spectators. Your job as an event manager is to satisfy the

A successful event requires planning.

needs of each of these groups. At times the needs, wants, and desires of these groups may initially seem to conflict. Because of these apparent conflicts, when planning and producing sporting events, sport managers would be wise to remember Gunny's (Clint Eastwood's character) famous admonition to his troops in the movie *Heartbreak Ridge*, "Adapt, improvise, overcome."

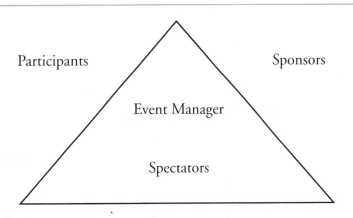

Participants   Sponsors

Event Manager

Spectators

Figure 2.1. Event Triangle

Steps in Planning and Producing the Event

This adaptive planning process includes the (a) achievement of identified goals/objectives by (b) coordinating the actions of people/organizations, while (c) recognizing the constraints of limited resources (Chelladurai, 2001). Planning involves deciding what you are going to do before beginning to do it. Planning is paying attention to details. Sounds easy, doesn't it? As a sport manager waits for her volunteers to arrive for their first meeting, she must know what she wants to accomplish. Here are some steps in planning and producing a sports event. (Note: Steps may not always occur in the described sequence.)

Agree Upon Event Goals.

Is the event intended to make money for the organization? How much money? Is the event designed to generate publicity for the organization? Is the event unique, unlike anything else ever done? Asking these types of questions enables the event management staff to conceptualize the event's purpose and focus. In addition, searching for answers to these questions helps frame the event-planning structure. Before spending time dealing with specific logistical concerns, a sport manager needs to define the event and its associated goals. Coming to a consensus about the event's goals focuses the event planning process toward achieving these goals.

Defining goals helps frame the event-planning structure.

Different basketball games may have different goals.

Identify Strengths, Weaknesses, Opportunities, and Threats.

As this questioning process takes place, both the organization's and the event's strengths and weakness need to be identified. Although event planners, even in ancient times, have probably always asked these types of questions, one of the first documented examples of this process was developed and used in the 1950s by U.S. military planners and was referred to as a strengths, weaknesses, opportunities, and threats (SWOT) analysis (Chelladurai, 2001; Graham, Neirotti, & Goldblatt, 2001; Slack, 1997). Many types of managerial functions call for a SWOT analysis, but performing a SWOT analysis is extremely important in event planning. Initially a SWOT analysis involves identifying an organization's or event's strengths and weaknesses. What is the group or organization good at doing? Do members have experience in planning and producing the event? If they have experience, this can often be a strength. If no one in the organization has ever organized and produced any sort of event, this is probably, at least initially, a weakness. Referring back to the wheelchair-basketball-game scenario at the beginning of the chapter, even if none of the sport management students has produced a wheelchair basketball game, perhaps some students have produced or worked at other sporting events. Perhaps some students have experience as student managers or trainers. Maybe some students have worked as security staff or concession-stand employees at a game.

> Identifying opportunities and threats involves looking outside the organization at the surrounding social, cultural, economic, and political environments.

When performing a SWOT analysis, managers need to move beyond just looking at an organization's strengths and weaknesses. The next two steps, identifying opportunities and threats, involve looking outside the organization at the surrounding social, cultural, economic, and political environments.

Although it is important to identify weaknesses and threats, it is just as important to recognize that identified weaknesses and threats can often be transformed into organizational strengths and opportunities if managers can learn to effectively utilize the environments that surround an event. For example, even though a fledgling student-run organization may not have specific expertise in managing a wheelchair basketball game (a weakness), the event still provides the organization excellent opportunities for media exposure and sponsorship opportunities not available from many other events. These opportunities arise from economic, social, cultural, or political situations that surround this type of event.

Threats are external to the organization. Threats may come in many shapes and sizes. A threat may be a similar event scheduled at the same time, or it may be the fact that many students commute and are not on campus at night. A threat may be economic, such as a lack of funding for the event. Whatever the results of the SWOT analysis, it is important that the event-planning staff moves on to the next step, generating alternative courses of action based on the SWOT analysis. In addition, plans of action must be measurable. A manager has to be able to evaluate the efficacy or success of any plan.

To help make a SWOT analysis more effective, it is a good idea to develop checklists that list and evaluate the organization's strengths, weaknesses, opportunities, and threats. Construction of these checklists should involve as many of the central members of the organization as possible. After the checklists have been developed, it's a good idea to have someone who was not involved in this process perform an evaluation and provide comments and suggestions.

Develop checklists that list and evaluate the organization's strengths, weaknesses, opportunities, and threats.

Develop and Monitor Planning Process.

After strategies for achieving an organization's goals have been completed, planning begins. Effective event planning necessitates completing critical tasks in a timely and efficient fashion. For example, in planning a wheelchair basketball game, insuring proper scoreboard-clock operation does not need to take place 3 months in advance, but it should be done more than 10 minutes prior to tip-off. One way to not run out of time and make sure that everything gets done is to plan in reverse. This reverse planning can occur through the use of Gannt charts, developed in 1917 by Ameri-

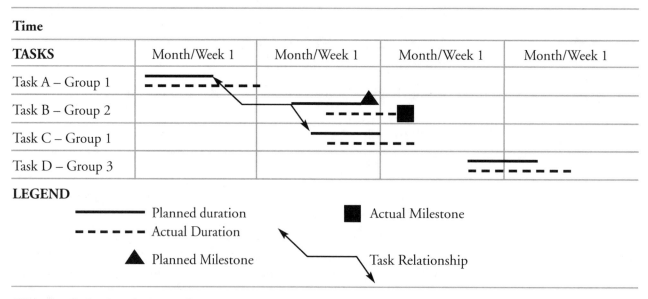

Time

TASKS	Month/Week 1	Month/Week 1	Month/Week 1	Month/Week 1
Task A – Group 1				
Task B – Group 2				
Task C – Group 1				
Task D – Group 3				

LEGEND

——————— Planned duration   ■ Actual Milestone

- - - - - - - Actual Duration

▲ Planned Milestone   Task Relationship

Figure 2.2. Sample Gannt chart

Some event tasks must be taken care of prior to tip-off.

can engineer and sociologist Henry L. Gannt. These charts are horizontal bar charts used in project planning and management. Gannt charts provide a graphical depiction of schedules that help to plan, coordinate, and track specific project tasks. These charts may be simple, created on graph paper, or more complex. Today, computer software programs or personal computer applications such as Microsoft Word, Project, or Excel can be used to construct a Gannt chart that graphically displays the relationship(s) between tasks, the planned and actual task duration(s), groups or persons responsible for task(s), and the milestones in a project/event.

After you have utilized your Gannt chart to plan your event from start to finish, mentally rewind back through your event to the first planning session (think of how the movie *Memento* unfolded in reverse), making sure you can identify the preceding event for each event in your planning sequence. Make sure to assign a completion date for each task/item/or event in the event planning cycle. Practicing event planning this way forces the sport manager to think in greater detail about the "nuts and bolts" of the event. Think about how much concentration and attention to detail it takes to drive a car in reverse. Planning this way is another example of thinking outside the box. Managers are less likely to forget things when they are forced to look at the event from this type of reverse perspective.

- Event checklists need to be developed to reflect the event's budget. Do not plan items the budget cannot support.

- Make sure to check items off the lists, but check back with the person(s) responsible for the item to confirm and reconfirm completion of the task(s).

- Design specific checklists for each facet of the event. Breaking the master checklist down into checklists for specific areas of the event helps each person in charge of that specific area monitor individual area(s) of responsibility.

- Make each checklist as specific as need be. It's better to be more specific than too general, but also keep in mind the nature of the event, possible threats, and their consequences.

- Recognize the existence of Murphy's Law: Anything that can go wrong will go wrong. Recognition of this law should guide the development of event checklists. Build flexibility and adaptability into the event checklist. Use *branch-chain thinking* (developing alternative outcomes based on changes in the external environment) in constructing of the checklist. As you build your event checklist, continually ask yourself, "What if. . .?"

Table 2.2 Event Planning and Production Suggestions

Manage Event Logistics.

After developing the event checklist, the next questions that face a sports event manager are "How do I check off checklist items?" and "Whom do I get to help get things done?" These questions involve managing an event's logistics. The phrase "The devil is in the details" sums up the challenge of managing event logistics. Assign specific duties to specific persons. Demand accountability for accomplishing the assigned tasks on time. Also, recognize people when they complete their tasks. If you are going to demand, then reward, too.

Develop a timetable and methods for effective communication. Make sure everyone involved in the event knows whom he or she should contact for information and answers. However, as part of the training process of staff and volunteers, empower event staff members to solve problems on their own. Make it clear to both staff and volunteers that they are expected and encouraged to be problem solvers within their job description parameters. Point out that not all situations require them to contact a supervisor. Explain that you expect them to recognize the difference between a situation they are qualified to handle and one that requires a supervisor's intervention. Throughout the training process, allow staff and volunteers to be active participants in the event-planning process. Encourage analysis and use, and where appropriate, their suggestions. This process helps develop critical thinking on the part of event staff and volunteers. If you, as the manager of the event, fail to practice this technique, you will become nothing but a firefighter, saddled with constantly putting out problem fires, thus decreasing your effectiveness and the overall likelihood of your event's success.

Train event staff to perform their jobs. Never assume any level of knowledge or skill. If staff members have not been trained, a manager does not know if they have the ability or motivation to perform their assigned tasks. With this in mind, developing checklists to train staff members on their individual duties and responsibilities is critical.

> When training event staff, never assume they have any level of knowledge or skill.

Figures 2.3-2.5 are examples of orientation/training completion checklists for staff members. Complete the checklists as staff members perform the tasks. It is important that the managers do more than simply ask staff, "Do you understand?" Staff members must actually *show* a trainer they can perform their duties.

Phase 1: General Orientation

Estimated Time to Complete:	[✔ =Done]
1. Explain the kind of organization we are.	[ ]
2. Describe who our customers are.	[ ]
3. Review our company/organization's history, traditions, and values.	[ ]
4. Describe our most recent changes: Past, present, and future.	[ ]
5. Describe who our competition is and how we position ourselves differently.	[ ]
6. Explain how we are organized (i.e., levels of management.)	[ ]
7. Explain how company/organization is unique or special.	[ ]
8. Review products and services.	[ ]
9. Familiarize employee/staff with vendors and suppliers.	[ ]
10. Tour the facility/event area.	[ ]
11. Introduce employee to people he/she will work with.	[ ]
12. Give employee copy of employee/staff handbook.	[ ]
13. Allow employee time to review handbook.	[ ]
14. Answer questions.	

Supervisor _____   Employee/Staff _____

Figure 2.3 Sample General Orientation Checklist

Estimated Time to Complete: *[✔ =Done]*

1. Summarize job description.   [   ]

2. Define major job responsibilities.   [   ]

3. Communicate job expectations and standards of performance.   [   ]

4. Explain introductory period.   [   ]
   - •Length of time   [   ]
   - • Define *conditional employee*   [   ]

5. Discuss employee benefits and eligibility requirements.   [   ]
   - •Insurance*   [   ]
   - •Vacations*   [   ]
   - •Holidays*   [   ]
   - •Sick leave*   [   ]

6. Discuss pay periods, rates of pay, and how figured.*   [   ]

7. Discuss payroll deductions (voluntary and involuntary).*   [   ]

8. Discuss overtime.*   [   ]
   - •Approvals required   [   ]
   - •How calculated   [   ]

9. Explain purpose of this orientation and training program.   [   ]

10. Emphasize company as equal employment opportunity employer.*   [   ]

11. Explain the performance evaluation system.   [   ]

12. Summarize company/organization rules.   [   ]
    - •Ethics   [   ]
    - •Alcohol and drugs   [   ]
    - •Personal appearance and name badges   [   ]
    - •Safety   [   ]
    - •Telephone use   [   ]
    - •Smoking   [   ]
    - •Parking   [   ]
    - •Visitors   [   ]

13. Respond to questions.   [   ]

Supervisor _____   Employee/Staff _____

* (Note: These elements may not be appropriate to certain events or organizations.)

Figure 2.4 Sample Job Orientation Checklist

Estimated Time to Complete: _____   *[✔ =Done]*

1. Review with the employee how to _____.   [   ]

2. Review with employee all emergency procedures.   [   ]

3. Review with employee _____ approval levels.   [   ]

4. Review with employee all _____ response codes.   [   ]

5. First review and demonstrate each procedure listed below.
Then determine if employee has acquired the ability to perform each
transaction by asking him or her to demonstrate it for you.

    • _____   [   ]
    • _____   [   ]
    • _____   [   ]
    • _____   [   ]
    • _____   [   ]
    • _____   [   ]

6. Demonstrate _____ procedures. Ask employee to demonstrate. [   ]

7. Explain _____procedures. Ask employee to review the procedures with you. [   ]

8. Review all _____procedures. (Refer to event manual.)   [   ]

9. Explain how to deal with _____. Familiarize employee with proper forms. [   ]

10. Discuss _____, its causes and preventive measures.   [   ]

11. Define and review _____ procedures.   [   ]

12. Answer questions.   [   ]

Supervisor _____ Employee/Staff _____

Note: Successful completion of this ORIENTATION DOCUMENT verifies that on (Date _____)
(employee/staff member) _____demonstrated the ability to perform the tasks listed above.

Figure 2.5 Sample Operations Orientation and Training Checklist

Once it has been determined that staff members have the ability to perform assigned tasks, the only real reason they do not perform these assigned tasks is a lack of motivation. Most often, event staff members possess the physical and mental abilities to perform their jobs. When they don't perform job correctly, it is because they have not internalized the importance of their performing their job correctly. In other words, they were not motivated to do their job. Because there are numerous types of motivation, including extrinsic and intrinsic motivations, one of the biggest challenges facing an event manager is discovering how to motivate and influence staff members.

It is important to note that volunteer orientation/training will often not include all of the elements contained in the staff examples in this chapter. Volunteer training, although often limited, should not be overlooked. Because volunteers have varied schedules, trainers must make the most efficient use of the limited time available for training. It is critical that volunteer training be "hands on." Keep volunteer responsibilities to a minimum. Trainers must ensure that volunteers perform the critical tasks required. In addition, leave any checklists with the volunteer as reference tools. Volunteers do not want to appear uninformed or unable to perform. Their primary motivation for volunteering is from a desire to contribute to a cause or from altruism. If they are asked if they understand what their duties and responsibilities are, almost every volunteer will say, "Yes." Meanwhile, they often have no idea what is expected of them, or they assume they can figure it out on their own.

Motivate and Influence Event Volunteers.

In order to manage volunteers who are not highly experienced in performing their tasks and duties, event managers must ensure a minimum level of volunteer competency through proper training. At the same time, managers must also motivate their volunteers. However, because volunteers are not paid, monetary compensation is not often available as a motivating force. Because many sporting events require volunteers to assume responsibilities in crucial areas, understanding the dynamics of motivating and influencing volunteer behavior by the use of nonmonetary means is critical. Even when all staff members are salaried employees, one of the primary challenges facing a sport event manager is finding an answer to the question "How do I motivate my event staff?"

In his book *Influence: Science and Practice*, Cialdini (1993) described several effective methods for influencing people's behaviors. Understanding the methods discussed in Cialdini's book and employing *influence jujitsu*—influencing without appearing to influence—allow an event manager to increase the likelihood that both volunteers and paid staff will work toward ensuring the event's success.

Cialdini's rules of influence include

Reciprocation.
Volunteers will try to repay, in kind, what you have provided that is of value to them. In other words, you need to provide reasons why your volunteers are obligated to repay you and your event by doing a great job. These reasons may be tangible or intangible benefits. Reciprocation motivators can include staff T-shirts, a staff party, the chance to rub elbows with celebrities, public recognition, a sense of belonging, or appeals to a volunteer's sense of purpose.

Commitment and consistency.
Once volunteers make the decision to commit to your organization and its goals, they will encounter personal

and interpersonal pressures to behave consistently with that commitment. Even though staff members are volunteers, a job description and a contract that clearly outlines their duties and responsibilities are advisable. Once volunteers sign on for a tour of duty, they are more likely to fulfill their obligations.

Social proof. Volunteers view a behavior as correct in a given situation to the degree that they see others performing it. To ensure that volunteers see correct behaviors, put well-trained and efficient staff members in positions to model proper behaviors. These staff members set the tone. In addition to volunteers, other staff members will see these *correct* behaviors and model them. Not every staff member needs to be a strong leader. Actually, you need followers who take their cues from these leaders and follow directions. If a manager is successful in convincing critical leaders to model appropriate behaviors and adhere to the event plan, chances are that event volunteers will follow suit.

Liking. Volunteers prefer to say yes to the requests of people they know and like. For an event manager, it's important to *not* alienate event staff or volunteers by being too demanding and autocratic. Correcting mistakes is important, but staff members, and especially volunteer staff, must also be encouraged. At a minimum, all members of the organization, both paid staff and volunteers, must respect management. If respect is present, liking often follows.

Authority. Volunteers will tend to follow the directions of genuine authorities because such individuals usually possess high levels of knowledge, wisdom, and power. Volunteers recognize and appreciate the inherent authority of an event manager who has developed a higher level of event knowledge and possesses a management plan that anticipates and deals with problems. Part of any management plan is to maintain a sense of control, to ensure calm among staff even when the event becomes hectic. To put it simply, even if you as a manager do not immediately know exactly what to do, don't panic. As quickly and calmly as possible, look at alternatives and work through them in search of an answer to the problem at hand. Maintain a calm demeanor. Remember: Even if you doubt yourself, don't let others see your doubt. Don't be afraid to admit mistakes, but also have a plan to address the mistakes and move forward.

Try to create an environment where all members of the organization, both paid staff and volunteers, respect management.

Scarcity. Opportunities seem more valuable to volunteers when they are less available. This limited-number tactic is useful to an event manager. Make sure volunteers feel as if they are part of an elite group – the event staff. In addition, make regular staff members feel valued. Although it is important to place time lines and deadlines on the completion of tasks, reward those who are first to complete their tasks. Have contests among the staff and volunteers, and reward those who are most efficient. Make sure that the time lines are reasonable, but also build in some leeway for completion for workers who don't meet the deadlines.

Draft and Conduct Pre-Event Briefings.

Anyone who has ever been part of an athletic event knows that coaches and players always meet before a game. Players may meet with individual position coaches. Players may meet among themselves. Then, the entire team meets just before kickoff, tip-off, or when the gun sounds. Why do teams meet just before athletic events? If a coach hasn't already prepared the team for the game, isn't it too late to solve problems just before game time? If the players have practiced and developed the skills necessary for success, is a rousing pregame pep talk going to magically make them run faster or jump higher? If they aren't already motivated to do their best, are

Dive Briefing Checklist	Yes	No
• Site (_____) • Topography, points of interest, hazards, depth		
• Divemaster's role		
• Entry and exit considerations		
• Dive procedures • Course to follow, safety stops, air reserves		

• Emergency procedures
     • Protocols
     • Buddy separation
     • Low-air/out-of-air
     • Diver recall procedures		

• Signal review		
• Roster/Buddy check		

• Environmental & aquatic life
     • Hazards
     • Diver responsibilities
     • Discourage feeding
     • Take only memories…		

• Pre-dive safety check		
• "Divers are responsible for their own profiles"		

**Figure 2.6 Sample Scuba-Diving Briefing Checklist.
(Courtesy Belize Divers)**

clichés going to suddenly instill a sense of purpose? The answer to each of these questions is "No!" But most coaches would never eliminate meeting with their team just before a game. Most event planners also recognize the need to meet with their event staff before an event.

Why conduct pre-event briefings? More than anything, such briefings allow all event team members to make sure that pre-event checklists have been completed, upcoming logistics are coordinated, and the event plan is on schedule. These meetings also increase the likelihood of any last-minute oversights being caught and corrected. Each pre-event briefing involves reviewing the highlights of the specific event plan one final time before the event begins. It serves to refocus the attention of event staff members on their duties and assigned responsibilities.

Pre-event briefings may be developed for a wide variety of events and activities. Figure 2-6 is an example of a pre-event briefing checklist for a specific specialized recreational activity/event - a scuba dive from a boat. This example can be helpful to future sport event managers; it breaks down a 5-minute event (the briefing) that takes place before a scuba dive into a series of items that must be completed. Once the staff member and the participants jump off the boat and go underwater, it is hard to communicate. You cannot easily change a scuba diving plan once it has begun. Just as dive guides shouldn't surprise their scuba diving customers with changes in plans while they are underwater, good event managers will not surprise their staff members with new plans or schedule changes unless it is necessary. A pre-event briefing is not the time to make drastic changes in an event's schedule or reassign staff duties. It is a time to make sure all of the staff is all on the same page. Remember: If staff members don't know what to do by now, they never will!

Pre-event briefings are also final pre-event opportunities to cement the culture of professionalism that began when the organization held its first brainstorming session. The number of pre-event briefings needs to be determined by the overall event manager well in advance. An event's complexity helps establish how many briefings are needed. Each pre-event briefing needs to be concise and clear. Regardless of an event's complexity, there should be at least three pre-event briefings: (a) one overall briefing for all event staff members, (b) one briefing with the overall event manager and all supervisors, and (c) at least one briefing conducted by all supervisors with their individual staff members.

Track the Event in Real Time

One common event-planning error is to lose track of the event as it unfolds. Checklists are linear, and managers have a tendency to want to work down a list from the top to the bottom. On the other hand, events sometimes unfold in a nonlinear fashion that requires adaptability and improvisation by the event staff and managers. However, because something unexpected happens, event checklists and plans should not be abandoned. Abandoning well-designed event checklists because something unexpected happens makes as little sense as throwing a road map out the window because you have to take an unexpected detour around some road construction. If an event's planning is solid, the event itself will most likely unfold according to plan. If nothing goes according to plan, then perhaps the plan was deficient. Keep that in mind during postevent debriefings.

When possible, it is a good idea to set benchmarks within an event to allow staff supervisors to assess the event's status. It is critical for supervisors to periodically communicate with managers to allow ongoing event assessment. Although it is imperative for event managers to monitor their supervisors, an efficient manager will refrain from constantly interceding in the supervisor and event staff management. Because an overall event manager cannot be everywhere at once, she must trust her staff members to do their jobs. If the event's plan is sound, including solid training and motivation of staff members, it is likely that the event will be successful.

To help ensure an event's success, managers should train supervisors to track the success and failure of each phase of the event and let supervisors and staff members know that although perfection is not expected, they must prevent the same problem from continually recurring. By encouraging supervisors to freely share both event failures and successes, future event supervisors can better avoid similar problems at future events. Staff members should be encouraged to log event successes and failures as soon after they occur as possible. This will help ensure that these items are not forgotten. It is not important that *everything* be written down, but if *nothing* is written down, too much is forgotten. In addition, something that seemed catastrophic during the event may not seem as bad afterward. Through a judicious real-time tracking of the event, the postevent evaluation process will be more meaningful.

> Set benchmarks within an event to allow staff supervisors to assess the event's status.

Develop and Conduct Postevent Debriefings.

Just as coaches meet with their teams before the game, they also meet with their teams after the contest. This postgame meeting allows a coach to go over the good and bad things that occurred during the game. If the team achieved its goals, the coach congratulates the players. If the team didn't achieve all of its goals, a good coach still discusses the many positive aspects of the game. In addition, the coach often uses this postgame talk to address methods of correcting the deficiencies in the team's performance and working to maintain the team's cohesion. Similarly, a good event manager will conduct postevent debriefings.

If one of the organization's goals is to conduct the event on an annual basis, then discussing the good and bad occurrences during an event will help in the planning for future events. As the saying goes, "Those who do not learn from the mistakes of the past are doomed to repeat them." By reviewing event checklists and supervisor logs, a manager can begin to evaluate an event. Managers should look for event positives and negatives, think of ways to improve and streamline all phases of the planning and production of the event, make amendments or changes to the checklist as soon as possible, and engage in thorough discussions of the benefits and drawbacks of making a change in event protocol.

Before changes are made in an event's future plans, managers should determine whether a failure occurred because of faulty planning or because of an external environment that was different than anticipated. Will the change allow for adaptation to the external environment? Will the external environment be the same or different at the next event? The problem should be discussed with the staff members who actually encountered the problem. These staff members should be involved in plans to ensure the problem does not recur. Staff members who adapted and improvised to deal with the problem during the event are a great resource for developing possible long-term, permanent solutions.

Once a sport event manager has decided that a change needs to be made, she should not put off making changes to her checklist or procedures. If she does not make necessary changes immediately, they are often forgotten, and the same problems may recur during future events. Once the change has been made, care must be taken to begin the process of insuring that the solution or change becomes part of the organization's culture—the way the organization does things.

Perform Event Cleanup and/or Closeout.

As any college student knows, nobody likes to be the last one at a party. Why? Because the last person at the party always has to clean up. One of the hardest parts of any event is the cleaning up, closing out, and/or shutting down of the event site. The fans have gone home, the teams or participants have received their rewards, and the press has left to file their stories. All that is left is the mess! The adrenaline of the event has dissipated; the glamour is gone. Just as actors must go back to their dressing rooms and slowly remove their makeup, designated event staff members must pack up the event. They must clean up the kitchen or put away the toys.

An event manager needs to plan this event cleanup process so that it is as efficient and painless as possible. This process of postevent wrap-up must be planned as carefully as the rest of the event. If this process is too long, too taxing, or too dreary, the event manager risks alienating volunteers, damaging equipment, and ending the event on a sour note. Managers must remember that the motivation and adrenaline that the event generated are over, so insuring that staff members and volunteers still do things correctly depends on maintaining staff motivation and professionalism. Shoddy cleanup procedures cannot be tolerated. Shortcuts in event cleanup can negatively impact an event's profitability and the prospects for future events.

> An event is not over until the cleanup is completed.

Managers should develop checklists that cover this entire process. All event planning should include a thorough discussion of the postevent cleanup and closeout process. An event's staff must truly believe that the event is not over until the cleanup is completed. It is critical that a sport event manager stay upbeat during the cleanup process. An event's staff will follow their supervisor's lead, so a manager must ensure that supervisors also stay upbeat during this process. Conducting a complete and thorough event cleanup and closeout allows for a seamless transition to the accounting and reconciliation process.

Reconcile the Event (Settlement).

The process of accounting and reconciliation (settlement) actually begins during the event cleanup. Accounting and reconciliation include dealing with equipment used during the event that must be properly inventoried and insuring that procedures for returning any equipment rented, or warehousing equipment the organization owns, are followed. The accounting and reconciliation process begins during the immediate postevent cleanup but includes much more.

Settlement involves more than just the monetary balancing of the books. Although it's critical that the event budget be reconciled, there is much more to the process of settlement. Some questions that a sport event manager needs to answer during this process include the following:

- Did the event make money? How much money? Have all the bills been paid?

- If event participants received prizes or some sort of mementos, have all the prizes been distributed?

- Have all volunteers been publicly and personally thanked for helping? Have all participants been thanked for participating?

- Have all the results been communicated to the media?

- Have any sponsors been thanked publicly and personally? Have these sponsors been encouraged to be sponsors for the next event?

The process of accounting and reconciliation must start before the event begins. Again, develop checklists to ensure that planning is well conceived and the accounting process is completed according to the plan. Because this process occurs before the event's conclusion, it is more likely that there will be fewer volunteers available and that more of the workload will fall on a few organization members. With this in mind, prioritize the items and work steadily, but quickly, to complete the checklists.

The settlement process can be invaluable as a final evaluation of the entire event. As an event manager deals with an event's final loose ends, she can think back through the entire event. By going over the entire event again, an event manager can increase future event-planning efficiency. As time passes, an event manager can gain useful insights into her personal performance and the event staff's performance during all phases of the event. Taking part in accounting and reconciliation allows an event manager to better plan future events.

Summary

1. Event planning and production are the processes of getting things done (accomplishing goals) through people.

2. Event management involves satisfying the needs of event participants, sponsors, and spectators.

3. The planning process includes achieving identified goals and coordinating the actions of people/organizations, while recognizing the constraints of limited resources.

4. An event SWOT analysis consists of identifying the Strengths, Weaknesses, Opportunities, and Threats associated with a particular event.

5. Reverse planning for an event can be accomplished through the use of such planning formats as GANNT charts.

6. The use of event checklists is an excellent event-management strategy.

7. Most event staff members possess the ability to perform their assigned tasks. When they don't perform their task correctly, it is most often due to a lack of motivation.

8. Important rules of influence that an event manager should understand include reciprocation, commitment and consistency, social proof, liking, authority, and scarcity.

9. Pre-event briefings allow all event team members to make sure that pre-event checklists have been completed, upcoming logistics are co-ordinated, and the event's planning is on schedule.

10. Regardless of an event's complexity, there should be at least three pre-event briefings and three postevent debriefings. All the event staff members should attend organization-wide briefings and debriefings. There should be pre- and postevent meetings attended by the overall event manager and all supervisors. In addition, each supervisor should conduct a briefing and debriefing with individual staff members whom she directly supervises.

11. It is important to develop and complete "shutdown" checklists that cover the entire cleanup process following the actual event.

12. Accounting and reconciliation (settlement) involve more than the monetary balancing of an event's books.

Questions

1. What are the steps in event planning and production?

2. Why is it important to agree upon an event's goals at the beginning of the event planning and production process?

3. What is a SWOT analysis?

4. Develop a Gannt chart for this course's assignments.

5. What is an important element of staff training that is often over-looked?

6. Identify and give an example of each of the rules of influence discussed.

7. Why is it important to conduct pre-event briefings and postevent de-briefings?

8. Why is it critical that event managers develop "shutdown" checklists and ensure that they are completed?

9. Identify the critical elements in event accounting and reconciliation.

Chapter Three

Financing Facilities

Application Exercise   Laura Fitness, a student at Sports and Recreation University, has been asked, as a leader within the student body, to help study and, it is hoped, promote the construction of a new recreation facility. The University has 10,000 full-time students; its present facility is too small and does not have adequate equipment. As a sport management student, Laura is interested in learning as much as possible about the process while creating a successful endeavor. The process with which to help Laura will be explained further. After reading this chapter, please refer to the review questions to check comprehension and help solve Laura's task.

Introduction   Sport facilities have undergone unprecedented renovation and construction within the past few years. However, as costs continue to rise, the owners of professional franchises are not as willing or able to fund the entire project. For additional funding, owners have turned to the public. In addition, the lure of a new stadium has caused some professional franchises to entirely vacate their host city (Graney & Barrett, 1998). Two examples of this phenomenon involve the cities of Baltimore and Cleveland, which wanted to bolster their downtown areas by building new sports facilities.

Baltimore agreed to build a baseball park (now Camden Yards) and a football stadium to attract a new franchise as the Colts had covertly moved to Indianapolis (Graney & Barrett, 1998). In turn, Cleveland built Jacobs Field as their new baseball stadium and Gund Arena for their basketball team. The newly built facilities attracted new lifeblood into the downtown area, and fans turned out in droves to attend the games, which consequently drove up revenue production and allowed the signing of a number of quality players (Graney & Barrett).

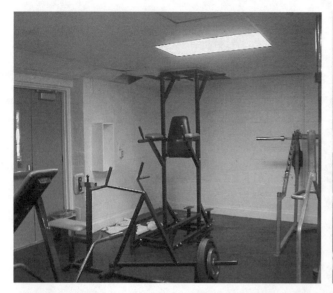

Many colleges and universities have replaced outdated recreation facilities with new, state-of-the-art complexes.

In an interesting turnabout, cities not willing to build new facilities have received threats from owners to move to other locations. This particular mode of thinking impacted the cities of Baltimore and Cleveland once again. As mentioned previously, although Cleveland had built new baseball and basketball facilities, a new football stadium was still wanting. Baltimore, on the other hand, had a newly constructed football stadium with no team. As a result, Baltimore made an offer to Art Modell, the owner of the Cleveland Browns, and he moved the team east. Although the fans in Cleveland were ferociously loyal to their team, today's economic factors require not only rabid fans to ensure success, but also a new state-of-the-art facility (Graney & Barrett, 1998).

Cities not willing to build new facilities have received threats from owners to move to other locations.

However, the overall value of these facilities has been hotly debated. New facilities have been thought to bring in dollars to the city, but perhaps they bring in only a feeling of pride and economic redistribution of wealth and not the creation of anything new (VanderZwaag, 1998). A discussion of how these facilities are funded, what appropriate planning consists of, and an examination of the public vs. private financing debate is the subject of this chapter.

Facility Financing

Facilities generally fall into two types—public and private (Graney & Barrett, 1998). When managing resources in the public arena, the objective is to keep public subsidy to a minimum, thereby expanding cash-flow possibilities (Regan, 1997). In the private sector, the emphasis is placed on shareholder wealth and healthy stock prices (Regan, 1997). However, the business world of today is rarely this cut-and-dried or neatly differentiated. In fact, many times, financing occurs as a combination of public and private financing. When deciding financial packages for a facility, many players are involved, and those involved are at the same time influencing and being influenced. For example, if a community determines a need for a facility, then that community will make selected governmental offices aware of the need. If successful, those government leaders will contact facility personnel to determine the best course of action for the construction and financing of the facility. In turn, the government may respond to the community by asking residents to vote for an increase of tax dollars to fund the facility.

Many cities around the country are building new sport facilities with the hope of significant economic gains to follow in their wake (Graney & Barrett, 1998). With this new growth comes different methods of financing to pay for the new arena, court, or field. Financing options can be very attractive to investors. For example, most funding plans are exempt from paying federal, state, or local income tax on interest earned on "qualified municipal securities (munis)" that are issued (Regan, 1997, p. 43). Therefore, without paying interest on that particular income, the borrower can sell bonds at a reduced interest rate (Regan, 1997).

Some of the most common methods of acquiring financing include bond issues "backed by general obligations and/or dedicated revenues, lease appropriations bonds (certificates or participation), and tax increment bonds" (Regan, 1997, p. 44). State and local governments may be interested in building facilities to attract tourist dollars and entertainment revenue on one end, but they also can earn cash through financing. By issuing bonds, the government helps to finance other programs such as the upkeep of roads, water, sewer, and other needs. Because these bonds are issued by local governments and are free from interest on taxes, they are referred to as *municipals* or *tax exempts* (Regan, 1997). Two important types of bonds are called *general obligation* and *revenue.*

Bonds

General obligation bonds are backed by the local, state, or regional government and usually require *ad valorem,* or property, taxes (Graney & Barrett, 1998; Regan, 1997). In this instance, the taxes are issued based on the property value. Therefore, the higher one's property value, the more taxes would be issued. General obligation bonds usually have a higher credit rating with lower size and lower issuance costs because a debt reserve fund is not always required (Regan, 1997). Revenue bonds are payable from a specific source of funds, such as a tax on revenues from hotels, restaurants, or cigarettes. As a governmental pledge is required, these bonds require higher debt service reserve, debt services coverage ratio, and they have a higher interest rate than other bonds (Regan, 1997).

> Facilities can be financed through parking garages, land donation, and funding of site improvements.

Other types of public funding include *certificates of participation* (*COPs*) and *tax increment financing* (*TIF*). With a COP, the government first creates a corporation to build and buy a facility. Next, this corporation issues COPs to raise money for the facility. Last, the government leases back the building. The lease payments then help to pay back the bonds (Regan, 1997). The aforementioned scenario takes place without a vote from the public, and although a COP is a type of a bond, it is not backed in full by the government entity and, as a result, is rated a full step lower than a general obligation bond. This type of arrangement is usually popular during times of recession as real estate values and property taxes are waning (Regan, 1997). Tax increment financing is based on the increased values of property surrounding the new facility. The increases in property taxes from the surrounding area are then used to repay the bonds. As a result, site selection in this type of arrangement is very important (Regan, 1997).

Other ways to finance, or help publicly finance, a facility may be achieved through parking garages, land donation, funding of site improvements, and the like (Regan, 1997). However, a recent trend is that toward a cooperation of public and private financing.

Public and Private Cooperation

Public and private cooperation financing can be achieved in a scenario whereby the public sector implements the project funding and the private sector commits project-related revenue resources (Regan, 1997).

Premium seating	Merchandise revenues
Building rent	Advertising rights
Corporate sponsorship	Concessions revenue
Lease payments	Naming rights
Vendor/Contractor equity	Food and beverage serving rights
Parking fees	

Note. From "Financing Facilities," by T. H. Regan, 1997, in *Sport Facility Management,* M. L. Walker and D. K. Stotlar, (Eds.), p. 46

Table 3.1. Revenue Streams From the Private Sector

By using both public and private financing, both entities share in the responsibility, and both can benefit in the end. Examples of facilities that have used the public/private financing options to their advantage include the Alamodome in Texas, Coors Field in Colorado, the Delta Center in Utah, and the "Big Stadium" in France (Regan, 1997). The Alamodome publicly financed city revenue bonds, which were backed by a 1/2% sales tax and had private contributions of arena revenues. Coors Field had public bonds secured by a sales tax in the Denver area of 1/2 of 1% along with private naming rights and arena revenues. The Delta Center again used tax financing bonds and private naming rights. Last, the "Big Stadium" in France used a combination of land, state, region, and city taxes along with private donations and club seating (Regan, 1997).

Issuer or owner	Cost estimator
Facility management	Designer/Contractor
Feasibility consultant	Construction Manager
Examination accountant	Senior underwriter
Business plan consultant	Co-underwriter
Financial advisor	Bond Council
Architect	Issuer's legal counsel

Note. From "Financing Facilities," by T. H. Regan, 1997, in *Sport Facility Management,* ed. M. L. Walker and D. K. Stotlar, p. 49.

Table 3.2. Example of a Typical Financial Team

Financial Team

Of obvious importance are the relationships between public and private entities to ensure that varying and sometimes competing interests are met so that the goal, financing a facility, can be met.

Other Factors

In addition to the financing team stated above, there are various factors to keep in mind when planning to finance and construct a sport facility. These considerations can help to attract financing by showing a well-thought-out plan and in the end will, it is hoped, ensure a successful endeavor.

Things to Keep in Mind When Constructing a Sports Facility

1. Purpose of the facility. Who uses the facility? Is it multipurpose? Is there a broad base of participation?

2. Needs of the community for which the facility is designed. What are the desired activity areas and educational requirements? Philosophy, goals, and programs should be examined.

3. Predesign factors. This should include space programming, scheduling dates (start, completion, phases, etc.) and setting up a cost model (structure, finishes, floors, mechanical costs).

4. Who comprises the planning committee? Include potential users and a representative from each program area

5. Use of consultants. Should an experienced consultant be hired? An experienced planner will save time, money, and effort. Few architects have experience in building sports facilities.

6. Building materials: encapsulated, pre-fabricated, steel, etc.

7. Site and geological factors. Considers zoning and environmental impact analysis.

8. Legal concerns and risk management. Looks at the proper placement of activity and program areas.

9. Money to build. How much money will the project require? A cost assessment should be completed.

10. Money to finance. How will the necessary funding be obtained? Who is financially responsible for this project? Identify possible sources.

11. Money to maintain. How much money will be needed to operate the facility once it is completed?

12. Architectural firm. Who will it be? Are they reputable? Have they built similar facilities?

13. Future trends. Are there foreseeable changes in programs, enrollments, and demographics?

14. Computerization. Should computerized systems be designed for specific functions such as security, programming, or laboratories?

15. Access for the disabled. Is the building totally accessible?

16. Energy-efficient design. Explore possible uses such as solar, south-facing design, skylights, or thermal storage systems.

17. Flexibility of design. Is the building designed for multipurpose use?

18. Building codes. Are there any discrepancies between the planned design and local building codes?

19. Adequate space. Does the facility fulfill the space requirements according to the established standards?

20. Alternatives. Consider all the possibilities and evaluate the existing facilities. Explore renovation and rental as well as new construction. Perhaps there is available space underground or over traffic areas.

21. Environment and climate. Should attention be paid to the local conditions and development of appropriate facilities? Is there greater need for indoors or outdoor space?

22. Miscellaneous. Don't forget about acoustics, aesthetics, video stations, etc.

(quoted from Walker, 1994, p. 180-181)

The importance of teamwork cannot be overstated. From public officials to private representatives, every link is important to the strength of the armor and, therefore, the facility proposition. Once the facility is completed, however, you must keep in mind daily operational expenditures. Additional money for items such as salaries, equipment, maintenance, and repairs is a strict necessity (Regan, 1997). A consistent cash flow for these items may be provided from funding sources such as sales tax, hotel tax, or lottery revenues (Regan, 1997). Whatever the chosen source, daily operations must be included in the overall project plan. Without them, the facility cannot be a viable institution.

Sales tax, hotel tax, or lottery revenues can provide necessary cash flow for everyday expenses incurred by the facility.

Cash Flow

Cash is defined as "cash in the bank and all short-term liquid investments that can be readily converted to cash" (Regan, 2001, p. 402). For example, money market funds, treasury bills, commercial paper, and securities with less than 3 months maturity are all considered cash equivalents. In the seasonal business of sport, it is important to have adequate cash flow for the variety of operations that encompass a sport facility. In a college athletic department, for example, cash flow helps to finance sport expansion, postseason play, and regular stadium maintenance (Regan, 2001). Cash flow is defined as "reported net income plus amounts charged off for depreciation, depletion, amortization, extraordinary charges to reserves that are bookkeeping deductions, and not paid out in actual dollars and cents" (Regan, 2001, pp. 401-402). Cash flow information, or statements, provides information about money coming in and going out during a particular time. Armed with this information, it is possible to

- Assess the team's ability to generate a positive future net cash flow

- Assess the sport enterprise's ability to meet its obligations

- Assess the difference between net income and cash receipts and disbursements

- Assess the effects of both cash and noncash investing and financing during a period (Regan, 2001, p. 402).

Classifying cash receipts and cash disbursements is accomplished by categorizing cash flow into investing, financing, or operating activities. Investing activities encompass loans made or payments received on existing loans, the purchase or sale of securities or other entities, and the sale or purchase of fixed assets. Financing activities involve borrowing, paying dividends, repaying debt, buying treasury stock, and issuing securities.

Cash sales or collections on ticket receivables

Cash sales or collections on licensed merchandise

Cash receipts from returns on loans (interest income) or divided income

Cash received from licensees and lessee

Receipt of a litigation settlement (i.e., between city, team, owner, and players)

Reimbursement under an insurance policy (strike insurance, etc.)

Note. From "Financing Sport," by T. H. Regan, 2001, in *The Management of Sport: Its Foundation and Application* (3rd ed.), ed. B. L. Parkhouse (Boston: McGraw-Hill), pp. 402-403.

Table 3.3. Examples of Cash Inflows

Cash paid for raw materials and merchandise for resale

Principal payments on accounts payable arising from purchase of goods

Payments to suppliers of operating-expense items (insurance, advertising, supplies)

Player and personnel salaries/wages

Payment of taxes

Payment of interest expense (bonds or loans)

Lawsuit payment (collusion settlement)

Cash refunds to customers for merchandise, ticket sales, or service

Charitable contributions

Note. From "Financing Sport," by T. H. Regan, 2001, in *The Management of Sport: Its Foundation and Application* (3rd ed.), ed. B. L. Parkhouse (Boston: McGraw-Hill), p. 403.

Table 3.4. Examples of Cash Outflows

Operating activities are those that are not investing or financing activities. In general, accounts payable and accounts receivable are operating activities. Cash flow from these activities usually relates to the effects of transactions in computations of profits (Regan, 2001).

Managing cash flow is an important concept for sport managers because items such as investment opportunities, player salaries, and future expansion of facilities all depend on it.

Public v. Private Financing

As discussed earlier, facilities may be funded either publicly or privately, or both. Each scenario has its benefits as well as its share of detractors. In fact, the issue is vehemently debated. Proponents of public financing argue that a new stadium brings in new jobs and attracts new fans, who support radio and television stations as well as local hotel, bar, and restaurant establishments (VanderZwaag, 1998). In addition, smaller towns that attract a professional team can establish themselves as "major league cities," attracting tourists and generating a sense of pride for their community. In terms of economic impact specifically, it has been said that adding a new stadium brings in millions of dollars per year not only in stadium revenue, but also in jobs that are created, the money that is respent, and the taxes collected, called the *multiplier effect* (VanderZwaag, 1998).

However, the opposition to public financing states that the numbers are not quite so clearly delineated. The opposition argues that new stadiums do not attract more money; they only redistribute what is already there. In addition, if people are going to the games rather than a movie or the zoo or another attraction, then those other activities lose out. Furthermore, the costs of the stadiums are so great that the increased revenue cannot repay the debt. Finally, opponents argue that the jobs created and tax revenue generated are relatively small, because the jobs are mostly minimum wage and the tax base is not expanded significantly (VanderZwaag, 1998).

The debate continues, with the only certainties being that new stadiums continue to be built and threats to move a major league franchise constitute a successful scare tactic used by owners for public subsidy support.

College Facilities

Due to competition for institutional funds, financing collegiate facilities is of specific importance. The first step is to research the particular college's policy toward athletics and determine goals and objectives of that institution and potential relationships with surrounding groups and activity leaders (VanderZwaag, 1998). Within this preliminary planning stage would also include a determination of usage in the current facility, any new sports being added to the program, admission projection numbers, etc. Next, a development team should be established to first survey funding potential, followed by a formal capital campaign (VanderZwaag). Part of this team's responsibility would be to stimulate support from inside and outside the college community.

Student fees may prove a valuable funding resource.

Institution Management Team Member/Planning Unit

Marketing/Public Relations

Financial Consultant

Personnel from the Athletic Department

(VanderZwaag, 1998)

Table 3.5. Development Team Members

As mentioned above, competition for funds in this arena will be keen. Various sources are available:

1. *Institutional Funds.* These are funds specifically appropriated for facilities. The appropriation would come from the state in the case of a public college or university, from the school district for a public school, or from the trustees for a private institution.

2. *Revenue from intercollegiate athletic events.* This source applies to relatively few institutions in terms of the entire collegiate spectrum.

3. *Special fund-raising drive.* In many cases, this is basically in the form of alumni support. However, this source is by no means limited to alumni for most institutions.

4. *Student fees.* As noted later, this is a growing source of funding particularly for recreational facilities.

5. *User fees.* This was typically used more frequently outside the school and college environment, but the potential for development is also there in this setting.

6. *Corporate funding.* This may also be tied in with the special fund-raising drive. (VanderZwaag, 1998, p. 180).

Although this is certainly not an exhaustive list of the funding available, the categories do give a general sense of where monies may be available. The next section will explore a few of these areas more in-depth.

Student Fees

As more people become interested in sporting activities, it behooves the facility planner to investigate student fees as a viable resource for funding. Many times, students will vote to increase their fees and are interested in "open recreation" time as opposed to controlled activity (VanderZwaag, 1998). For example, before arrangements were made to build a recreational center at the University of Kansas, students were limited to using the recreational facilities before 8:00 a.m. or after 5:00 p.m. During the day, activity classes were held in the gymnasium, and only students enrolled in an activity class could participate. Interestingly enough, even though hours were limited and sporting activities were growing in popularity, a new recreation center was first voted down by the students and was not approved until years later. According to VanderZwaag (1998), this problem could potentially be alleviated through proper planning. It is advisable to first study the needs of the students in-depth. Next, organizing student leaders into campaign leaders in favor of the new center will help public relations. Finally, the timing of the campaign should fall into two time slots. The first would be 6 to 8 weeks after the fall term begins. At this point, students are somewhat financially secure and still enthusiastic about the semester. The other time to campaign for a new center would be about a month before spring graduation. In this scenario, the increase in fees would not apply to the seniors, and the proposal might find more support from them. Of course, the danger with this proposition is that the seniors may also be more inclined to vote down the proposal, because they will not get to use the new facility.

User Fees

This plan, which has also been called, "pay as you go" or "pay as you play," can be attractive if there are a number of outside groups who will use the facility. However, there are also a number of concerns. For example, what will be the assessment on students, and will that assessment be different from fees assessed to faculty and staff? In addition, how will the fee structure be developed to accommodate outside user groups (VanderZwaag, 1998)? To best answer these questions, it is imperative that a cost containment scenario be devised so that total expenses are taken into consideration and that whatever the fees are, expenses can ultimately be met.

> Corporate funding, along with other sources of revenue, can be a win-win situation for all if it is done with foresight, proper planning, and solid relationship building.

Corporate Funding

Corporate funding can be a very viable option in the financing of facilities. Surrounding businesses are generally inclined to have their name displayed in some fashion. The downside, however, is that companies will generally exert some influence over the facility unless strict guidelines are developed. Other potential problems involve tax laws. For example, the 1986 Ruling 86-83 limits tax deductions if the donor is receiving preferential seats in return. In addition, tax deductions have been reduced to 80% for contribution to athletic programs. Furthermore, leases on skyboxes are no longer deductible (VanderZwaag, 1998). However, even with these problems, corporate funding, along with other sources of revenue, can be a win-win situation for all if it is done with foresight, proper planning, and solid relationship building.

Overall, facility funding involves many people, concepts, and time. It is an endeavor not to be taken lightly, but one that can provide wonderful experiences and great rewards.

Summary

1. Facilities generally fall into two types: public and private (Graney & Barrett, 1998). When managing resources in the public arena, the objective is to keep public subsidy to a minimum, thereby expanding cash flow possibilities.

2. Most funding plans are exempt from paying federal, state, or local income tax on interest earned on "qualified municipal securities (munis)" that are issued.

3. Some of the most common methods of acquiring financing include bond issues "backed by general obligations and/or dedicated revenues, lease appropriations bonds (certificates or participation), and

tax increment bonds." General obligation bonds are backed by the local, state, or regional government and usually require *ad valorem*, or property, taxes. General obligation bonds usually have a higher credit rating with lower size and lower issuance costs as a debt reserve fund is not always required. Revenue bonds are payable from a specific source of funds, such as a tax on revenues from hotels, restaurants, or cigarettes.

4.   Other types of public funding include certificates of participation (COPs) and tax increment financing (TIF). Tax increment financing is based on the increased values of property surrounding the new facility. Other ways to finance, or help publicly finance, a facility may be achieved through parking garages, land donation, funding of site improvements, and the like. However, a recent trend is toward a co-operation of public and private financing.

5.   Cash is defined as "cash in the bank and all short-term liquid investments that can be readily converted to cash."

6.   In the seasonal business of sport, it is important to have adequate cash flow for the variety of operations that encompass a sport facility. Cash flow is defined as "reported net income plus amounts charged off for depreciation, depletion, amortization, extraordinary charges to reserves that are bookkeeping deductions, and not paid out in actual dollars and cents."

7.   Proponents of public financing argue that a new stadium brings in new jobs and attracts new fans, who support radio and television stations as well as local hotel, bar, and restaurant establishments, adding to the multiplier effect. The opposition argues that new stadiums do not attract more money; they only redistribute what is already there. Finally, opponents argue that the jobs created and tax revenue generated are relatively small, because the jobs are mostly minimum wage and the tax base is not expanded significantly.

8.   Due to competition for institutional funds, financing collegiate facilities is of specific importance. Competition for funds in this arena will be keen. Various sources are available, including institutional funds, revenue from intercollegiate athletic events, a special fund-raising drive, student fees, user fees, and corporate funding.

9.   Overall, facility funding involves many people, an array of concepts, and a good deal of time. It is an endeavor not to be taken lightly, but one that can provide wonderful experiences and great rewards.

Laura Fitness, a student at Sports and Recreation University, has been asked, as a leader within the student body to help study and, it is hoped, promote the construction of a new recreation facility. Please address the following questions to help Laura in her project.

1. What are the steps that should be taken in planning and financing a new facility?

2. What are the finance options available?

3. What are the possible pitfalls of these funding options?

4. If this facility were to be financed using a combination of public and private funds, describe the various scenarios and resources available.

5. Would you suggest that bonds be used or another funding source, and why?

6. How would you characterize a debate, which may be set off in the private v. public financing scenario?

7. How important would cash flow be in this endeavor?

8. What time of year would you suggest to propose this to a vote by the student body?

9. Whom would you have on the planning committee?

10. If corporate funding were a possibility, what arrangements could you make to help ensure that control remained with the school and not the sponsors?

11. Judging from what you know about your school, what would be the important factors to include at a recreational facility at your school?

Chapter Four

Privatization

Your employer, OroMark, has been hired by Genro County, TN, to manage the newly constructed minor league baseball stadium for the local team, the Genro Hilltoppers. The county owns the stadium, but your company has been retained to manage all phases of stadium operations. You have been appointed facility manager. The previous stadium was owned and operated by the county government. Your duties include developing, planning, and overseeing public-private partnerships necessary for efficient stadium operations. To accomplish these tasks, you must determine which facility functions should be handled by the county and which ones your company will assume. In developing your plan, you may interview local facility managers and employees of private companies involved in providing facility management, research the Internet, and use material in this text and your class notes.

Today, many phases of facility management have been privatized. (Photo courtesy of Jay Bratschi.)

Over the last three decades, taxpayers and politicians around the world have come to realize that governmental resources are not limitless. In the late 1970s and early 1980s, this reality was reflected in the election of conservative leaders in the United States (Ronald Reagan), Great Britain (Margaret Thatcher), and other Western countries. Although citizens have become increasingly unwilling to pay increased costs for public services, they still demand such amenities. In response, governments at all levels—local, state, and federal—have looked to the private sector as an option for providing these services. This concept, often termed *privatization*, describes this shift in the balance of the production of goods and services from the state to the private sector. Glover (1999) described privatization as any form of public service delivery that involves the commercial or not-for-profit sectors in the delivery of public services. Starr (1988) contended that privatization is a fuzzy concept that covers a great range of ideas from the reasonable to the impractical.

> Privatization is the shift in the balance of the production of goods and services from the state to the private sector.

In the sport industry, privatization has occurred most frequently in facility construction and event and facility management. However, trends toward privatization in the sport industry have not always mirrored developments in other industry sectors.

During the 1990s, four out of every five dollars spent on stadium construction came from public sources. Forty-four of the 49 existing professional baseball and football stadiums were financed with public funds (Reason Public Policy Institute [RPPI], n.d.). This reflected an increasing reliance on public financing of stadiums. However, **management** of these *publicly* financed and constructed facilities was increasingly *privatized*. Since 1975, when management of the Louisiana Superdome was effectively privatized, municipalities and stadium districts have overwhelmingly turned to private facility and event management companies to manage publicly constructed facilities, park maintenance, and recreational services. By 1995, 33% of U.S. cities contracted park and recreation management services (RPPI, n.d.).

Although privatization is the most commonly used term to describe this trend, more accurately the term *public-private partnership* should be applied. The use of the term public-private partnership to describe this general overall movement recognizes that privatization is only one of many techniques or approaches to public-private partnerships.

Implicit in a shift to public-private partnerships are some changes in governmental public policy. Four types of policy transformations can lead to increased privatization partnerships. First, any time public programs or services are discontinued or scaled back, a type of privatization will occur. When government gets out of the business of supplying a service, a private entity will emerge to meet the demand, unless there is no demand for the services or programs. Second, government may explicitly transfer public assets to the private ownership by selling or leasing public lands, infrastructure, or enterprises. Third, instead of producing the service, government may finance the private sector service provider through a type of public-private financial partnership (see *contracting out* or *vouchers*). Fourth, a type of privatization may occur as a result of deregulation of the previous services that functioned as public monopolies. (Deregulation has occurred in the U.S. airline industry, as well as energy and phone utilities.)

Rationale for Utilizing Public-Private Partnerships

As the preceding paragraphs illustrate, the drive for public-private partnerships is grounded in the fundamental belief that government can, and should, do more with less. The philosophy that forces (or relationships that shape private markets) can, and should, apply to government bureaucracies as a cornerstone of the development of public-private partnerships. Fundamentally, the goal of any form of privatization is increased efficiency and effectiveness of service production and/or delivery. The rationale for developing public-private partnerships in sport and recreation settings answers the question "Can a private *vendor* (service provider), in partnership with the government in some fashion, produce and/or deliver *better* swimming lessons, games, or hot dogs than can the government working alone?"

The notion of "better" necessarily involves the availability of choices. If there is only one place to obtain a hot dog, there is no chance for one hot dog vendor to be better. In order to incorporate market principles into the sport and recreation industry, more competition and choices must be available to the consumer. If there are available choices, then competition can exist. Once competition is introduced, existing public or private service providers are forced to respond to consumers' wants, needs, and desires.

Competition forces service providers to respond to consumer needs or face extinction. If a local parks and recreation agency can't respond to the lower costs and/or increased perceived value of gymnastic instruction provided by a private gymnastics academy, the agency may face losses in prestige, budget, and participation. Increased responsiveness not only increases efficiency, but it also increases effectiveness by satisfying customer needs and is beneficial to both the customer and the agency. Even when there is no natural competition available, quasi-competitive mechanisms can be implemented to reproduce the benefits of competition in a monopolistic setting.

Another way in which competition increases an agency's efficiency and effectiveness is through rewarding innovation. Government monopolies may often stifle creativity and innovation through the development of moribund bureaucracies. Traditionally, government organization encourages agencies to increase the size of their departments, which results in an oversupply of services and service providers and a lack of service quality. (Think about going to get a driver's license.) Just the threat of competition and options is often enough, according to public choice theorists, to promote more effective and efficient services. What, then, are some types of public-private partnerships that can be developed to meet sport and recreation consumers' needs?

> Contracting out or outsourcing is when the government contracts a private company, organization, or agency to produce and/or provide a service.

Types of Public-Private Partnerships

No matter what configuration they take, public-private partnerships involve a reconfiguration of the provision, production, or delivery of a service (Heilman & Johnson, 1992). In 1988, Starr wrote, "Many things seem to be public and private at the same time in varying degrees or in different ways" (p. 6). There are many types of public-private partnerships that can be utilized to provide goods and services to sport and recreation consumers.

Contracting out or *outsourcing* involves the government competitively contracting with a private company, organization, or agency (either for profit or not for profit) to produce and/or provide a service. An example of contracting out would be a municipal stadium district's hiring a food service vendor to provide stadium concessions. Another closely related example of a public-private partnership is *franchising.* Franchising is very similar to contracting out, but it involves a private firm's being given the exclusive right to provide a service within a certain geographic area. An example would be one food service vendor's obtaining exclusive rights to all concessions at a stadium.

Commercialization occurs when the government gets out of the "business" of providing a particular service completely and allows the private sector to take on the function of providing the service. This is process is also called *service shedding.* Often, when local or county governments have decided to no longer sponsor youth baseball programs, nonprofit youth baseball associations have assumed the task of providing this service. *Management contracts* entail the management of a facility being contracted out to a private company. Today, many private companies manage publicly owned arenas, convention centers, and stadiums. *Self-help*, or transfer to nonprofit organization, is the process by which a community group and/or neighborhood organization acquires either ownership or management of traditional government assets or services. The community group or organization directly benefits from the service and is, therefore, motivated to increase efficiency and effectiveness. Often times, the beneficiaries turn over management of the asset or service to a not-for-profit organization. Self-help public-private partnerships often involve parks, zoos, museums, arenas, and recreational districts (RPPI, n. d.).

Tax expenditure privatization occurs when the government, through tax code provisions, offers incentives to organizations to produce a public service. Certain infrastructure projects, such as stadiums and arenas, may make use of such tax incentives. Another economic-based privatization concept is *vouchers*. Through the issuance of vouchers, the government pays for the service, but individuals are given some sort of redeemable certificates with which to purchase the service on the open market. The government subsidizes the consumer, but does not provide the service or impede consumer choice. Theoretically, consumers have the incentive to "shop around," and service providers are motivated to supply high-quality, low-cost services (RPPI, n. d.).

Examples of Public-Private Sport Partnerships

In recent years economic activity has increased dramatically in the sport industry. This activity has often been the result of innovative public-private partnerships. Examples of such partnerships involving event management and promotion, infrastructure development, and stadium financing and construction offer insights in how governments and private organizations have worked together to achieve sport event goals.

Event Promotion and Management

A seminal event in sport event management was the 1984 Los Angeles Olympics. For the prior hundred years, Olympic Games were strictly public/government projects. The Southern California Olympic Organizing Committee (SCOOC) and its progeny, the Los Angeles Olympic Organizing Committee (LAOOC), were both groups of private citizens whose mission was to secure and promote the Games as a *private* event. The LAOOC bid was revolutionary because it proposed that the Los Angeles Games would not involve massive public works projects (venue construction) and would not require federal/government subsidization. At the time, most observers doubted that the LAOOC could pull it off. However, the 1984 Games closed with a record $230-million surplus. The 1984 Los

> Every successful event must have superior infrastructure and creative event management.

The 1984 Olympic Games were a successful public-private partnership. (Photo courtesy Ball-parks.com)

Angeles Olympics is an excellent public/private partnership example (Catherwood and Van Kirk, 1992).

What were the secret ingredients to the LAOOC partnership's success? They really aren't secret but are critical to the success of any large privately funded and managed sporting event: superior infrastructure, creative event management, great television ratings and revenue, and phenomenal corporate sponsorship dollars. Although every event cannot have the last two ingredients, every successful event needs to possess the first two ingredients.

Infrastructure and Privatization

The secret to the success of the 1984 Games was the infrastructure of the LAOOC, which reflected involvement and commitment from local and state governments, civic and community groups, influential business leaders, key politicians, high-profile celebrities, and local and national media. Although the LAOOC was a *private* entity, the infrastructure reflected a true *public-private partnership* (Catherwood & Van Kirk, 1992). By having both public and private "movers and shakers" from throughout Southern California involved and supportive, tasks were accomplished and rough spots were smoothed over. Both the public and private sectors were caught up by the community spirit of the bid. This spirit overcame the initial reluctance and concerns of the International Olympic Committee (IOC) that a private bid was doomed to fail.

The second secret ingredient was creative private management. *Ueberroth, Usher & Company*, headed by Peter Ueberroth and Harry Usher, was hired by the LAOOC to merchandize, promote, market, and manage the '84 Olympics as no previous Olympics had been. Their innovative approach to event management was symbolized in their market economy approach to the Olympic Torch Run. Torch-relay runners were charged a fee to participate. Corporate sponsors were solicited. Initially, several media reports were critical of this commercialized approach, but, as the torch relay progressed, it evolved into a marketing and promotional bonanza for the Games (Catherwood & Van Kirk, 1992). The run generated an emotional

Many sport stadia, such as Invesco Field at Mile High, have been constructed since 1988.

connection between the public- and the privately-funded and managed Games. This connection led to increased ticket sales and sustained and positive media coverage. By the time the torch reached Los Angeles, the *public* was solidly behind the first *private* Olympic games (Catherwood & Van Kirk).

Sports Stadium Financing and Construction

As was discussed earlier, most of the stadium construction in the 1990s has been financed from public sources. However, there have been a few notable exceptions to this trend. Pacific Bell Park was financed through nam-

Construction of Invesco Field at Mile High was accomplished through a limited public-private partnership.

ing rights, sponsorship, and concession rights (Pacific Bell paid $50 million in naming rights' fees.), charter-seat sales, and bonds pledged against increased revenue from future Giants' games. In Denver, the Nuggets (NBA) and Avalanche (NHL) are tenants in a private $150+-million arena (Pepsi Center) financed and built by Ascent Entertainment. Ascent matched its initial investment with increased first-year arena revenues from hockey and basketball games (80 games) and additional events, including rodeos and concerts. Additional revenue sources available were $17 million in revenue from luxury boxes and club seating; $20 million in naming rights from Pepsi; and $20 million from parking, concessions, and advertising (RPPI, n. d.). It should be noted that although the financing and construction of the Pepsi Center were private ventures, the City and County of Denver provided tax incentives, infrastructure, and other support for the project.

Private Sport Facility and Event Management

Another development in public-private partnerships in sport facility (arenas; stadiums; and convention, exhibition, and trade centers) and event management has been outsourcing the management of these public facilities to private management corporations. Two examples of the response for professional management of these facilities are SMG and Global-Spec-

> A current trend in public-private partnerships in sport facility and event management is to outsource the management of these public facilities to private management corporations.

Figure 4.1 highlights some major privately financed sport facilities built in North America since 1988. It should be noted that although the financing for these facilities was private, there were still various public-private partnerships developed to assist with stadium and/or arena financing and construction or renovation.

City	Facility	Tenant(s)	Est. Cost*
Boston	Fleet Center	Celtics/Bruins	$160
Chicago	United Center	Blackhawks/Bulls	$180
Denver	Pepsi Center	Avalanche/Nuggets	$150
Detroit	The Palace at Auburn Hills	Pistons	$70
Milwaukee	Bradley Center	Bucks	$80
Minneapolis	Target Center	Timberwolves	$113
Montreal	Molson Center	Canadiens	$230**
New York City	Madison Square Garden	Knicks/Rangers	$200
Philadelphia	CoreStates Center	Flyers/76ers	$235
Phoenix	America West Arena	Suns	$100
Portland	Rose Garden Arena	Trailblazers	$260
Sacramento	Arco Arena	Kings	$65
Saint Louis	Kiel Center	Blues	$130
Salt Lake City	Delta Center	Jazz	$78
Vancouver	GM Place	Canucks	$180**

Note. Source: RPPI, n. d.

* Cost in millions (includes land, site preparation, and construction, administration costs).

** Canadian dollars.

Figure 4.1 Privately Financed Sport Facilities in North America (since 1988)

trum. These corporations partner with both municipal and private facilities to provide the expertise to manage many arenas throughout the world.

The single largest facility management company today is SMG. SMG is composed of two equal principals: the Hyatt Hotel Chain and ARAMARK Corporation. As of 2003, SMG manages 156 facilities for both municipal and private clients throughout the world. This includes 63 arenas, 7 stadiums, 31 performing arts centers, 44 convention centers, and 11 other recreational facilities. Overall, SMG controls more than 1.4 million seats in entertainment venues privately managed by the firm (www.smg.worldcom). Global Spectrum, a division of the Philadelphia-based sports and entertainment company Comcast-Spectacor, is the second largest public event facility management company. Founded in 1994, Global-Spectrum presently manages 31 facilities in North America. Both SMG and Global-Spectrum provide clients with a wide range of service options including turnkey management and/or consulting for preopening/design and construction phases of a new facility, as well as the ongoing operations for an existing facility (www.global-spectrum.com).

Possible Benefits and Drawbacks of Privatization

As has been discussed in this chapter, one of the trends in facility management is privatization. Privatization has its proponents and its critics. As with many things in life, both sides have some convincing arguments.

Benefits

Proponents of privatization point out that private management companies offer economic efficiency, quality services, an increase in the number of jobs, and workforce stability. Economic efficiency arguments are centered on a discussion of *economies of scale*. A private company (e.g., a concession vendor) can perform the same service for several municipalities or stadiums, justifying the costs in necessary equipment and the recruitment and training of a specialized labor force. The labor costs associated with a private-sector provider are often lower, not only because private workers will often be paid less than municipal government workers, but also because the private sector has more flexibility in its hiring practices, and seasonal or part-time employees may not receive benefits. All these factors increase the economic efficiency of privatizing event and facility management.

In addition, as a result of increased competition, it is argued that privatization improves the quality of services provided. Because service providers or contractors are always aware of the possibility of their contract's not being renewed, the *discipline of market forces* is assured (Heilman & Johnson, 1992). From this point of view, increased competition naturally leads to improved service effectiveness. Privatization proponents argue that private sector employees who are not dedicated to providing a quality product or service can be terminated much more easily than can civil servants entrenched in a government bureaucracy.

Another privatization benefit cited is an increase in meaningful private sector jobs. The private sector contractors can hire any workers displaced by privatization. These jobs will be meaningful jobs, not the municipal government jobs lacking in the opportunity for rapid advancement and increased responsibilities. Finally, the threat and impact of strikes are greatly decreased by privatization, because the provision of goods and services is decentralized. The public is no longer at the mercy of large public service unions (RPPI, n. d.).

Drawbacks

Opponents answer each argument in favor of privatization. Privatization critics contend that privatization is actually economically inefficient, decreases the quality of services provided, and leads to lower paying jobs devoid of benefits.

Privatization opponents argue that it doesn't make sense that the private sector can deliver the same service cheaper than the public sector, while making a profit. Opponents argue that the process of contracting out is inefficient and costly. Public entities must prepare and manage the bidding process, draft contracts, and monitor performance. Even when a private contractor provides goods or services, the government entity is still responsible for quality control. If the product or service is deficient, or the private contractor goes out of business, the public sector must step in and perform the job or go through another bidding process. In addition, many costs associated with privatization are hidden. Often, public equipment and services are provided to contractors, and managers and other public employees are needed to monitor the private sector (Glover, 1999; Starr, 1988).

An example of a possible problem in financing stadiums utilizing private entities is the selling of naming rights to stadiums. If a city or other public entity is depending on the revenue from a naming rights deal, what happens if the private company that has paid for the right to name the stadium is unable to fulfill its contractual obligations (payment) because it goes out of business (PSINet, Enron, TWA)? In addition, what if having the stadium's name associated with a company becomes a liability (Enron)? The public sector is faced with unanticipated costs associated with these eventualities.

> One possible problem with private entities financing stadiums is the sale of the naming rights.

An associated drawback of privatization cited by opponents is that it is frequently hard or impossible to actually monitor quality. In addition, because private companies are often motivated by profit maximization, maintaining consistent quality throughout their workforce may be undermined. For example, in an attempt to increase profits, a stadium concession vendor may look to pay minimum wage salaries, buy lower cost and inferior products, or hire an insufficient number of employees. Finally, as a result of economies of scale, the municipality may be at the mercy of the large, private service provider who has a virtual monopoly on the desired products or services (Glover, 1999). If the municipality no longer possesses the ability to provide the goods or services, it does not have the option of taking over the functions if the private contractor proves to be unsatisfactory.

Regardless of whether privatization is seen to be a blessing or a curse, it is part of today's sport event and facility management landscape. The sport event/facility manager must operate in a world where she will be asked to deal with satisfying the demands for traditionally public services, while encountering a resistance to taxes. A judicious use of privatization strategies can help managers run their events or facilities efficiently, while being accountable to the needs of the public.

Summary

1. In the sport industry, privatization has occurred most frequently in facility construction and in event and facility management.

2. Although financing of recently constructed professional football and baseball stadiums in the United States has primarily come from public sources, management of these facilities has increasingly been privatized.

3. The drive for public-private partnerships is grounded in the fundamental belief that government can, and should, do more with less.

4. The goal of any form of privatization is increased efficiency and effectiveness of service production and/or delivery.

5. There are many types of public-private partnerships that can be used to provide goods and services to sport and recreation consumers.

6. The 1984 Los Angeles Olympic Games were revolutionary because they did not involve massive public works projects or federal government subsidization.

7. Important ingredients of the success of the 1984 Olympic Games were an infrastructure that reflected a public-private partnership and creative private management that promoted, merchandized, marketed, and managed the games.

8. Proponents of privatization point out that private management companies offer economic efficiency, quality services, and an increase in the number of jobs and workforce stability.

9. Privatization critics contend that privatization is actually economically inefficient, decreases the quality of services provided, and leads to lower paying jobs devoid of benefits.

10. Regardless of whether privatization is seen to be a blessing or a curse, it is part of today's sport event and facility management landscape.

Questions

1. What factors might explain the increase in public funding or stadiums in the United States in the 1990s?

2. What political or social forces have influenced the increased reliance on privatization in sport event and facility management?

3. How did the 1984 Olympic Games differ from any previous Olympic Games? Why was this important? Has this development been a good thing for the Olympic movement? Why or why not?

4. Identify and discuss some types of public-private partnerships. For each form identified, highlight advantages and disadvantages.

Chapter Five

ADA Requirements

Application Exercise
As a facility manager for Old School Arena (OSA), Jeff Martinez has not made any changes to his facility to accommodate individuals with disabilities. Recently Jeff has had several complaints by various disabled individuals, and he may be facing a lawsuit if certain adjustments are not made. Recently, Jeff hired a sport management graduate as the new assistant manager. The new hire, Steve Rightway, has working knowledge of the ADA. Jeff has given Steve complete responsibility to undertake the necessary renovations. Currently, OSA has four 2800 square foot floors, with no elevators and two staircases within. OSA has two parking spaces for the disabled that measure 8' X 8'. The restrooms are on the ground floor immediately next to OSA's storage facility.

Introduction
President George H. W. Bush signed the Americans With Disabilities Act (ADA) into law in 1990 (G. B. Fried, 2000). The ADA protects individuals with disabilities from discrimination. Specific to sports facilities, the law states that managers must provide "reasonable accommodations" for individuals with disabilities (Fried). Various groups, including the Paralyzed Veterans of America, have used the reasonable accommodation provision during litigation. With a membership of 17,000, the group has challenged new facilities to ensure that persons in wheelchairs have adequate seating. The ADA regulations require that people in wheelchairs have various options for seating prices, that they not be isolated, and that their lines of sight be comparable to those of other areas and not obstructed by standing fans (Fried). For a newly constructed stadium with over a 300-person capacity, a minimum of six seats for the disabled should be available in more than one location (Miller, 1997). In addition, building codes and state and local laws may determine guidelines for the disabled. Some of these may include provisions for a certain spacing between

seats (usually 17-20 inches) or handrail necessity based on the number of steps (Fried).

The ADA has mandated that reasonable accommodations be made toward those with disabilities. Examples of reasonable accommodation may be ramps, railings, and certain types of listening systems. Persons with disabilities must be granted access to the event equal to that of all other patrons. Therefore, in its simplest form, a patron must be able to enter through the front door (Graham, Goldblatt, & Delpy, 1995).

Specific to the ADA is Title III, which prohibits discrimination of access or participation related to facilities (Miller, 1997). The ADA was designed to prohibit discrimination based on callous assumptions or generalizations. This chapter will further discuss the law, its history, and its application.

The primary goal of the Americans With Disabilities Act was to mainstream and incorporate people with disabilities into society as much as possible to ensure equal opportunity (Fried, 2000). From a historical perspective, the ADA began with the Occupational Safety and Health Administration (OSHA). In 1970, OSHA created specifications for equipment, maintenance, and safety in construction (Seidler, 1997). Also in the 1970s, Congress was interested in creating opportunities for individuals with disabilities (Wolohan, 2001a). The first of the laws created was the Rehabilitation Act of 1973. Section 504 of the Rehabilitation Act states:

No otherwise qualified handicapped individual in the United States, shall solely by reason of his handicap, be excluded from participation in, be denied the benefits of, or be subjected to discrimination under any program or activity receiving Federal financial assistance. (quoted in Wolohan, 2001a, p. 510)

History of the Americans With Disabilities Act

In addition, under this auspice, facilities receiving federal assistance had to meet strict accessibility standards (Seidler, 1997). Public Law 94-142 established appropriate free education for children in an environment that is least restrictive (Seidler). Under Section 504 guidelines, "qualified handicapped persons" are protected from discrimination (Carpenter, 2000. p. 187). A "qualified handicapped person" is one who

1. Has a physical or mental impairment which substantially limits one or more major life activities,

2. Has a record of such an impairment, or

3. Is regarded as having such an impairment. (Carpenter, p. 187)

In addition, "major life activities include 'caring for one's self, performing manual tasks, walking, seeing, hearing, speaking, breathing, learning, and working'" (Carpenter, p. 187).

The Amateur Sports Act of 1978, also referred to as Public Law 95-606, followed the Rehabilitation Act legislation (Seidler, 1997; Wong, 1994). Although broadly based to coordinate and increase amateur participation in athletics, the act also called for "encouragement and assistance to 'amateur athletic programs and competition for handicapped individuals'," among other items (Wong, 1994, p. 165).

The Americans With Disabilities Act

The Americans With Disabilities Act (Public Law 101-336) has been called the most sweeping and most far-reaching piece of legislation to positively affect those with disabilities (Seidler, 1997; Wolohan, 2001). The Act decrees the full accommodation of disabled persons in language that is clear and enforceable (Seidler). A disabled person is someone who

1. Has a physical or mental impairment that substantially limits one or more of his/her major life activities;

2. Has a record of such impairment; or

3. Is regarded as having such an impairment. (Miller, 1997, p. 131)

Persons with disabilities must be granted equal access to an event.

The first classification above relates to conditions or diseases such as AIDS, cancer, mental retardation, and it is generally what people associate with the scope of ADA (Miller, 1997). The second classification would allow an individual to show, through medical records, that they should be covered under the ADA. Third is the classification that represents and prohibits a stereotype or preconceived notion about someone with a disability. Although physical impairments are easier to discern and provide accommodations for, mental conditions are more difficult to accommodate. A major factor of disabilities covered under the ADA is that the condition "substantially limits one or more" of primary life activities such as eating, breathing, learning, and walking (Miller, 1997, p. 132; Seidler, 1997, pp. 196-197).

In total, the ADA has five components, which encompass discrimination in employment, state and local government concerns, public accommodation, telecommunications, and a final miscellaneous category (Miller, 1997).

The sport manager needs to be cognizant of making facilities available to all persons in a reasonable manner.

Specific to sport facilities, Title III of the ADA provides no individual shall be discriminated against on the basis of disability in the full and equal enjoyment of the goods, services, facilities, privileges, advantages, or accommodations of any place of public accommodation by any person who owns, leases, or operates a place of public accommodation (Wolohan, 2001a).

Persons interested in pursuing a Title II claim must prove the following:

1. The individual is disabled;

2. The sport business represents a "private entity" operating a "place of public accommodation"; and

3. The person was denied the opportunity to "participate in or benefit from services or accommodations on the basis of his disability," and that reasonable accommodations could be made which do not fundamentally alter operations of the sport business. (Miller, 1997, p. 153)

In plain language, the sport manager needs to be cognizant of making facilities available to all persons in a reasonable manner. The ADA does not require separate facilities for those with disabilities; in fact, the intent is to grant access and interaction with all. In this way, the ADA influences the equipment, programs, and design of facilities so that "reasonable accommodation" may be made (Seidler, 1997).

The Justice Department has identified accessible restrooms for each gender as a major priority.

Another term worth defining is that of *public accommodation*. Public accommodation has been defined and related to sport facilities as affecting interstate commerce (Fried, 2000) and

Places of Lodging—Example: Ski Resorts, vacation hotels, motels renting six or more rooms

Establishments serving food, drink—Example: Sport Bars, lounges in health clubs

Places of public gathering—Example: Auditoriums, convention centers, lecture halls

Sales or rental establishments—Example: Athletic equipment stores

Sport Facilities
and the ADA

Service establishments—Example: Sport medicine clinics, sport masseuse, professional sport agent business, and insurance offices

Public transportation terminals, depots, or stations (not including facilities related to air transportation)—Example: Arenas, stadiums providing transportation from parking lot to area of event

Places of public display or collection—Example: The Baseball Hall of Fame

Places of recreation—Example: Parks, zoos, and amusement parks

Places of education—Example: Nursery schools, elementary, secondary, undergraduate, or postgraduate private schools

Social service center establishments—Example: Day-care centers

Places of exercise, recreation—Example: Gymnasium, health clubs, bowling alleys, golf courses.   (Miller, 1997, p. 152)

Under ADA requirements, all places of public accommodation must remove all barriers to access as long as such access is "readily achievable." Readily achievable is somewhat difficult to define, but generally speaking, if services cannot be provided, new services need to be created. In addition, new construction must meet ADA standards unless it is impractical to do so. Furthermore, requirements of the ADA apply to facilities that are owned by individuals in the government, nonprofit, or private sectors (Fried, 2000).

Readily Achievable

The regulations for present facilities differ from those for facilities that are undergoing significant renovation or are newly constructed. In the case of a new facility or one undergoing major renovations, the guidelines for ADA standards are quite clear (Seidler, 1997). However, those covering present facilities are more complicated. Many times, it is difficult to determine whether the removal of structural barriers is "readily achievable." However, if mats, or boxes, or the like obstruct a hallway, the removal of these barriers to allow a wheelchair to pass would constitute "readily achievable" (Miller, 1997).

1. The nature and cost of the action;

2. The overall financial resources of the site or sites involved; the number of persons employed at the site; the effect on expenses and resources; legitimate safety requirements necessary for safe operation, including crime prevention measures; or any other impact of the action on the operation of the site;

3. The geographic separateness, and the administrative or fiscal relationship of the site or sites in question to any parent corporation or entity;

4. If applicable, the overall financial resources of any parent corporation or entity; the overall size of the parent corporation or entity with respect to the number or its employees; the number, type, and location of its facilities;

5. If applicable, the type of operation or operations of any parent corporation or entity, including the composition, structure, and functions of the work force or the parent corporation or entity.

Table 5.1. Five-Part Test to Determine if Facility Is "Readily Achievable"

Note. From *Sport Business Management* by L. K. Miller, 1997 (Gaithersburg, MD: Aspen), pp. 155-156.

Installing ramps

Making curb cuts in sidewalks and entrances

Repositioning shelves

Rearranging tables, chairs, vending machines, display racks, and other furniture

Repositioning telephones

Adding raised markings on elevator control buttons

Installing flashing alarm lights

Widening doors

Installing offset hinges to widen doorways

Eliminating a turnstile or providing an alternative accessible path

Installing accessible door hardware

Installing grab bars in toilet stalls

Rearranging toilet partitions to increase maneuvering space

Insulating lavatory pipes under sinks to prevent burns

Installing a raised toilet seat

Installing a full-length bathroom mirror

Repositioning the paper towel dispenser in a bathroom

Creating designated accessible parking spaces

Installing an accessible paper cup dispenser at an existing inaccessible water fountain

Removing high pile, low density carpeting

Installing vehicle hand controls

Table 5.2. The Following Remedies for Various Barriers Have Been Designated
Note. From *Sport Business Management* by L. K. Miller, 1997 (Gaithersburg, MD: Aspen), p. 157.

Newly Constructed Facilities

Newly constructed facilities, or any facility of public accommodation occupied after January 16, 1993, must meet the strict guidelines of the ADA (Miller, 1997). For example, new buildings must install an elevator when the building has more than three stories and when each floor has more than 3000 square feet. In addition, half of all drinking fountains must be accessible to people in wheelchairs when there is more than one fountain per floor (Miller, 1997). Interestingly, or amazingly, the ADA guidelines are not all-inclusive. However, professional standards may ensure accessibility in these areas. If they do not, the ADA guidelines mandate that at least one area of the aforementioned facilities be accessible (Miller, 1997). For example, a specific machine in an exercise room must be accessible to those with disabilities.

Alterations

On the subject of facility alterations, the regulations take into account that not all alterations need to meet ADA requirements. For example, in a gym, primary function areas, such as the exercise room, would have to meet ADA standards, whereas nonprimary function areas, such as the mechanical room, would not. In addition, the "path of travel" to a primary function area should meet ADA requirements. Furthermore, the law stipulates that accommodations do not need to exceed 20% of the cost of renovation (Miller, 1997).

An accessible entrance

An accessible route to the altered area

At least one accessible restroom for each sex or a single unisex restroom

Accessible telephones

Accessible drinking fountains

Table 5.3. Alterations Prioritized by the Department of Justice

Note. From *Sport Business Management* by L. K. Miller, 1997 (Gaithersburg, MD: Aspen), p. 159.

Other alterations may include, but are not limited to, removing seats and leveling the floor to incorporate wheelchairs, installing communication aids such as telephone devices for the deaf (TDDs) and Braille placards (Fried, 2000).

> ADA regulations are not intended to impose undue hardship on the sports business owner but to ensure equal access.

Planning for accessibility for the disabled may start in the venue parking lot.

Cost. It should be remembered that the ADA calls for renovations or alterations or additions that are "readily achievable" (Fried, 2000). Therefore, the regulations are not intended to impose undue hardship on the sports business owner but rather to ensure inclusion and equal access. Therefore, an expense that would impose undue hardship can be avoided, such as major structural renovation. However, all other efforts must be made to make accommodations when reasonable. Other options for ADA compliance and cost reduction can be achieved through tax deductions. For example, according to G. B. Fried (2000), the following codes are worthy of note:

Internal Revenue Code 190. Up to $15,000 of ADA allowable expenditures can be deducted. Capital expenditures are considered material over $15,000.

Internal Revenue Code Section 44. Small businesses with fewer than 30 employees and less than $1 million in sales can receive a credit of 50% of the accommodation's cost, as long as the total cost is between $250 and $10,250 in one year.

Exemptions

Truly private organizations are exempt from ADA requirements (Miller, 1997). However, if a private institution had a restaurant open to the public, invited nonmembers to participate in tournaments, or advertised in a public medium, it would no longer hold private status. Other factors that determine privacy include substantial fees and exclusivity of membership (Miller, 1997).

In a similar vein, religious organizations are also exempt from ADA legislation. However, if a private organization, such as a sport camp, were to rent or lease the religious facility for an event, that camp would have to provide accommodation under ADA guidelines (Miller, 1997).

Case Law

The landmark case involving ADA legislation, specifically Title III accommodation for sports programs, was *Anderson v. Little League Baseball, Inc.* (Fried, 2000). In this case, Little League Baseball enacted a policy prohibiting wheelchair-bound coaches due to the potential collision between a player and a coach. Under scrutiny from the court, it was found that the Little League's position was based upon stereotypes and misconceptions. In fact, the Little League had not taken any steps to assess the merits of its own rule. As a result, the rule was abolished (Fried, 2000).

From a practical sense, this case shows that rules cannot be made arbitrarily (Miller, 1997). For example, persons in wheelchairs could not indiscriminately be prohibited from participating in a cardio boxing class. Direct evidence must be shown for a person with a disability to be excluded from an activity. If the evidence does not exist, the facility faces the possibility of a lawsuit and, perhaps more damaging, a public relations nightmare.

Another case directly linked to Title III of the Americans With Disabilities Act was *Montalvo v. Radcliffe* (1999). In this case, the plaintiff, a 12-year-old boy, wanted to take karate lessons with his friends. On his application, the plaintiff and his parents stated that he was in good health and free from disease. However, later that day the owner of the karate school received an anonymous phone call that the plaintiff had AIDS. The plaintiff's parents vehemently denied the accusation at first, but later admitted its truth. They were afraid the plaintiff would not be able to participate in karate lessons with his friends if the truth were known. The defendant disallowed the plaintiff from participating with other students, because there was significant chance of blood exchange from the physical blows, but he offered to teach the plaintiff privately. The Montalvos rejected this offer and consequently sued.

After examination of the facts, it was determined that "a place of public accommodation is entitled to exclude a disabled individual from participating in its program 'where such individual poses a direct threat to the health or safety of others'" (*Montalvo v. Radcliffe*, 1999, in 42 U.S.C. Sec. 12182(b)(3)). Therefore, even though the karate school was a place of public accommodation, it was unreasonable to change the method of instruction so significantly as to protect all participants from harm. As a result, in this case, the plaintiff's exclusion from participation did not violate Title III of the ADA.

> Accommodation must be balanced with practicality and safety concerns.

For the sport manager, the lessons to be learned from the previous cases are that one must certainly not eliminate someone from a particular activity based on stereotypes or fear. In many cases, accommodations can be made that do not substantially alter the activity. However, it must also be remembered that accommodation needs to be balanced with practicality and safety concerns. If one approaches activities with common sense and an open mind, accommodation can be effective and practical, and it can positively impact participants from many walks of life.

Planning and Accommodations

Solutions to ADA accommodation begin with careful examination of the current state of affairs. You could hire a consultant or simply appoint a person within the facility to research and audit the situation. That person should review applicable ADA requirements, listen to the needs of the customer, and travel a path similar to the one that someone with a disability might journey (Fried, 2000). Next, documentation should be prepared as to what was found, what can be done, and the dates for completion of renovation. This material serves two purposes: one, it sets a timeline for completion of the task at hand; two, it provides documentation if an ADA lawsuit were to arise alleging improper adherence to legislation (Fried, 2000).

When planning a facility that is accessible to those with disabilities, it is important to be cognizant of the wheelchair-bound, but not to limit your thinking to only one type of disability (Seidler, 1997). For example, it is also important to recognize the needs of those on crutches and of those with visual, hearing, speech, mental, and physical weakness impairments (Fried, 2000; Seidler). For the facility manager, it may be a worthwhile exercise to put yourself in the position of a person with a disability and tour your facility. Start in the parking lot in a wheelchair and attempt to access all primary locations within the facility; then try the same maneuvers on crutches, blindfolded, etc. This could also be an eye-opening exercise for your staff. In addition, training your staff on the issues of persons with disabilities can be a very worthwhile experience. It may be necessary to bring in a consultant or perhaps to simply discuss the issues and how persons with disabilities should be treated (Seidler). Finally, follow-up and regular checks to ensure that accommodations are adequate are helpful in preventing a lawsuit, and more important, in maintaining an environment where all patrons have equal access to facilities (Fried).

Specifics

The following are potential areas to be cognizant of when determining ADA compliance. This list is not all-inclusive. Rather, it is a point of departure.

Parking area. Make sure that there are adequate spaces for people with disabilities and that the area between the spaces is large enough to maneuver a wheelchair between vehicles. Provide signs to direct patrons to the nearest accessible entrance.

Entranceways. There should be a minimum of 60" X 60" of level space to allow for adequate maneuvering. All doors should be relatively easy to open. Doormats should not impede entrance. Automatic door openers should be positioned so that the doors do not hit an individual when opening. Floors should be covered with a nonslip surface or carpeting.

Stairs. Stairs should be constructed of a nonslip surface. The railings should extend 12" at the top and bottom of stairs. Handrail height should be between 34" and 38" and less than 1 1/2" diameter.

Elevators. Visual and auditory travel direction signals must be available. Call buttons need to be 42" from the floor and unobstructed. Doors should open 32" wide. The elevator itself should be no more than 1/2" from level on any floor. Handrails should be 34" to 36" above the elevator's floor. The control panel should be no more than 48" above the floor.

Public restrooms. Mirrors and paper towel dispenser should be 40" from floor. Toilet stalls should have an area of 30" x 48" in front for adequate maneuvering. Markers and signs should direct patrons easily to the facility.

Telephones. Dial and coin slot should be no more than 48" from the floor. Receiver cord should be at least 30" long. Phone directories should be usable at wheelchair level. The handset should have an amplification mechanism as well as TDDY capabilities.

Water fountains. Fountains should be at least 27" high and 17"-19" deep. Control buttons should be easy to manipulate (Fried, 2000)

Sports Participation and the ADA

Specific to various sports, Stein (1998) has suggested several accommodations noteworthy for the facility and sport manager.

Track and field. In track and field, position the starting pistol in the downward, rather than the toward-the-sky position, to make it easier for a deaf runner to see the smoke from the gun or perhaps equip the starter with a beacon as well as the gun to signify the start of a race. In addition, partially blind runners can be given communication devices to wear so that a coach can guide them around the track. Furthermore, it may be possible for athletes to compete in events such as the shot put with coaches in the circle and with appropriate tie-downs. For expediency, an official could allow the athlete to complete all of his or her preliminary throws in succession.

Swimming. In swimming, you could permit starting in the water rather than in blocks or holding a person's ankle until the starting gun sounded.

Tennis. In a tennis double's match, it may be possible for two people in wheelchairs to follow the same rules as their able-bodied counterparts.

The aforementioned suggestions are not meant to be exhaustive or exact stipulations, but rather suggestions to achieve reasonable accommodation.

> When reasonable accommodation can be made and the idea of stereotyping can be eliminated to some degree, the purpose of the ADA will have begun to take shape.

Final Thoughts

The primary goal of the Americans With Disabilities Act was to mainstream and incorporate individuals into society as much as possible to ensure equal opportunity (Fried, 2000). When reasonable accommodation can be made and when the idea of stereotyping can be eliminated to some degree, then the purpose of the ADA will have begun to take shape. It is up to the facility manager to be cognizant of areas where accommodations can take place, evaluate their reasonableness, and, if appropriate, take action. Doing so will not only prevent lawsuits, but can also make the facility a more open and welcoming venue for all who enter.

Summary

1. President George H. W. Bush signed the Americans With Disabilities Act (ADA) into law in 1990.

2. The ADA protects individuals with disabilities from discrimination. Specific to sports facilities, the law states that managers must provide "reasonable accommodations" for individuals with disabilities.

3. The overarching goal of the Americans With Disabilities Act was to mainstream and incorporate individuals into society as much as possible to ensure equal opportunity. Specific to the ADA is Title III, which prohibits discrimination of access or participation related to facilities.

4. In 1970, OSHA created specifications for equipment, maintenance, and safety in construction. Also in the 1970s, Congress was interested in creating opportunities for individuals with various disabilities. The first of the laws created was the Rehabilitation Act of 1973. Following this legislation was another piece established as the Amateur Sports Act of 1978, also referred to as Public Law 95-606.

5. The Americans With Disabilities Act (Public Law 101-336) decrees the full accommodation of disabled persons in language that is clear and enforceable.

6. Disability, as defined by the ADA, is "a physical or mental impairment that substantially limits one or more of an individual's major activities of daily living such as walking, hearing, speaking, seeing, learning, and performing manual tasks."

7. The ADA influences the equipment, programs, and design of facilities so that "reasonable accommodation" may be made.

8. Public accommodation has been defined and related to sport facilities as affecting interstate commerce, places of lodging, establishments serving food and drink, places of public gathering, and sales or rental establishments, among others.

9. Under ADA requirements, all places of public accommodation must remove all barriers to access as long as such removal is readily achievable.

10. Determination of readily achievable can be performed through a five-part test developed by the Department of Justice. In addition, the Department of Justice has identified examples of removal to barriers, which are readily achievable.

11. A newly constructed facility, or any facility of public accommodation occupied after January 16, 1993, must meet the strict guidelines of the ADA. In addition, the "path of travel" to a primary function area should meet ADA requirements. Furthermore, the law stipulates that accommodations do not need to exceed 20% of the cost of renovation.

12. Interestingly, or amazingly, the ADA guidelines are not all-inclusive. For example, exercise equipment, bowling alleys, and golf courses are not covered. However, professional standards may ensure accessibility in these areas.

13. It should be remembered that the ADA calls for renovations or alterations or additions that are readily achievable. Therefore, the regulations are not intended to impose undue hardship on the sports business owner but rather to ensure inclusion and equal access.

14. Truly private organizations are exempt from ADA requirements. However, if a private institution had a restaurant open to the public, invited nonmembers to participate in tournaments, or advertised in a public medium, it may no longer hold private status (L. K. Miller, 1997).

15. A landmark case involving ADA legislation, specifically Title III accommodation for sports programs was *Anderson v. Little League Baseball, Inc.* From a direct practical sense, this case shows that rules cannot be made arbitrarily.

16. Solutions to ADA accommodation begin with careful examination of the current state of affairs.

17. When planning a facility that is accessible to those with a disability, it is important to be cognizant of persons in wheelchairs, but to not limit your thinking to only one type of disability (Seidler, 1997). Furthermore, follow-up and regular checks to ensure that accommodations are adequate are helpful in preventing a lawsuit and, more important, in maintaining an environment where all patrons have equal access to facilities.

18. Specific guidance from the ADA can help establish guidelines for compliance in structure and various activities. However, ultimately, it is up to the facility manager to be cognizant of areas where accommodations can take place, evaluate their reasonableness, and, if appropriate, take action. Doing so will not only prevent lawsuits, but can also make the facility a more open and welcoming venue for all who enter.

As you remember, Jeff Martinez, the owner of Old School Fitness (OSA) had concerns that his facility would not meet the standards of the Americans With Disabilities Act. Therefore, he asked his newly graduated assistant manager, Steve Rightway, for help. Please review the case at the beginning of the chapter along with the following questions for a comprehensive check and critical analysis of material covered.

Questions

1. Jeff Martinez received word that he might be sued for ADA violations. How could such a suit originate?

2. Would Jeff be obligated to install an elevator?

3. Are the parking spaces large enough for those with disabilities?

4. What potential problems could arise with the restroom's proximity to storage facilities?

5. How can you identify someone with a disability as expressed by the Americans With Disabilities Act?

6. What would constitute measures that are not "readily achievable"?

7. How would you go about training your staff in being cognizant of helping those with disabilities?

8. What are options for deferring some of the cost of renovation?

9. What is your first priority in making ADA alterations according to the text?

10. What stereotypes may exist for Jeff Martinez that Steve Rightway may have to overcome?

11. If a wheelchair basketball league were to be formed, and games played in Mr. Jeff Martinez's facility, what alterations to "able-bodied" basketball rules might have to be made?

12. What would be an appropriate method of follow-up for Steve after alterations had been made to ensure that proper procedures were being followed?

Chapter Six

Hiring Personnel

Eisha Brown, the manager of Summer Sport Camp, had just received news that her swimming director of 7 years, Steve, had left to start his own camp. With only 2 weeks until the start of the summer season, Eisha had to act quickly to hire another swimming director.

The first thing that Eisha did was to create a job announcement. The trouble was that because Steve had managed the swimming program for so long, Eisha did not know exactly what the program entailed. However, she put together what she could from memory and posted the announcement at several local businesses. In it, Eisha included the title of the position, the qualifications required, the details of the job, the pay rate, and the contact person for further information.

Eisha received several interested applicants and sorted through their various credentials. She chose three individuals whose experience and credentials seemed to match the position most closely. The first, Jason, had been a lifeguard for several seasons at Eisha's camp. Eisha knew Jason was a good worker, but she wasn't certain if Jason, a high school junior, was ready for the added responsibilities of the new position. The second candidate, Cole had been an aquatic director 10 years ago and wanted to get back in the business after taking some time off to help raise his two children. Eisha was not sure that Cole could juggle the responsibility of a family and the swimming position. The third candidate, Martina, had been a swimming director at a camp in another state the previous year. However, in that camp, there had been accusations of improper conduct toward campers. Unfortunately, Eisha could not get in touch with the director of the out-of-state camp to check on Martina's credentials, and her own camp was slated to begin in 2 days.

The various issues raised above will be discussed in depth in the following chapter. Keep this case in mind, and we will refer to it at the end of the chapter for a follow-up discussion.

Introduction

Sound hiring practices can significantly influence the health of the sport facility in terms of its other employees, its customers, and its economic stability. Sport organizations normally are very people oriented. Customers are cognizant of employee turnover and may, in fact, frequent a particular facility due to its personnel and the service they provide (Fried & Miller, 1998b). A facility manager should be aware that numerous lawsuits have arisen over instances where employees were not promoted or were discharged inappropriately (Fried & Miller, 1998b). Loss of productivity and ill feelings born from inadequate hiring decisions affect the entire institution (Billing, 2000). Moreover, the economic impact in hiring a new employee equates to approximately 15% of that person's salary (Fried & Miller, 1998b). It is much less costly from a legal, organizational, and customer-focused standpoint to apply good hiring practices up front rather than explain poor hiring decisions in the courtroom. A good hiring decision can lead to a healthy, inspired business (Miller, 1998). Therefore, hiring appropriate personnel is of prime importance because their influence is felt at many levels within the business (Billing, 2000). The following chapter will examine what those hiring practices consist of and how to help ensure that the right person is ultimately employed.

Human Resources

Human resource management (HRM) "involves all the ways in which employees interact in both the formal and informal context of the organization" (Billing, 2000, p. 5). In addition, HRM "is the study of systems and activities in organizations that influence employee behavior" (Linnehan, 2001, p. 111). The overall goal of human resources is to help the organization meet its short-term and long-term objectives (Linnehan). HRM may involve the functions of evaluation, motivation, promotion, and retention (Billing, 2000). Arguably, however, the most important function is that of staffing and selection.

The Job Itself

Before facility managers embark upon the hiring process, many steps are necessary to help gain the best employee possible. First and foremost is a job analysis. Recommended by the EEOC, a job analysis includes the tasks and roles associated with that particular job (Fried & Miller, 1998b). A specified list of responsibilities will help in recruiting the new hire and ensuring that the person selected for the job knows what is expected (Fried & Miller, 1998b). Also involved in this process is a determination of where the job fits in relation to the organizational chart and how this job relates to the overall schema of the organization (Billing, 2000). Employees and managers should be jointly involved in this analysis (G. Fried & Miller, 1998b). The more information gathered up front, the more satisfying result in the end.

> A job analysis details the tasks and roles associated with a particular job.

Writing the Job Description

Job descriptions should be explained to include the major responsibilities, whom the person reports to, and whom the person supervises. In addition, the description should give an overview of what that particular job entails (Billing, 2000). Although job descriptions may vary depending on a particular situation, job descriptions have five basic components.

Job Title

Essential Job Duties and Responsibilities

Job Qualifications

Starting Date

Name and Address of the Contact Person

Table 6.1. Basic Components of a Job Description

Note. From "Creating the Job," by G. Fried & L. Miller, in *Employment Law: A Guide for Sport, Recreation and Fitness Industries,* ed. H. Appenzeller, 1998 (Durham NC: Carolina Academic Press, p. 39.

In addition, common terms to describe a particular job may include, "supervise, train, host, organize, plan, schedule, life, carry, reach, diagram, maintain, clean...." (Fried & Miller, 1998b, p. 39).

The categories of essential job duties and responsibilities and job qualifications have been debated and in some instances taken to court to be resolved. Employers are advised to pursue descriptions that match *bona fide occupational qualifications* (BFOQ). Discrimination in hiring is acceptable, but it must be based on BFOQ criteria (Fried & Miller, 1998a). For example, if a job in a sport facility required heavy lifting as one of the duties, then eliminating applicants who could not lift a certain amount of weight would be acceptable, as long as the amount lifted corresponded directly to the duties at hand.

Well-thought-out and well-written job descriptions help to attract a focused applicant pool, prepare the interviewer and interviewee for specific questions, define employee and employer expectations, keep the new employee on task, and prevent them from doing too much and getting burned out or from overstepping their boundaries, provide information on promotion and evaluation to prevent duplication of effort, and potentially alert an employer that a certain position may not need to be filled due to changes in technology, customer base, etc. (Fried & Miller, 1998b).

> External recruitment requires the release of a position announcement.

What would you include in a job description for security personnel at your venue?

Finding the Employee

Recruiting employees is performed through numerous channels. Examples of various channels include external and internal recruitment options (Fried & Miller, 1998b). External recruitment consists of employment agencies, college placement centers, want ads, professional associations, internships, and unions (Fried & Miller, 1998b). This type of recruitment will be handled through a position announcement, which is a "public advertisement of positions to be filled" (Billing, 2000, p. 7). The announcement should include the primary duties of the position as well as salary, how to apply, benefits, qualifications, and the closing and starting date (Billing).

Employment agencies are beneficial due to direct outsourcing, avoidance of bulky EEOC record keeping, and potential transference of hiring liability. The downside, however, includes expense, loss of control, and legal responsibility for discrimination by the agency (Fried & Miller, 1998b). College placement centers are beneficial in that a number of potential candidates are all at a central location, the placement center can do a preliminary sorting of resumes, and expenses are kept to a minimum by having the recruiters travel rather than the candidates. Want ads in newspapers, journals, and the Internet provide viable locations for job advertisements. By placing ads in a variety of locations, you are actively recruiting applicants from many walks of life. Diversity can help a business in many ways and at the same time complies with EEOC statutes (Fried & Miller, 1998b).

Internships are generally a wonderful way for the employer to become acquainted with the employee and vice versa. It is an opportunity for both parties to try the job for a limited amount of time with no guarantees from either side. However, if the intern is hired, the employer gains a valuable employee, and the intern gets a foot in the door of the sport industry. From a legal standpoint, employers need to be cognizant of the fact that they are liable for any negligent conduct by the intern (Fried & Miller, 1998b).

Internal recruitment, or filling a position from within (Billing, 2000), has distinct advantages such as improving morale; it creates less risk by promoting an employee who has already demonstrated competence or ability, costs less in time and money, and it promotes loyalty (Fried & Miller, 1998b). However, the disadvantages include creating chaos by promoting someone above their ability, creating tensions among coworkers, increasing homogeneity, failing to generate outside or disparate opinions and the like. (Billing, 2000; Fried & Miller, 1998b). It has been suggested, when possible, to solicit applications from both inside and outside of the organization (Billing, 2000).

> Applications forms should be simple and straightforward.

Gathering Information

The application process can be timely, costly, and potentially litigious. In some instances, an application form is used. In others, resumes and cover letters are required. In still other cases, employers may receive unsolicited applications. In the sport industry, as people clamor for even an entry-level job, employers should be aware of the liability of this type of applications. The EEOC requires that all accepted resumes be kept on file for 2 years (Fried & Miller, 1998c).

Applications forms should be simple and straightforward, gathering all necessary information (Fried & Miller, 1998c). In addition, a closing date for the particular position should be stated, because the EEOC requires re-examination of a candidate's file for other jobs that may open in the future (Billing, 2000; Fried & Miller, 1998c).

General categories on an application include (Fried & Miller, 1998c)

Name. Asking a person's name is perfectly acceptable. However, asking for a prefix, such as Ms. or Mrs. is not acceptable because it relates to marital status and, therefore, is private and potentially discriminatory.

Work history. You may ask about a person's work history, his or her supervisor's name and contact information, and past salary.

Discriminating questions. Alerting applicants that you have a policy against nepotism is acceptable; however, questions relating to gender, height, religion, national origin, etc., are not.

Residence. It is permissible to inquire about an applicant's length and place of residence. However, it is not acceptable to ask if the person owns or rents or if he or she has lived abroad.

Age. Applicants may be asked to verify that they are at least 18 years of age, but may not be asked a birth date or when they graduated from high school because that can be perceived as age discrimination.

Dependents. You may not ask about the candidate's dependents in the hiring process.

Photo. You may not ask for a photograph of candidates until they are hired and then only for legitimate reasons such as security provisions.

Citizenship. Asking about citizenship is not permitted. However, you may ask about foreign language ability.

Arrests. You may not ask about arrests, but you can ask about prior convictions if they are job related. Furthermore, if an applicant is denied a job based on a prior conviction, the employer must be able to show how this would negatively affect performance.

Relatives. Nepotism may be an exclusionary rule. Once hired, it is permissible to ask for names and addresses of relatives in case of an emergency.

Military service. An employer may inquire into an applicant's position, duty, and experience in the Armed Forces.

Association. Information about associations that an applicant may belong to may be gained as long as they do not refer to age, sexual orientation, religion, ancestry, etc.

Medical. Medical questions that were routine at one time have been banned by the EEOC.

Before an interview, it is advisable to review the Equal Employment Opportunity Commission guidelines (Fried & Miller, 1998c). For example, the EEOC has specified that the following questions may ***not*** be used in a job interview or on an application:

1. Have you ever had or been treated for any of the following conditions or diseases? (Followed by a checklist identifying various conditions or diseases).

2. Please list all conditions or diseases for which you have been treated in the past three years.

3. Have you ever been hospitalized, and if so, for what?

4. Have you ever been treated by a psychiatrist or psychologist and if so, for what conditions?

5. Have you ever been treated for any mental condition?

6. Is there any health-related reason why you may not be able to perform the job for which you are applying?

7. Have you had a major illness in the last five years?

8. How many days were you absent from work last year due to illness?

9. Do you have any physical defects, which preclude you from performing certain kinds of work, and if so, please specify the defect and the specific work limitations.

10. Do you have any disabilities or impairments that may affect your performance in the position for which you are applying?

11. Are you taking any prescription drugs?

12. Have you ever been treated for drug addiction or alcoholism?

13. Have you ever filed for worker's compensation insurance coverage?

(Fried & Miller, 1998c, pp. 60-61)

Once the employment questions have been established to meet accepted guidelines, the applications should be grouped logically and concisely. In addition, a statement that confirms that the organization is an Affirmative Action/Equal Opportunity Employer (AA/EOE) is advised (Fried & Miller, 1998c).

As an employer moves to the interview, various conditions that are not illegally discriminatory should be developed. These criteria can help to "weed out" the undesirables and keep the good prospects. It is recommended that no more than five candidates be selected for interviews due simply to cost in time and money (Fried & Miller, 1998c). Applicants not selected for an interview should be sent a rejection letter in a timely fashion. Those selected for an interview should be called and alerted. Arrangements should be made by the employer for interview, food, and lodging. Accommodations and meals should be above average, but not extravagant (Fried & Miller, 1998c). In addition, an itinerary should be made available to the candidate.

Interviews may be structured, semistructured, or unstructured (Fried & Miller, 1998c). A *structured interview* includes rigid questions, a *semistructured interview* allows for follow-up questions, and an *unstructured interview* has no set plan. Each technique has its advantages and disadvantages depending on the situation. Preparation for an interview generally consists of first examining the job description, then reviewing the application, writing sample, test scores, references, etc. (Fried & Miller, 1998c).

> To keep cost in time and money to a minimum, no more than five candidates should be selected for interviews.

Special circumstances. If one is interviewing for a position that will have the responsibility of working with children, special consideration is warranted, and special guidelines should be followed (Fried & Miller, 1998c). A course of action may include

1. Follow-up with what hobbies are listed and if they are appropriate for someone of similar age and background. This can be a concern when dealing with [a] potential child sexual abuser.

2. Follow-up with what the applicant's attitudes are towards children.

3. Be cognizant of appropriate and inappropriate nonverbal queues given by the interviewee.

4. Be cognizant of potential problems if the applicant is single with no "age-appropriate" romantic relationships. You cannot ask if an applicant is single, but if he/she provides information, you are free to utilize such information in helping to make appropriate hiring decisions.

5. Be cognizant of potential problems if all activities and interests center on children.

6. Be sensitive, but also cautious, when an applicant was sexually abused as a child. An interviewee should not be asked about such matters, but the interviewee might offer such information. If the information is offered, and the interviewee has received or continues to receive treatment for the mental anguish, then they could be protected by the ADA.

7. Be cognizant of potential problems if the applicant is fearful of the adult world.

8. Be cognizant of potential problems if the applicant sees children as "pure," "innocent," and/or "clean."

9. Be wary if the applicant is overanxious to get the position.

10. Deny any applicant who is willing to bend the rules to allow overnights or other actions that might violate the employer's policies or rules.

11. Deny any applicant who abuses alcohol or drugs. Such actions are not discriminatory based on the critical need to properly supervise children which cannot be effectively accomplished when an applicant is under the influence.

(Fried & Miller, 1998c, p. 70)

To expedite the process of interviewing candidates for a position where they will be working with children, the following questions may help to provide information leading to a qualified candidate:

1. Why are you interested in the position?

2. How would you describe yourself?

3. Have you ever had to discipline a child, and how did you do it?

4. Why do you like to work with children?

5. What traits do you think you have that qualify you to supervise children?

6. What about the position/job appeals to you the most/least?

7. Are you familiar with the issues associated with child sexual abuse?

8. Have you read our policy statement concerning sexual abuse?

9. What do you think about the policy?

10. Have you ever been convicted of a criminal offense including criminal driving violations?

11. Have you ever worked in a position for which you were bonded?

12. How do you relate with children?

13. Are you aware of any problems or conditions that could interfere with your ability to care for children or in any way endanger any child under your care? (Fried & Miller, 1998c, pp. 71-72)

The aforementioned questions are to be used as a guide, not as hard and fast rules. However, by utilizing questions such as those mentioned, taking careful notes, and perhaps taping the interview with the interviewee's permission, a potential employer can find out very relevant information about the potential candidates.

Tests. The polygraph (or lie detector) test is no longer a viable tool in the interview process since it was made illegal by the federal government in 1988 (Fried & Miller, 1998c). Therefore, besides the aforementioned interview questions, other tests may be conducted to determine the fitness of a particular employee. Personality tests may be very valuable, and in fact, even the less expensive tests have merit. Drug testing, if it can be shown to have a link to the safety of the employee and the person under the employee's care is perfectly legal (Fried & Miller, 1998c). For example, a gym supervisor or a lifeguard could certainly warrant a drug test. However, it is important to be fair in testing. To that end, if drug testing is to be performed, no discrimination should be involved that would conspicuously exclude any group. In addition, applicants must be given notice of the test. Finally, if physical performance tests are used, such as being able to lift a certain amount of weight, the test must directly relate to the job at hand, and there must be no other way to perform the job (Fried & Miller, 1998c).

The interviewer. The interviewer is a critical link in the hiring process. This person can either promote or inhibit growth of the company. Good interviewers possess skills such as poise, maturity, freedom from biases and extreme opinions, and the ability to listen well and to think objectively and critically (Fried & Miller, 1998c).

If possible, two people should be present at each interview not only in the event that a discrimination case should arise but also as a means of assessing and checking reactions to an interview with a colleague. The interviewer should be very familiar with the institution's sexual harassment policy. In addition, if permission has been received beforehand, taping the interview may be wise from a legal as well as hiring standpoint. Prior to the interview, check the candidate's identification, but be careful not to gather restricted information. Use background checks, the police, and other means to further examine the individual's history. If anything on the application or what a candidate says during the interview seems out of place, make sure to address the discrepancy and ask follow-up questions. Finally, to assist in the affirmative action evaluation, ask the candidate how he or she learned of the position opening (Fried & Miller, 1998c).

> Taping an interview may be wise from a legal as well as a hiring standpoint.

Even the best interviewer may be fooled from time to time. That is why it is important to seek the opinions of others acquainted with the candidate. The reference check is of great importance (Fried & Miller, 1998c).

Checking the References

References can be checked either before or after the interview. References serve three purposes: They verify information cited on a resume, can alert an employer to potentially dangerous or dysfunctional behavior, and can help in the overall screening and hiring process (Fried & Miller, 1998c). References can be potentially problematic if former employers are unwilling to give information or leery about giving unfavorable information that could be used by former employees as grounds for a defamation lawsuit based on a negligent referral (Fried & Miller, 1998c; van der Smissen, 2001a). On the other end of the spectrum, if employers refuse to give information and the employee is subsequently hired and found to be incompetent, the present employer may decide to sue the former employer for failing to disclose important information about a poorly performing employee. To combat these competing ends, legislation has been enacted in many states to limit liability of those granting references.

Insert a waiver in the job application allowing reference checks to be made.

Be consistent on the number of references you call per applicant.

Ask similar questions of all references.

Ask only legitimate and legal questions.

Table 6.2. Ways to Avoid Reference Check Situations

(Fried & Miller, 1998c)

Still another suggestion for reference checks would be to provide former employers with a questionnaire that has been reviewed by the appropriate human resources personnel for its validity, legality, and direct application to the job at hand (Fried & Miller, 1998c).

Discrimination

Title VII of the Civil Rights Act of 1964

The Civil Rights Act of 1964 provides for equality in a general sense (Fried & Miller, 1998d). Title VII, a part of the 1964 act, addresses employment situations. Specifically, it is stated in Title VII:

i. It shall be an unlawful employment practice for an employer—

    a. To fail or refuse to hire or to discharge any individual, or otherwise to discriminate against any individual with respect to his compensation, terms, conditions, or privileges of employment, because of such individual's race, color, religion, sex, or national origin. (quoted in Fried & Miller, 1998d, p. 116)

Furthermore, Title VII applies to employers with 15 or more employees working 20 or more weeks per year (Fried & Miller, 1998d). The two types of discrimination within Title VII involve disparate treatment and disparate impact. *Disparate treatment* involves open discrimination based on religion, race, color, gender, or national origin (Fried & Miller, 1998d). *Disparate impact* addresses the consequence of a specific employment practice. For example, a job advertisement that, without logical rationale, required applicants to be a certain height or have a certain strength level would be held invalid. An example of a logical reason is called a *bona fide occupational qualification* (BFOQ). For example, if one were to hire only people who could successively lift 75 lbs. for a moving corporation, and lifting such weight was a central part of that job, then lifting a certain amount of weight could be a legal discriminating factor even if this were found to be a gender issue (Fried & Miller, 1998d).

Negligent Hiring

Negligence falls under the general body of law called *torts* (Wong, 1994). As such, it is an "unintentional act that injures" (van der Smissen, 2001b, p. 37). That is, although unintended, something that a person did or did not do resulted in another person's being hurt. Specifically, negligence is defined as

> the failure to exercise the standard of care that a reasonably prudent person would have exercised in a similar situation; any conduct that falls below the legal standard established to protect others against unreasonable risk of harm, except for conduct that is intentionally, wantonly, or willfully disregardful of others' rights. (Garner, 1999, p. 1056)

The elements used in a court of law to determine negligence consist of "duty, breach of duty, causation, and damages" (Garner, 1999, p. 1056; for more information related to negligence, please see chapter 9, "Facility Negligence").

> Reasonable efforts must be made to check the backgrounds, references, and qualifications of applicants.

Specifically related to hiring practices, negligent hiring is a potential problem for employers. "Negligent hiring occurs when the employer knows, or should have known, of an applicant's dangerous or violent propensities, hires the individual, and gives the employee the opportunity to repeat such violent behavior" (Fried & Miller, 1998e, p. 159). As an employer, it may be impossible to check for every circumstance and each situation for all prospective employees. However, reasonable efforts must be made to check the backgrounds, references, and qualifications of applicants (Carpenter, 2000). More to the point, one third of all resumes have falsely contrived information (Miller, 1998). Therefore, adequate background checks are very important. If this has not been done, the employer may be guilty of negligent hiring (G. Fried & Miller, 1998e).

Final Negotiations

Once a final candidate has been selected, the process of salary negotiation and benefits allocation begins. As an employer, you need to be cognizant of being honest about the working conditions, promotions, and personnel. If you are not, the employer may be guilty of fraud (Fried & Miller, 1998f).

After the offer has been made and accepted, an employee manual should be provided. This manual should be typeset so that it is easy to read, with some graphics, a color-coded table of contents, and perhaps a question and answer section (Fried & Miller, 1998f). In addition, some manuals may require the signature of the new hire to prove that he or she has, in fact, read the manual.

The contents of the manual or handbook should have, among other items, company history, philosophy, and mission, organizational chart, EEO/affirmative action statement, working hours/days, pay, raises, benefits, and sexual harassment policy (Fried & Miller, 1998f). Furthermore, the handbook will need to be updated and revised at regular intervals (Fried & Miller, 1998f). Finally, a contract is prepared, and signed, and the employee begins work on the agreed-upon date (Fried & Miller, 1998f; for an expanded look at contracts, please see chapter 7, "Contracts"). As a final suggestion, if at any time, it is found that the applicant falsified information on the application, the person should be terminated. If an employee is not terminated, and he or she performs a service inadequately or criminally—an outcome that could have been known by the discrepancy in the resume—the employer could be liable for negligent retention (Fried & Miller, 1998c).

Summary

1. Sound hiring practices can significantly influence the health of the sport facility related to its other employees and, ultimately, its customers. Sport organizations in particular are very people oriented. Therefore, hiring appropriate personnel is of prime importance because their influence is felt at many levels within the business.

2. Before facility managers embark upon the hiring process, many steps are necessary to help gain the best employee possible. First and foremost is a job analysis. Recommended by the EEOC, a job analysis includes the tasks and roles associated with that particular job. A specified list of responsibilities will help in recruiting the new hire and ensuring that the person selected for the job knows what is expected.

3. Once the employment questions have been established to meet accepted guidelines, the applications should be grouped logically and concisely. In addition, a statement that confirms that the organization is an affirmative action/equal opportunity employer (AA/EOE) is advised.

4. Medical questions that were routine at one time have been banned by the EEOC.

5. If you are interviewing for a position that will have the responsibility of working with children, special consideration is warranted, and special questions should be asked.

6. Before an interview, it is advisable to see the Equal Employment Opportunity Commission guidelines.

7. The interviewer is a critical link in the hiring process. This person can either promote or inhibit growth of the company. Good interviewers possess skills such as poise, maturity, freedom from biases and extreme opinions, the ability to listen well and to think objectively and critically.

8. Reference checks can be conducted either before or after the interview. References serve three purposes: they verify information cited on a resume, can alert an employer to potentially dangerous or dysfunctional behavior, and can help in the overall screening and hiring process.

9. Last, a contract is prepared, and signed, and the employee begins work on the agreed-upon date. If all has been done properly, it is hoped that the employer and employee will be satisfied.

Questions

At the beginning of this chapter, we looked at the case of Eisha Brown, the summer camp manager who was looking for a swimming director. To review the case and the material presented in this chapter, please address the following questions:

1. How would you write the job announcement for the swimming director?

2. Where else could Eisha have posted the announcement?

3. What specific qualifications would you look for in an application/resume?

4. From the three finalists, are there any mistakes that Eisha may be possibly making?

5. Is there any way to solve some of the problems that Eisha faces with respect to Martina?

6. What steps in the hiring process has Eisha forgotten?

7. Who would be your perfect candidate for the job?

8. From the finalists selected, whom would you hire and why?

Chapter Seven

Contracts

Preferred or premium seating has been a mainstay in sport facilities built within the last ten years. Premium seating is generally located in a luxury suite with excellent sight lines of the game, and it entitles its patrons to services and amenities such as special parking, wait-staff, and restaurants. This type of seating is among the most expensive and usually requires holders of the seats to agree to a multi-year contract. Facility managers have attempted to ensure these agreements are upheld because money from premium seating is the most important source of revenue for facility operation and construction (Wong, 2000). Due to the expense and longevity of this type of contract, patrons may attempt to cancel the agreement prior to the end of its term.

A specific case that revolves around these contractual issues is *New Boston Garden Corporation v. Baker* (1999). In this case, Baker signed a 3-year, 18-page contract that entitled him to sit in a type of luxury seat, called a club seat, to watch the NBA's Boston Celtics and the NHL's Boston Bruins (Wong, 2000). For this privilege, he agreed to pay $18,000 per year. Before the contract terms were up, he breached the agreement due to marital problems, a son's being diagnosed with cancer, and the teams' performing at a substandard level. In fact, due to the teams' poor performance, more than 2,000 seats went unsold per game (Wong, 2000).

As you might imagine, with so many unsold seats, the New Boston Garden Corporation (NBGC), the management group for the Celtics and Bruins, was in dire need of money, including revenue from club seats. Therefore, NBGC sued Baker for breach of contract.

If you were to decide this case, how would you proceed? What confounding factors make this a difficult case? How would your perspective and arguments change depending on which side of the issue you chose? Please keep these questions and the case in mind as we explore contracts as they relate to facilities.

Introduction

In today's litigious society, contracts have become a ubiquitous facet of the business world. In sports, and for the facility manager specifically, contracts are an important and many times necessary fact of life. As a general rule, most relationships involving contracts involve personal service or goods (Carpenter, 2000). More specifically, contracts may be used for television and sponsorship coverage, contest scheduling, equipment purchases, player and coaching assignments, facility leases, licensing agreements, limiting liability with insurance coverage, officials for games, injuries on the field, and scholarships, just to name a few (Wilde, 2001; Wong, 1994). As this chapter unfolds, it should be noted that legal representation should be sought for all-important contractual matters. However, the contract concepts in this chapter can give an overview, provide information, and help you avoid troubling situations (Wilde). Furthermore, by examining the principles involved in a contract, the facility manager is in a more advantageous position to explain his or her needs to legal counsel, thereby establishing a well-written, well-served contract. The contract itself should represent the worst-case scenario to prevent mishaps. Although this may seem like overkill to some, the reality of a poorly written contract can have sweeping ramifications, not the least of which is the common occurrence of dispute resolution involving ambiguity of contract terms settled against the party who drafted the original document (Sharp, 1996).

Contract law is primarily based on common law (court decisions) except where it has been codified. The Restatement and Second Restatement of Contracts, 1932 and 1982, respectively, are prime examples. However, more to the point, the Uniform Commercial Code (UCC) governs commercial transactions in all states but Louisiana (Wilde, 2001). Of specific interest to the facility manager is Article 2 of the UCC. This particular section addresses the sale of items including game tickets and sporting goods (Wong, 1994). According to the UCC in Article 2-201, goods sold in an amount of more than $500 must have a written contract, or the sale is unenforceable (Sharp, 1996; UCC, 1972; Wilde, 2001; Wong, 1994). In addition, facility lease agreements, real estate sales, coaching contracts, long-term scheduling contracts, and other matters not performed within a one-year period of time need to be in writing (*UCC*, 1972, Section 2-201; Wilde; Wong, 1994). As a general rule, it cannot be stressed enough that administrators should have all important matters spelled out in written contracts (Wilde). A paper trail of information can help avoid conflicts, aid in the speed of resolution, and help increase the chances of winning if the situation presents itself in a court of law. Therefore, it behooves the wise facility manager to pay close attention to the following concepts and to use them judiciously.

Definition of a Contract

Many people associate contracts with promises. To a large degree, this association is accurate, but not completely so. A promise may begin the process of a contract, but does not complete the deal (Wilde, 2001). A contract is defined as "a promise, or set of promises, for breach of which the law gives a remedy, or the performance of which the law in some way recognizes as a duty" (Wilde, p. 364). In addition, a contract is seen as "an agreement between parties which is enforceable under the law" (Wong, 1994, p. 64). It can be either oral or written, and it includes a promise to perform an act (Wong, 1994).

Types of Contracts

Bilateral Contract. In this type of a contract, each party promises to perform an act on the condition that the other party will also perform an act (Wilde, 2001). Within this type of agreement, a conditional exchange of promises has been met (Wong, 1994). For example, one person would pay $1, 000 to a facility manager if the manager would lease gym space for a specified day and time.

Unilateral Contract. In this particular case, there is not an exchange of promises (Wong, 1994). In this example, only one party promises to perform an act, whereas the other party is not bound to accept the offer. However, if the other party does accept, then the first party is obligated to hold up its end of the deal (Wilde, 2001). For example, between games during a volleyball match, spectators may be invited to participate in a game of skill to see who can serve a volleyball into a specified area for a prize. This is a unilateral contract because the spectators are not required to participate, but if they do, and if they win the game of skill, then they are legally entitled to receive their prize.

What type of contract did the NCAA and the Georgia Dome enter into for the 2002 Men's Final Four?

Specifically, a contract involves the concepts of meeting of the minds (Carpenter, 2000), offer, acceptance, consideration, (Sharp, 1996; Wilde, 2001), legality, capacity (Sharp; Wong, 1994), and intention to create legal relations (Wilde, 2001).

Meeting of the minds. From a conceptual standpoint, the buyer and seller must agree to what is being bargained over. If one or both parties are unclear about what has been agreed to, the contract is not valid (Carpenter, 2000).

Offer. An offer is defined as a conditional promise made by one party to another party (Sharp, 1996; Wilde, 2001). The offer may cease to exist if the other party does not act in a reasonable time or if the allotted time has elapsed (Carpenter, 2000). In a related manner, an offer can be revoked at any time unless there has been an agreement to keep the contract open for specified amount of time; this is called an *option contract* (Carpenter). For this scenario, the buyer pays the seller to keep the contract date open for a certain length of time. If the buyer decides to decline the offer, that person loses the money paid for the option. However, the seller is bound to the terms if the buyer accepts under the agreed time constraints (Carpenter).

An offer will generally include "1) the parties involved, 2) the subject matter, 3) the time (and place) for the subject matter to be performed, and 4) the price to be paid" (Wong, 1994, p. 65).

> Only upon "offering" to pay for a product does the contractual relationship begin.

Confusion will sometimes arise as to what constitutes a valid offer in the sport business world. Many times the legality of the offer will depend on the specific situation. Nevertheless, there are some offers that can be discussed in general. For example, offers that are made in "jest" are not considered legally binding offers (Wong, 1994). Likewise, an advertisement is not an offer; rather it is an invitation to buy (Carpenter, 2000). Only upon "offering" to pay for a product does the contractual relationship begin (Carpenter). In the same vein, price quotes are not an offer as they are more of an opinion (Wong, 1994). However, "first come, first served" would be considered an offer (Wong, 1994, p. 67).

Acceptance. Once an offer is made, that offer can be accepted only by the party to whom the offer was presented (Sharp, 1996; Wilde, 2001; Wong, 1994). The affirmation can be in words or actions, and it must be agreed to in the same terms as was originally offered (UCC, 1972, Section 2-206; Wilde, 2001). If the offeree changes terms, the original contract is void, and the new contract would be considered a counteroffer (Wilde). In addition, if the offer is rejected outright, if there is a significant passage of time, or if the other party dies or is incapacitated, the offer would no longer be valid (Wong, 1994).

Consideration. Consideration, also called "legal detriment" (Wong, 1994, p. 69), is an "exchange of value" between bargaining parties (Sharp, 1996, p. 187). In addition, "there must be a mutual exchange of consideration" for a valid contract to be formed (Wilde, 2001, p. 365). Even in a unilateral contract, there is consideration, because the person performing the act is said to have met consideration requirements (Wilde).

On the other hand, an article that you receive unsolicited in the mail is considered a gift. Therefore, without mutual consideration, there has not been a contract formed, and the sender cannot legally ask to be compensated (Carpenter, 2000).

Within the concept of consideration arises another notion: *mutuality of obligation.* Under this premise, consideration given by both parties needs to be equivalent, but need not be identical (Wong, 1994). In other words, if land to be used for the lacrosse team's competition field were leased for the sum of $1.00, the compensation would not be identical. However, consideration could be considered equivalent and mutuality of obligation met if the lacrosse field carried the benefactor's name prominently on the scoreboard.

Legality. The courts will not enforce a contract that relies on illegal actions (Sharp, 1996; Wong, 1994). For example, contracts with unlicensed professionals, loan sharks, or gamblers will not be enforced (Sharp). Specific to sports, a contract between two people to switch urine samples in order to help an athlete pass a drug test or an agreement between friends to help an athlete pass an American history class and remain eligible would not be enforceable.

> A business does not have the capacity to enter into a contract, but the facility manager, as an authorized agent, does.

Capacity. Capacity is defined as "the ability to understand the nature and effects of one's actions" (Wong, 1994, p. 71). Generally speaking, a person who has reached the age of 18 and is mentally sound possesses the capacity to enter into a contract (Sharp, 1996; Wong, 1994). A minor (generally, someone under 18) or a person who is mentally incompetent (due to alcohol or drug consumption) may enter into a contract, but it is only binding against the other party, not the minor (Wilde, 2001). Therefore, contracts with minors are a "one-way street" and should be entered into with due caution (Carpenter, 2000, p. 113). On a related topic, a business such as a facility does not have the capacity to enter into a contract because it is not a person. However, the facility manager, as an authorized agent, does have capacity (Wilde, 2001).

Intent and specificity. Finally, there must be serious intent on the sides of both parties for a contract to be enforceable (Wilde, 2001). If the other requirements of a contract have been met, but the parties never intended to create a legally binding document, then there is no contract (Wilde). In addition, the terms of a contract must be precise enough to be followed (Carpenter, 2000). If not, the contract will be considered void.

Errors in Contracts

Misrepresentation. A contract can be voided if the facts were intentionally or unintentionally construed. However, this process must take place in a reasonable amount of time (Wilde, 2001).

Undo influence/duress. If a person has been unfairly persuaded to enter into a contract, the person who was in the less powerful position can generally void a contract. Under similar circumstances, if a person were forced into forming a contract by fear of life and limb or through economic hardship, that contract is considered voidable (Wilde, 2001).

Mistake. In the case of a mistake, the parties could be allowed to rewrite the contract (Sharp, 1996). However, unless the mistake was mutual or if a unilateral mistake is unconscionable, a mistake is not cause to void a contract (Wilde, 2001). The courts will investigate to see the varying explanations for the mistakes and make a ruling on the merits of the individual case (Wong, 1994). The lesson here is to be very careful when drafting a contract, because mistakes could come back to haunt you.

Integration and parole evidence. Many times a contract will contain an integration clause that states that the signed contract will be upheld "as is," and no other previous agreements that would add to or detract from the contract will be allowed. If this clause is in place, the Parole Evidence Rule states that no other information, even if it were discussed beforehand, will be considered binding if that information is missing from the signed document (Wong, 1994). In sum, the contract will be upheld as written.

Breach of Contract. A breach of contract is a "failure to perform a duty imposed under the contract" (Wong, 1994, p. 74). In other words, a breach is a failure to follow the guidelines set forth in the document itself.

Damages

To remedy a situation if a contract is broken, the courts may award compensatory packages or liquidated damages (money) in order to fulfill the obligation (Carpenter, 2000; Sharp, 1996; Wilde, 2001). The amount of compensation to be paid in a breach situation is determined at the time of the contract, not at the time of the breach (Carpenter). In addition, if a contract is broken, the courts may order that the person carry out the terms of the contract, when appropriate, called *specific performance* (Wilde, 2001).

In the coaching world, one resolution to a breach of contract may be to prevent the coach from rendering her service elsewhere if she were to breach her contract with the original university (Wilde, 2001). For example, in *New England Patriots Football Club, Inc. v. University of Colorado* (1979), the coach was prevented from hiring out his services to the university until his contract expired with the Patriots.

Delegation of Duties

If one party is unable to fulfill the contract as promised, the individual may delegate his or her duty to another party. However, if the second party is unable to meet the contract specifications, the first party may still be held liable (Wong, 1994). For example, it would be reasonable for a facility manager to contract with a sporting goods supplier for an order of premium leather basketballs. If the supplier could not fill the order, it would be legal to delegate the duty to another supplier. However, if the second supplier could not or did not fill the order, the original supplier would be liable for a breach of contract.

Defenses to Breach of Contract

There are three ways in which a contract can legally be dissolved (Wong, 1994). The first, "*impossibility of performance,*" exists when the matter originally contracted for was destroyed or became illegal, or when one of

Before putting fans in the stands, facility managers must ensure that all contractual obligations have been met.

the contracted parties died (Wong, 1994, p. 75). The second, *frustration of purpose*, exists when the value of the matter contracted for has become worthless due to unforeseen circumstances (Wong, 1994). *Impracticability* is the last breach of contract defense available. It is rarely used, but refers to a situation in which the cost of fulfilling a contract has dramatically increased. Examples of when this defense may be successful would be in a time of war, embargo, or crop failure (Wong, 1994).

> Monetary awards are generally the easiest and quickest forms of restitution for facility managers.

Breach of Contract Remedies

The most often used breach of contract remedy is monetary award (Wong, 1994). From a facility manager's perspective, monetary awards are generally more favorable, create less disgruntlement, and resolve the situation more quickly than other forms of restitution (Wong, 1994). However, specific performance may be utilized if monetary damages will not fully compensate the injured individual (Sharp, 1996). For example, if someone contracted to purchase a Michael Jordan Chicago Bulls basketball jersey and the owner of the jersey suddenly decided not to sell, the money to be paid would not necessarily allow someone to buy another such jersey because it might not be available in that price range. Therefore, the court may order that the jersey be sold as agreed in the contract. In employment cases, however, specific performance is generally not sought, because the courts see this as a form of involuntary servitude (Sharp, 1996).

Facility, Game, Event, and Sponsorship

In today's world, the facility manager may be asked to supervise a number of tasks, from the initial setup before a game to sponsorship acquisition to agreements between competitors (McMillen, 2001). To ensure that the aforementioned items are handled with diligence, care, and understanding, the formation of a contract is advised. In addition, the planning and foresight associated with contracts of this sort help to establish prudent risk management programs (McMillen).

Facility Contract

A facility contract allows the contracted person(s) to use the facility for a set period of time, for a set fee, and for a designated purpose (Sharp, 1996). An important facet of this type of a contract is an indemnification agreement. This type of agreement holds the facility owner harmless for the events contracted, and a provision that the contracted persons possess insurance for the event is usually required (Sawyer & Smith, 1999; Sharp, 1996). Contracts of this nature must be very specific as to the responsibilities of all parties involved. For example, considerations should be given to rent amount, method of payment, services provided by rental, promotion, setup, personnel, time of event, warm-up policy, potential for conflict with multiple lessees, radio and TV arrangements, and insurance (Wong, 1994).

Game Contract

A game contract is generally between two schools, which identify one game or a series of games to be played (McMillen, 2001). Included in this contract would be such items as location, date, time, provisions as to officials, guarantees (remuneration), broadcast rights, complimentary tickets, and termination clauses with compensation in the event of nonperformance in mind (Sharp, 1996). In addition, an option for renewal and locker room arrangements may be included (Sawyer & Smith, 1999).

Event Contract

An event contract includes more than a single game. It is associated with multiple affairs surrounding an event (McMillen, 2001). For example, an event contract for a particular conference tournament may, on the surface, appear to be a single-event proposition. Upon further examination, however, the event contract for the conference tournament includes many games and may include other items such as pre- and postgame activities, facility lease agreements, and sponsorship opportunities (McMillen, 2001).

> Facility managers should be wary of standard form contracts.

Issues to Consider

In developing game and event contracts, it is important to include event personnel, lease agreements, jurisdiction, and the use of licensed merchandise. Event personnel may consist of security, officials, emergency care professionals, and concessionaires (McMillen, 2001). Lease agreements must be in writing and may include items such as parking, maintenance, and merchandise (McMillen; UCC, 1972, Section 2-201). The state in which a particular game is played will affect the effectiveness of the contract. Therefore, it is essential that the state of jurisdiction be agreed upon when entering into the contract to avoid potential disputes at a later date (McMillen). Furthermore, licensed merchandise can generate large profits for an institution and should be protected legally through a license agreement (McMillen). Other items that may require a contract include concessions, merchandise, and services, such as medical and emergency care. In the aforementioned events, the astute facility manager should be wary of a standard form contract used by the supplier because such contracts are generally disadvantageous to the purchaser (Sawyer & Smith, 1999).

In times past, the Latin phrase, *caveat emptor* (let the buyer beware) was a doctrine that held that one buys at one's own risk. However, modern statutes and cases have changed the scope and sentiment of the rule (Garner, 1999). At present, *caveat venditor* (let the seller beware) reigns supreme (Garner, p. 215); restrictions and responsibility have gone to the seller. A more detailed description of the current state of affairs follows.

Goods Contracts

The UCC is a set of suggested laws that add uniformity of regulations to the states for business transactions (*West's Encyclopedia*, 1998). The guidelines help set standards between the seller and buyer. Article 2 of the UCC is particularly important to facility managers (Carpenter, 2000). Specific to Article 2 are the concepts of "implied warranty of merchantability, and implied warranty of fitness for a particular purpose" (Carpenter, p. 120).

Uniform Commercial Code

An implied warranty is not written, but understood. Therefore, provided you have bought a product from a merchant who regularly sells that particular type of merchandise and that particular product is merchantable, it is possible to be reimbursed if the product is unacceptable (Carpenter, 2000).

Implied Warranty of Merchantability

Pass without objection in the trade under the contract description

In the case of fungible goods, are of fair average quality within the description

Are fit for the ordinary purposes for which such goods are used

Run, within the variations permitted by the agreement, of even kind, quality and quantity within each unit and among all units involved

Are adequately contained, packaged, and labeled as the agreement may require

Conform to the promises or affirmations of fact made on the container or label if any.

Table 7.1. Qualities of Merchantable Products

(*UCC,* 1972, Section 2-314, p. 82-83)

If the product meets the previous criteria, but its quality is found to be severely lacking, the buyer has a legal right to be reimbursed, even if a receipt sold with the product explicitly denies that any warranties exist with the product, implied or explicit (Carpenter, 2000).

This particular type of warranty relies on advice given from a seller about a product (Carpenter, 2000). For this type of warranty to be effective, the goods must have been purchased from a seller who is regularly involved in the sale of that type of product and the seller must have known that the

Implied Warranty of Fitness

buyer might use the product for a specific use and that the buyer was making the decision to purchase that particular product based on the seller's information (Carpenter, 2000; UCC, 1972, Section 2-315). The implication from this type of warranty is that the facility manager needs to train her personnel adequately so that customers receive good advice about product purchases. In addition, the facility manager, who may purchase uniforms, sporting goods, or market the facility logo in order to protect her business adequately, should know the UCC as well as she knows the rules of any particular sport (Carpenter).

Both types of warranties discussed previously have the potential to be defeated if the merchant has labeled the product "as is" or with similar language (Carpenter, 2000, p. 121). It always behooves the buyer to follow the concept of *caveat emptor* and pay attention to the fine print (Carpenter).

Products and Strict Liability

The inclination to proceed from *caveat emptor* to *caveat venditor* has its roots in the 1916 case, *Macpherson v. Buick Motor Co.* (Garner, 1999). After this case, the doctrine became that "a buyer, user, consumer or bystander in proximity to an unreasonably dangerous product, and who is injured in person or in property by its dangerous propensities, may recover in damages from the manufacturer or intermediate seller" (Garner, 1999, p. 1225-1226).

Products liability is defined as

1. A manufacturer or seller's tort liability for any damages or injuries suffered by a buyer, user, or bystander as a result of a defective product. Products liability can be based on a theory of negligence, strict liability, or breach or warranty.

2. The legal theory by which liability is imposed on the manufacturer or seller of a defective product (Garner, p. 1225).

Products liability arises when someone is injured due to the use of a particular product (Carpenter, 2000). Facility managers may have patrons or employees involved in an injurious situation with products, and therefore, products liability is an important concept to understand. It may be possible to recover in a products liability claim under the doctrines of negligence, strict liability, and breach of warranty (Carpenter, 2000). A negligent product would be one in which the manufacturer did not use reasonable care in the design, production, packaging, labeling (failure to warn), and testing of that product (Carpenter; Wolohan, 2001b). Strict liability is a means to recover if it can be proven that the product, although not negligent under the legal definition, did possess a defect at the time of sale that was unreasonably dangerous and was what caused the injury (Carpenter, 2000). A breach of warranty can exist if a particular product was promoted to hold up to a certain standard and failed. This warranty can be either express or implied (Carpenter). An *express warranty* is one in which specific claims are made regarding the product (Wolohan, 2001b). For example, if a basketball rim had the claim that it met standards for breakaway rims but, in fact, would break under minimal force, that failure would be considered a breach. An *implied warranty* is the presumption that if a merchant sells a product, it will be reasonably safe (Wolohan, 2001b). However, if the product has been misused or altered by the consumer, the breach of warranty theory may no longer apply (Carpenter, 2000).

Strict products liability is defined as products liability arising when the buyer proves that the goods were unreasonably dangerous and that

> (1) the seller was in the business of selling goods, (2) the goods were defective when they were in the seller's hands, (3) the defect caused the plaintiff's injury, and (4) the product was expected to and did reach the consumer without substantial change in condition. (Garner, 1999, p. 1226)

Strict liability is also known as "liability without fault" (Wolohan, 2001b, p. 18). In general, the courts will find for the injured party if the product could have been made in a safer way (Wolohan, 2001b). On the other hand, in order for a manufacturer to win a product liability case, it should be shown that the product, given cost and usefulness, has been made as safe as possible.

The magnitude and seriousness of the danger in using the product.

The likelihood of injury.

The obviousness of the danger.

The product's utility to the public and the individual user.

The technological and economic feasibility of a safer design.

The ability to avoid injury by use of instructions or warnings.

The ability to have avoided injury by careful use of the product.

Table 7.2. Seven-Part Test Used to Settle "Risk-Utility" Debate

Note. From "Sports Law Report: Watch Your Step; Quinton Won Its Case, but the Effects of Product-Liability Law Are Wide-Ranging," by J. T. Wolohan, December 2001, in *Athletic Business 25*(12), p. 18.

Contracts drawn up by facility managers should be reviewed by an attorney.

The Contract Form

Contracts drawn up by facility managers should be reviewed by an attorney prior to execution and at least once per year thereafter. In addition, a facility manager needs to provide the attorney with as much information about the situation as possible to put that particular facility in the best legal stance possible (Wong, 1994).

Given the guidelines above, the following are general clauses found in most contracts (Wong, 1994, p. 78):

Opening. Identifies the parties to the agreement and also the date of the contract and its effective date.

Representations and warranties. Contains information regarding the rights and qualifications of the parties to enter into an agreement and also any express or implied warranties regarding the subject matter of the contract.

Operational language. Contains the subject matter of the contract. The precise rights and duties of the parties under the contract are explained.

Other clauses. Certain other clauses may be included, depending on the nature of the contract. Compensation, rights to arbitration for any disagreements, and the right to assign the contract are typical examples of other clauses.

Termination. Discusses the length of the contract and the means of ending the agreement.

Entire agreement and amendments. Details the comprehensiveness of the contract and its relation to other agreements and also the methods by which the contract can be amended.

Closing. Contains the signatures of the parties to the contract, any acknowledgments, and the signatures of any witnesses.

Summary

1. In today's litigious society, contracts have become a ubiquitous facet of the sport business world. Contracts may be used for contest scheduling, equipment purchases, player and coaching commitments, facility leases, licensing agreements, and teams' or officials' failing to show for a game, just to name a few.

2. By examining the principles involved in a contract, the facility manager is in a more advantageous position to explain his or her needs to legal counsel, thereby establishing a well-written, well-served contract.

3. Contract law is primarily based in common-law court decisions, save various codifications. For example, the Uniform Commercial Code (UCC) and its specific application to facility managers within Article 2 address the sale of items such as sporting goods and game tickets.

4. A contract is seen as "an agreement between parties which is enforceable under the law."

5. Two main types of contracts are called bilateral and unilateral.

6. The elements of contract include the following concepts: meeting of the minds, offer, acceptance, consideration, 2001) legality, capacity, and intention to create legal relations.

7. Some common errors within contracts include misrepresentation, undue influence/duress, and mistakes.

8. To uphold a contract as written, an integration clause is included, and the parole evidence rule invoked.

9. A breach of contract is usually remedied by a damages amount.

10. Facility, game, event, and sponsorship contracts are important to ensure that all events are handled with diligence, care, and understanding.

11. For contracts involving goods, *caveat emptor* has been replaced by *caveat venditor.*

12. Within the scope of goods contracts, the concepts of implied warranty of merchantability and implied warranty of fitness as they relate to UCC Art. 2 are of paramount importance. In addition, products liability would be of specific concern to a facility manager if an injury to a patron or employee were to occur.

13. The contract itself involves an opening, representations and warranties, operational language, other clauses, termination, entire agreement and amendments, and a closing.

14. It is hoped that by gaining knowledge of the elements of a contract and the various types and situations under which contracts apply, the facility manager can use these principles to a distinct advantage.

Case Study Revisited

Questions

The case of *New Boston Garden Corporation v. Baker* involved a multiyear contract dispute centering upon preferred or premium seating (Wong, 2000). Due to personal problems and team performance, Baker attempted to dissolve his 3-year, $18,000 contract. The facility was against this because revenue from premium seating is the most important source of funding for facility operation and construction (Wong, 1994). A breach of contract claim and lawsuit followed.

The decision in this case is compounded due to the confounding and colliding factors of personal life and private interest. Certainly, the personal problems of Baker were not to be dismissed. However, personal claims alone are not enough to warrant a breach of contract. For NBGC these claims may have been a source of public relations trouble, but they were of limited merit legally.

Baker's arguments would most certainly have been based upon personal turmoil. In addition, Baker argued that he offered to amend the agreement to buy fewer tickets, or have the contract terms shortened (Wong, 2000). In addition, Baker was upset that NBGC did not adequately advertise to sell its premium seating or reduce its prices despite a poor season (Wong, 2000). This practice may have helped Baker to sell his seats to someone else, had the NBGC allowed it.

The arguments from NBGC stemmed from a breach of contract claim alleging that a valid agreement had been entered into and the requirements of a contract had been met (Wong, 2000). Consideration had been exchanged, NGBC had the seating available, Baker did not fulfill his part of the bargain, and NGBC suffered damages as a result (Wong, 2000). On appeal, NGBC won, and Baker was ordered to pay restitution (Wong, 2000).

From a practical perspective, fans must understand that there are no warranties or representations in such a contract that guarantees a winning team (Wong, 2000). On the facility manager's side, by the same token, if a contract is poorly worded, the courts will award judgment against the creator of the contract (Wong, 2000). In this particular contract, the wording was clear and the contract upheld. Therefore, proper language and suitable counsel are always important in such an undertaking. In the end, frequent and appropriate communication between the patron and the facility manager, including addendums or adjustments to contracts, will, it is hoped, keep these and other types of cases out of court.

Chapter Eight

Risk Management

Six months ago, the facility director at Cushing Coliseum, an 18,000-seat multipurpose arena in Tinsel, Oklahoma, hired you as the risk manager. The Coliseum is home to an AF2 League team called the Scissor-Tailed Fly-Catchers, as well as a minor league hockey team, the Oklahoma Thrushes. Cushing's facility director hired you specifically because during the interview you spoke of the ability to present a viable risk management plan.

Your objective is to choose one of the teams and provide specific event risk management information as requested that would pertain to your specific game. This information may be gleaned from interviewing or observing a member of a facility management team. Further information may be obtained from newspaper articles, the Internet, any of your class notes, this text, your professors' reserve materials, etc. How the plan will be implemented is up to you, but remember you are the risk manager, so if the plan does not work, it is your reputation (and job security) that will be affected. Include all information required to make this decision.

Some of the items listed below may not be relevant based upon the particular event risk management plan, and some information will need to be created. You need to include all of the following:

Date and type of event. When will the event take place? Will it be an AF2 game or a hockey match? Who will the opponent be? Will it be a preseason, regular season or postseason game?

Risk management. Who is in charge of managing the plan? How is the plan communicated to the facility employees? What are five of the most common risks that occur at coliseum events? What are their classifications? What is the most significant treatment used to reduce the risks?

How do you plan on dealing with inherent risks to your event? Are all staff members aware of the risk management plan? Do they have any input?

Insurance. What types of insurance have you as the risk manager secured?

Staffing needs. Does a policy manual exist? What type of personnel and staffing needs exist for the game? Do you need to utilize volunteers? Where will they be recruited? Will you use independent contractors? In what areas?

Facility considerations. How many spectators do you anticipate for the event? When will the doors open? Who makes the decision to open the doors? How many locker rooms will be used? Where are they located in relationship to the arena floor? What happens in case of a power outage? Are there any hidden dangers of which the patrons need to be made aware? Do adequate numbers of restrooms exist?

Maintenance. Who provides the maintenance? What types of maintenance are available?

Business operations. Who will handle the cash? How will the money be transported from the box office, concession stands, and merchandise stands to the bank? Is there a cash pick-up from the stands during the event? Who will count the money?

Evaluation of the event. When will the evaluation take place? Who will be present? Is a standard form used? How long are the evaluations kept? Does a show or event file exist? What constitutes the file?

Introduction to Risk Management

Research illustrates that the number of lawsuits involving sport and recreational activities from 1977 to 1987 increased 150% (Fried, 1997). A large amount of this litigation may have been avoided with the implementation of a proper risk management plan. The impact of the facility industry has shifted in the past decade. Ten to 15 years ago, existing facilities dealt with a minimum number of events whose influence was most often on a regional basis. Today, the number of facilities has grown exponentially, and they schedule sporting and entertainment events that have global implications. Examples of these events include World Cup Soccer, NBA and NHL Championships, World Wrestling Entertainment events, NCAA tournaments, PGA Golf Championships, major concert tours, conventions, and trade shows. These various events have become extremely popular and have resulted in increased attendance and accompanying media coverage.

Risk management is the control of financial and personal injury loss from sudden, unforeseen, or unusual accidents and intentional torts.

Due to the tremendous increase in the number of events being staged worldwide, many in the sport and entertainment industry have recognized event management as a growing profession. Although event managers must be proficient in many areas in order to successfully stage an event, no area is more important than understanding and implementing an effective risk management plan.

Definition of Risk Management

Risk management has been defined as the control of financial and personal injury loss from sudden, unforeseen, unusual accidents and intentional torts (Ammon, 1993). Wong and Masteralexis (1998) termed it "a management strategy to maintain greater control over the legal uncertainty that may wreak havoc on a sport business" (p. 90). Other academics (Mulrooney & Farmer, 1998) explained risk management as "reducing exposure to danger, harm, or hazards leading to lawsuits" (p. 273). The loss or "risk" can be either physical or financial in nature. For example, sport facility managers must continually attempt to minimize patron injuries such as "slip and falls" that create the potential for lawsuits. In addition, financial losses may occur due to incidents such as vandalism, poorly written contracts, stolen equipment, and accidents in the facility parking lot due to poor lighting. The first goal of a risk manager must be to reduce the possible monetary losses while effectively managing a sport facility. This goal may sound easy, but it becomes a very complicated and difficult task.

The DIM Process

The DIM process has been utilized as a potential tool to establish a proper risk management program (Ammon, 2001). This simple process involves three basic steps: (a) *d*eveloping the risk management plan, (b) *i*mplementing the risk management plan, and (c) *m*anaging the risk management plan. The steps used in creating a risk management plan are similar no matter the type of facility. Thus, facility managers at fitness centers, aquatic parks, municipal golf courses, or minor league baseball parks would use the same fundamental concepts. The DIM process, when used as an anticipatory technique rather than as a reactionary procedure, will assist any organization in diminishing the chances for litigation (Ammon, 2001).

Developing the Risk Management Plan

Developing a risk management plan consists of three separate steps: (a) identifying the risks, (b) classifying the risks, and (c) selecting treatments for the risks.

Identifying the Risks

In the identification stage, the facility manager must differentiate various risks or losses that may occur during any given event. Conducting surveys of the attendees, carrying out inspections of the facility, talking to the present employees, or asking experts in the field who have similarly sized facilities are some of the more germane methods used to identify these risks.

> A well-trained staff can help the risk manager identify potential risks.

Each facility has primary and secondary factors that must be addressed in order to reduce the possibility of losses. Primary factors are included in the *standard operating procedures* (SOPs) of every sport facility, and each facility manager must consider these factors when trying to reduce risks (Farmer et al., 1996).

The facility staff is included among the primary factors. A well-trained staff, educated about proper risk management procedures, can help the risk manager to identify potential risks. Unfortunately the facility staff may also be risks themselves. For example, an improperly supervised ticket taker in a basketball arena may allow friends to enter without paying the admission fee. A poorly trained usher in a football stadium may step beyond his or her responsibilities to provide information and attempt to break up an altercation between drunken spectators. A fatigued personal trainer in a fitness facility may not provide a proper spotting technique for a client. A cashier hired with no background check may steal money from the concession stand. In each of these situations, the staff members themselves have become the risk. Risk identification for the facility's staff begins when interviewing prospective employees. The sport facility manager needs to demonstrate special vigilance to ensure that each employee is properly screened before being hired (see chapter 6). This precaution is paramount if the employee will be working with children or large sums of money (Farmer et al., 1996).

Once primary factors are identified, the sport facility manager must be watchful for secondary risks. A list of secondary risk factors that are applicable to most sport facilities include weather, event or activity type, patron demographics, and facility location. Many of these risk factors affect and interact with each other. This can be demonstrated through the following example.

A high school football game has been scheduled for the coming weekend. Several elements need to be identified. In what part of the country is the high school located? What time of year is it? Obviously, a game played in a southern state early in the season may have to contend with hot, humid weather. A game in a northern state, later in the season, may have cold, snowy conditions. For example, if heat and humidity are a factor, liquids need to available for both spectators and players. If a snowstorm approaches the stadium, the parking lot and sidewalks must be cleared, so patrons do not fall and injure themselves.

Risk identification may include design flaws. (Photo courtesy of Todd Seidlerbe.)

What time of day will the game be played? Research has demonstrated that sporting events held under the cover of darkness have more crowd problems than do those played in the light of day (Ammon, 1993). Is the game between two fierce rivals or is it a nonconference affair between teams who have not played each other before? Extra precautions must be implemented if problems have occurred at previous sporting events between the two schools. All of these examples are real-life risks that have occurred at football stadiums throughout the country. If the activity were an intercollegiate women's basketball game, a completely new set of risks or potential losses would need to be identified.

Risks may occur in a variety of locations including privately or publicly owned buildings, professional or intercollegiate entertainment facilities, and outdoor or indoor sport settings. Each facility, school, clinic, event, and program is different and has its own unique risks or areas of potential loss. Therefore, monitoring these risks needs to be constant and ongoing. It is important to remember that when identifying risks, special considerations should be taken, because the risk could involve either a financial loss or personal injury.

The sport facility manager has now identified potential risks or losses that may arise due to a high school football game. However, as mentioned earlier, developing a risk management plan is a three-step process. The second step is to classify the risk. The purpose of this stage is to determine the severity of loss arising from the risk and the frequency of occurrence of the risk.

Classifying the Risks

Once the risks or losses have been identified, they must be classified. The risk manager takes each of the previously identified risks and appraises it in terms of frequency and severity. The frequency of the risk is dependent on the number of times the risk or loss may occur. The risk manager will select each identified and assign a frequency of "often," "average," or "seldom." The severity of the risk is determined by the intensity of the loss and may be classified as "high," "moderate," or "low." The level of severity and amount of frequency are determined by the risk manager, based on his or her previous experience. It is important to remember that both financial as well as personal injury losses need to be classified in terms of their frequency and severity (Kaiser & Robinson, 1999).

Every activity is classified in a distinct manner, and each is dependent on the risks considered inherent to the activity. Inherent risks normally are the risks or potential losses that are associated with that activity or sport. If the inherent risks were deleted, the resulting activity would be different from the original. For example, an inherent risk in rock climbing is falling. An inherent risk in football would be the collisions that occur between players.

What risks can be identified at a baseball game? How do you classify these risks?

The facility manager should eliminate noninherent risks as much as possible because the courts will not accept an "assumption of risk" defense if the spectator did not know, understand, and appreciate the inherent risk (van der Smissen, 1990). For example, in an age-group soccer program, a sprained ankle would be classified as "often" in frequency and "low" in severity because a sprained ankle is common to the game of soccer. However, for those individuals participating in an aquatics program, a sprained ankle would probably be classified as "seldom" in frequency. The difference is because a sprained ankle would *not* be an inherent risk for those engaged in an aquatics program.

A matrix can be created that allows a consistent approach to the classification process. The matrix below (Table 8-1) gives the facility manager nine different categories in which to classify a risk once it has been identified. Nine categories are sufficient; too many categories create unnecessary complexity. By placing the identified risks in the matrix, the risk manager would have successfully completed the classification stage. It should be noted that risk assessment is an ongoing process always subject to change. For example, as previously mentioned, one week a high school football game may be played during the afternoon, and the next week the game may be held at night. Alternatively, one week's game may be against a weak opponent with no play-off implications whereas the next week's game may be for the conference championship. The risk manager must be aware of such changes and assess each risk accordingly. Below is a matrix with some risks from a high school football game placed in their proper categories.

	HIGH LOSS	MODERATE LOSS	LOW LOSS
OFTEN	None	Incorrect change given to spectators	Spills at concession stand
AVERAGE	Severe knee or shoulder injury to player	Slip and falls in/ around stadium	Spectators evading the admission fee
SELDOM	Paraplegia/death of player or spectator	Heat exhaustion or frostbite	Vandalism of stadium

Table 8.1. Risk Category Matrix

Treating the Risks

The final stage in developing the risk management plan is to determine a treatment for each identified and classified risk. The treatment of identified and classified risks usually depends on the sport facility manager's knowledge of when certain losses are likely to occur. Although it is often difficult to determine the severity and frequency of losses involved, a risk matrix can also assist in this identification process.

Avoidance. Risks should be *avoided* when they are severe, cause a high degree of loss, and occur frequently. A facility or risk manager should identify the risk before it occurs and avoid it completely. Scheduling an event or allowing an activity that has previously caused property damage and/or personal injury at other facilities would not be prudent (Farmer et al., 1996). For example, if a certain concert has the reputation for incurring heavy "moshing," the sport facility may wish to avoid scheduling the event. A sport facility manager is also an effective risk manager if he or she does not allow the event or activity to take place, thereby eliminating all potential and probable losses (Mulrooney & Farmer, 1995).

A risk matrix can help identify the severity and frequency of losses.

Transfer. The second type of risk treatment, *transfer*, occurs with average-frequency/high-moderate severity types of hazards. Although some risks are identified as problem areas, they should not always be considered immediate concerns and therefore do not have to be avoided. The question then becomes why transfer some risks and avoid others? First, the combination of severity and frequency may not be large enough to warrant avoiding the risk. Nevertheless, the risk may be large enough to cause substantial monetary damage to the sport facility. One option would be to transfer the risk to someone who is willing to take the risk. In this situation, the risk manager would pay an insurance company a yearly premium to cover any physical or financial damages that may occur (Farmer et al., 1996). Therefore, the definition of insurance is the transfer of risk from one individual or group to another group (Mulrooney & Ammon, 1995). A comprehension of the following terms is prudent to understand the basics about insurance:

> adjuster: a representative of the insurance company who determines the liability to the insurance company if a claim is made to cover a specific loss

> agent: an individual whose primary responsibility is to negotiate and sell insurance contracts to those seeking insurance

> deductible: the amount that the insured must pay on a claim before the insurance company pays on the claim

> claim: the act of the insured requesting payment from the insurance company due to the occurrence of an event included in the policy

> insurer: the company that agrees to pay claims according to the terms of the insurance contract

> insured: the individual or organization that carries the insurance in order to avoid large monetary losses due to occurrences at certain events

> policy: a contract between the insured and the insurer that provides the specific agreements on events covered, the amount covered, the premiums to be paid, etc.

> premium: a payment made by the policy holder to the insurance company to keep the policy in effect

There are many types of insurance in existence, and not all apply to the needs of a facility. The following two examples are types of insurance that facilities should carry in order to provide complete protection from potential risks.

Personal injury liability insurance. If a spectator, participant, or employee is injured by something the facility managers did or did not do, then the individual was injured personally and can sue to recover appropriate damages. Now, when talking about injuries, the reference is not limited to physical injury, but includes injury to a person's reputation or emotional well-being (Farmer et al., 1996). The following are examples of what could be covered under this type of insurance policy:

- During a fight in the crowd, the crowd management personnel eject the wrong person, causing the innocent patron to miss the entire event.

- When walking to her seat after half time, a patron is hit by a beer bottle that has been smuggled into the facility.

- A patron slips and falls on some nacho cheese that had not been cleaned up properly, ruining his new pants.

> At the urging of their insurance agencies, some organizations have begun to settle lawsuits rather than litigate the claims.

All of these incidents would be covered under the personal injury clause of the insurance policy. Although there is no "safe" amount of coverage, research has demonstrated that most facilities have at least $1,000,000 policies (Ammon, 1993; Ammon & Fried, 1998).

Paying the patron is not an automatic occurrence. A cost analysis process must take place between the facility manager, the facility's attorney, and the insurance company's adjusters (Farmer et al., 1996). Due to the litigious nature of our society and in order to reduce expenses, some organizations, at the urging of their insurance agencies, have begun to settle lawsuits rather than litigate the claims. Rather than fighting the lawsuit, being found innocent, and then paying an extravagant legal bill, many organizations are finding it cost-effective to settle out of court. Unfortunately, if the facility pays the claim, an innocent employee will not have the opportunity to prove his or her innocence. This can affect the employee's reputation for many years. "Sad as this scenario may be, it is a frequent occurrence. Justice and righteousness take a back seat to dollars and cents in the world of big business, and facility management is big business" (Farmer et al., 1996, p. 86).

Property insurance. The facility and its equipment represent a huge investment. This investment is at risk each time an event is held. When people come to the facility, certain individuals do not care what they damage or destroy. This is especially true if the facility schedules a concert where the patrons have been drinking. The combination of alcohol and an aggressive band often leads to significant amounts of damage to the walls, light fixtures, and bathroom stalls and sinks. The facility management must make a decision if the increased revenue from the concert is worth the potential damage that may occur to the facility. A solution may be property insurance (Farmer et al., 1996).

There are two basic types of property insurance to be considered. First, is *Named Perils* insurance. As indicated, this coverage will only be for certain events that are specifically mentioned in the insurance policy.

•Fire	•Lightning	•Vandalism
•Hail	•Malicious Mischief	•Smoke
•Explosion	•Tornadoes	

Table 8.2. Most Commonly Named Perils

Most of the events mentioned are natural occurrences and virtually uncontrollable. If more extensive coverage is needed, then an *All-Risk* policy is a better choice.

•Building Collapse	•Frozen pipes
•Burglary	•Falling objects

Table 8.3. Coverage That Might Be Included in an All-Risk Policy

Although this list is broader than the "Named Perils" list, items such as ordinary wear and tear, earthquakes, floods and general building deterioration would not normally be included. Thus, the name "All Risks" is somewhat of a misnomer because some exclusions will be specifically mentioned in the policy (Farmer et al., 1996, pp. 86-87).

Workers' compensation. Workers' compensation is another way to transfer some of the liability arising out of an injury. Workers' compensation provides benefits to an employee (workers' compensation applies only to employees) of a sport facility who suffers an injury in the course of and

Property insurance should be purchased to protect events as well as facilities.

arising out of an employee's employment. Sport facilities pay workers' compensation premiums much the same way that they would pay for other insurance premiums. Just as insurance policies have limitations on how much will be paid, workers' compensation claims also have limitations based on the type of injury suffered by the employee.

Additional types of transfer. Several other types of transfer exist including waivers, independent contractors, and indemnification clauses. A waiver will transfer the risk from facility management (service provider) back to the person who signed it. In most states, waivers are unenforceable for minors, although Colorado, California, and Ohio have begun under some circumstances enforcing waivers that have been signed by the minor's parent (Cotten, 2001).

> A waiver transfers the risk from facility management to the person who signs it.

Employees such as doctors, referees, and aerobic instructors are examples of independent contractors. These individuals are responsible for their own unemployment and liability insurance. Thus, most negligent actions would strictly become their sole responsibility (Mulrooney & Ammon, 1995).

Indemnification clauses are included in most contracts that facility managers sign with organizations that lease the facility. These clauses, sometimes called *hold harmless agreements* allow the facility to be compensated by the individuals renting the facility, if any damage occurs during the event. Thus, the risk during the event is *transferred* to the outside organization.

Retention. The third option that we have for treating risks is to keep or *retain* the risk. Any facility that decides to use retention becomes financially responsible for any injuries or financial risks that may occur. Sometimes retention is improperly termed self-insurance. Self-insurance does not shift the risk of loss to ***another*** as outlined in our definition; instead, the facility will allocate funds for specific risks, and these funds will be used exclusively for the payment of claims from these risks. In essence, the facility is simply paying the premium to itself. This is not, however, as easy as it sounds, nor is the loss minimized efficiently. It is important to note that the facility's business operations must include retention as a line item in the budget and accumulate a reserve or "pool" of revenue to pay for such injuries (Farmer et al., 1996).

Looking at the matrix (Table 8-4), we can see that risks to be kept and decreased are those that have low potential for loss. A sport facility can accept these risks because there is very little chance of incurring substantial losses. This, of course, assumes that once the sport facility manager decides to keep the risk, proper precautions are taken to decrease the occurrence and/or monetary losses associated with the risk (Mulrooney & Farmer, 1995). Normally this treatment is used for minor injury claims such as basic first aid treatment or ambulance service.

Reduction. Using the fourth and final treatment, a facility manager will try to *reduce* the risks. This treatment involves trying to reduce or restrict the risks, therefore diminishing the number of lawsuits. Requiring employees to undertake more training, using preventive maintenance instead of waiting for an accident to occur, and compiling extensive record keeping through the collection of accident forms, participation forms, and instructions are examples of reduction techniques (Ammon, 2001). These techniques need to become part of the standard operating procedures (SOPs). When a sport facility manager develops a risk management plan that will be the most efficient and effective way to decrease the occurrence of the risk, it becomes part of the SOPs. SOPs are systematic instructions that give detailed directions for appropriate courses of action, given the situation and the risks that arise (Farmer et al., 1996).

SOPs require proper facility maintenance. (Photo courtesy of Todd Seidler)

SOPs should always be used with risks that are transferred and risks that are retained. When a facility manager decides to retain the risks, he or she must be ready to develop SOPs that will ensure that each situation is handled in a manner that will reduce the chance of liability. No one SOP will work all the time. The fact that a facility will implement specific policies and procedures when certain events occur is a good indicator, in the case of a lawsuit, that reasonable care was taken to prevent any injury to patrons. If the risks are not reduced with the use of SOPs, more claims will occur. This will eventually cause the insurer to raise the facility premiums to cover the risks in question. By having SOPs to properly handle and possibly reduce the occurrence of risks, the insurer will not raise the premiums the sport facility pays to cover those risks. Thus, sport facilities can save money through properly managing transferred risks (Farmer et al., 1996).

	HIGH LOSS	MODERATE LOSS	LOW LOSS
OFTEN	Avoid	Transfer & Reduction	Transfer or Return & Reduction
AVERAGE	Avoid or Transfer & Reduction	Transfer & Reduction	Retain & Reduction
SELDOM	Transfer & Reduction	Transfer or Retain & Reduction	Retain & Reduction

Table 8.4. Risk Treatment Matrix

In order to develop SOPs for events that have not yet occurred, the facility manager must take great care to evaluate the potential risks. Because the event has not yet occurred, gathering adequate data to develop the SOP will be important. The manager may want to talk to various other facility managers to discover what they have done in similar situations (Farmer et al., 1996).

Implementing the Risk Management Plan

The next step in the DIM process consists of *i*mplementing the risk management plan. As discussed with the SOPs, communication is of paramount importance in order to put the risk management plan into practice. Each employee has a shared responsibility to insure the success of the plan. Therefore, each employee needs to be made a member of the risk management team. The facility manager (or risk manager) should ask for assistance and listen to suggestions made by the employees (Ammon, 2001).

> Each employee needs to be made a member of the
> risk management team.

As previously stated, communication of the risk management plan is critical for *i*mplementation, and the employees of the facility or organization are the primary group who need to be made aware of the plan. The easiest way to communicate the plan occurs when an employee is initially hired. Placing the risk management plan in the orientation handbook provides the new employee with a firsthand look. A note of caution: Do not place the entire plan in the notebook. It will be too comprehensive. Place only the sections that are pertinent to the individual employee. This will take a certain amount of organization on the part of the facility or risk manager, but will be an investment for the future (Ammon, 2001).

After several months of employment, in-services should be scheduled to update the facility workers about any new components involving the risk management plan. Additional insurance coverage, redesigned operational techniques, and new SOPs are often discussed and practiced during these in-services. Motivational techniques and team-building strategies may also be *i*mplemented during these sessions.

Managing the Plan

The final step of the DIM process is to *m*anage the plan. A risk manager or safety committee must be selected and provided with the authority to motivate and lead (Ammon, 2001). Some facilities will hire one individual to take on the responsibility of a risk manager. Other facilities, due to budget constraints, will divide the responsibilities among a group of current employees. Whichever system is chosen, the responsible party should monitor the risk management plan, implement changes, assist in fostering a genuine safety attitude among other employees, conduct inspections, review accidents, and supervise in-service training (van der Smissen, 1990).

The person or persons selected to take responsibility for the risk management plan should be chosen very carefully. First, they must recognize the need for such a plan. Second, they must understand that by managing risks properly, they are improving the spectators' overall experiences and ultimately the reputation of the facility, which translates into repeat customers. Without comprehending the connection between these two elements, the success of the risk management plan is questionable (Ammon, 2001).

Facility management and ownership must also "buy" into the idea of risk management. They must be willing to assist the risk manager or safety committee with verbal and financial support. Without upper management's support, a risk management plan will not succeed. The risk manager or safety committee must be given the freedom to act independently, but within the philosophy of the facility (Ammon, 2001).

Inadequate storage needs to be avoided. (Photo courtesy of Todd Seidler)

Application of the DIM Process

The DIM model is easier to understand when applied to a real-life situation. Cynthia Sanford recently graduated with her undergraduate sport management degree. Having completed an internship in the aquatic program at a prestigious Southern resort, Cynthia was hired as the first director of risk management for the resort. One of her responsibilities was to create a risk management plan for the aquatic program. Cynthia's first priority was to develop her plan. After several weeks of reading the aquatic directors' previous reports, observing the aquatic programs at other resorts, talking to guests at the resort, and questioning the resort employees, Cynthia made a list of the risks she had identified. The resort's aquatic program included swimming lessons for the children of resort guests, and Cynthia determined that the lessons posed some potential problems that needed to be addressed. Most of the risks involved skin abrasions, small lacerations, varying degrees of sunburn, and the occasional jammed finger. After identifying the risks, Cynthia classified them as average frequency and low severity.

When selecting a treatment for the risks, Cynthia decided from among four options. First, she could have *avoided* the swim lessons, eliminating the chance for loss, but she believed the resort managers would not be receptive to eliminating the revenue produced by the lessons. In addition, the decision would be unpopular with the parents of the children and could potentially cause a large amount of negative publicity for the resort. Second, Cynthia could have secured an insurance policy that would *transfer* the risk to an insurance company. The resort, having gone through a hurricane the year before, was under a severe budget crunch, so this solution would not have been economically viable. Third, she could have *re-*

tained the risks and paid for any of the identified minor injuries from the resorts' operating budget. If Cynthia classified the potential injuries correctly, retention would have been a good choice. Finally, she could have attempted to eliminate the risks through *reduction* and SOPs. As discussed earlier, a combination of treatments is usually the best solution for identified risks. In Cynthia's situation, retention and reduction offered realistic yet achievable solutions for her identified risks. Cynthia would continue to *d*evelop her plan by identifying, classifying, and selecting treatments for the additional risks of the aquatic programs.

In our synopsis, Cynthia *i*mplemented her plan by providing an employee manual to each lifeguard at the beginning of the summer. The manual discussed how to provide proper medical services and explained aquatic program rules and regulations. In addition, she conducted training sessions about current techniques for both pool and open-water lifesaving. Cynthia implemented an emergency medical plan that trained the lifeguards on how to handle life-threatening medical emergencies.

To *m*anage her plan effectively Cynthia made certain that the resort owners supported the idea of risk management. Cynthia was hired with the understanding that her duties as director of the risk management program would include the necessary authority to carry out the various responsibilities of a risk manager. During her interview Cynthia made certain that the resort management was willing to financially assist to her in creating the risk management plan.

Risk management is a necessity for facility managers today. Even though many risks can be identified, classified, and treated, some hazards will still exist, and accidents will occur. It is unreasonable to expect a facility manager to eliminate all injuries and financial losses. However, by developing an extensive risk management plan, implementing the plan, and bestowing the authority to manage the plan upon a concerned risk manager, sport managers can diminish a number of dangerous risks (Ammon, 2001).

Summary

1. Many experts recognize event management as a growth industry, and risk management is acknowledged as an important component of a successful event.

2. Risk management is defined as the ability to control both financial and personal injury losses from sudden, unforeseen, unusual accidents and intentional torts.

3. The DIM process is a tool used to establish a proper risk management program and involves three basic steps: (1) *d*eveloping the risk management plan, (2) *i*mplementing the risk management plan, and (3) *m*anaging the risk management plan.

4. In *d*eveloping the plan, each risk is identified and classified by frequency and severity. Then it is assigned to a specific treatment. These treatments include avoiding the risk, transferring the risk, retaining the risk, and reducing the possibility of loss with standard operating procedures (SOPs).

5. Insurance is the most common method used to transfer the risk to another party.

6. Other types of transfer include waivers, independent contractors, and indemnification clauses.

7. When a facility retains a risk, it becomes financially responsible for any injuries or financial losses that may occur.

8. Requiring employees to use preventive maintenance, compiling extensive record keeping, and using signage are reduction techniques that become part of a facility's standard operating procedures (SOPs). SOPs give detailed directions for appropriate courses of action.

9. *I*mplementing the risk management plan pertains to the ability of communicating the plan to others, namely the facility employees.

10. Facility management and ownership must be willing to assist the risk manager or safety committee with verbal and financial support in order for them to *m*anage the plan.

Questions

1. Why is risk management so vital to facility managers in the 21st Century?

2. Identify and define the various stages involved in the DIM process.

3. How can a risk manager identify the risks in his or her facility?

4. Identify and provide an example for each treatment of a risk management plan.

5. Define SOPs and explain how they should be used in decreasing facility risks.

6. What is an inherent risk? Is it important to know if the risk is inherent? Why or why not?

7. What is self-insurance an example of? Why is it a misnomer?

Chapter Nine

Facility Negligence

Application Exercise

Alliah Jones, a recent sport management graduate, was a fitness supervisor at the Bigger Bodies Health and Fitness club (BBHF). As an employee of BBHF, she was responsible for (a) orientation of new members; (b) fitness program assessment, design, and follow-up; (c) proper exercise instruction; (d) maintenance and cleaning of equipment; and (e) general supervision of the weight and fitness area. One day, Alliah stepped out of the fitness and weight room to use the restroom. On the way back, she stopped to chat with the front desk personnel and get a sports drink from the pro shop. Upon returning to the fitness and weight room, Alliah discovered that a new patron of the club, Jose, had injured himself carrying a weight from a rack to the bench press. Apparently, the weight slipped out of Jose's hands and fell on his foot, causing him great pain. Alliah, certified in first aid, treated the injury. It was later determined that Jose had broken his foot in several places. To make matters worse, Jose was a competitive triathlete who had only recently taken up weight lifting in order to increase his potential for victory and sponsorship acquisition. Because Jose would be in a cast for six weeks and would lose a considerable amount of fitness and strength and his athletic career as a whole was jeopardized, he sued the BBHF club owner; Alliah, the fitness club manager; and the manufacturer of the weights. Use the information presented in this chapter to help answer the following questions. Further information may be obtained from newspaper articles, the Internet, any of your class notes, this text, your professors, and reserve materials, etc.

Supervising a weight and fitness area involves several important facility management concepts.

1. Does Jose have a case?

2. Is Alliah potentially responsible for Jose's injuries?

3. Was the club owner negligent?

4. What "duty" did the weight manufacturer have to Jose?

It is risky to work in the sports industry. All sports and physical activities have certain inherent risks—risks that are essential to the integrity of that particular sport or activity. Participants assume certain inherent risks, but sport event and facility clients expect certain duties from sport managers. They expect event and facility managers to be experts and protect them, whenever possible, from certain risks associated with a particular sport event or activity. These risks may range from an errant puck's leaving the rink and striking a spectator to a NASCAR stock car's crashing over a barrier at a racetrack. Although it is impossible to eliminate all risks from sport and recreational activities, all sport managers must be aware of the need to identify these risks and remove or reduce them whenever possible (see chapter 8, "Risk Management"). As a sport manager, it is important that you be aware of participant, spectator, and sponsor expectations and familiar with methods for removing or transferring potential liability exposures associated with sport and recreational activities from yourself and your organization (see chapter 2, "Planning and Producing the Event").

To gain an understanding of facility negligence, this chapter first presents the basic elements of negligence, as well as application of these elements to facility operations, including supervision, proper care, proper instruction, participant responsibility, vicarious liability, product liability, and transfer of liability through the use of waivers and releases. The ability to apply these concepts in the real world is important for a sport event/facility manager. With this in mind, you are encouraged to evaluate an actual liability release and express assumption of risk document using the concepts and guidelines outlined in this chapter (See *Practical Application*).

Negligence deals with "avoidable accidents."

Many sporting activities, including soccer, involve the risk of injuries from collisions. (Photo courtesy of *The Times Georgian* and Kendra Waycuilis.)

| **Definition of Negligence** | Negligence falls under the general body of law called torts (Wong, 1994). As such, it is an "unintentional act that injures" (van der Smissen, 2001b, p. 37). Negligence deals with "avoidable accidents" that should have been anticipated and prevented by taking reasonable precautions. When negligence is claimed, the injured party (plaintiff) is making the claim that even though a service provider (defendant) may not have meant to harm or injure the plaintiff, injury or harm did occur as a result of action or inaction on the part of the defendant. Thus, in simple terms, negligence, although unintended, is something a person did or did not do resulting in another person's being hurt. In legal terms, negligence has been defined as |

> the failure to exercise the standard of care that a reasonably prudent person would have exercised in a similar situation; any conduct that falls below the legal standard established to protect others against unreasonable risk of harm, except for conduct that is intentionally, wantonly, or willfully disregardful of others' rights. (Garner, 1999, p. 1056)

| **Elements of Negligence** | The elements used in a court of law to determine negligence consist of "duty, breach of duty, causation, and damages" (Garner, 1999, p. 1056). In order for a person to be held liable for negligent action, all four elements must exist (van der Smissen, 2001b). |

Duty

There are two major categories of duty. One is a general duty to act with reasonable care toward others so as not to create an unreasonable risk of harm (Coren, 1995). This general duty is what a reasonably prudent person would do. Another more specific duty arises from a legal relationship between a service provider and the other person. Within that relationship is the duty, or obligation, to protect the user from unreasonable risks that may injure or harm. In order for such an obligation to exist, there must be a relationship between a service provider and the injured party that requires the service provider to protect the person from unreasonable risk of harm (van der Smissen, 2001b).

In any particular situation where a level of professional expertise is involved, there may be many such relationships. There may be relationships between a particular person and manufacturers of equipment, an operator, vendor, or other organization, and a particular professional. These relationships involve types of specific duties. These duties require a professional to abide by specific standards of care established or adopted as the standards of professional behavior in the particular industry.

Determination of the existence of a relationship and the degree of care required is established by examining similar conduct of other professionals

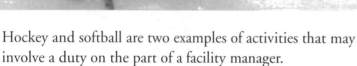

Hockey and softball are two examples of activities that may involve a duty on the part of a facility manager.

in the field and providing a safe environment for patrons (Wong, 1994). For example, in *Berman v. Philadelphia Board of Education* (1983), an 11-year-old hockey player was injured when hit by another player's stick in an after-school match. The court found that despite the fact that the Amateur Hockey Association did not require mouthpieces, the school board had a duty to protect its students from harm. Furthermore, the student's age precluded an admission of assumption of risk or contributory negligence. However, in *Scaduto v. State* (1982), the court found that no duty existed between college officials and an intramural softball player who tripped over a drainage ditch and fell while attempting to catch a fly ball. The court ruled that the student knew of the danger and assumed the risk when playing softball. Therefore, the college was not responsible for the student-athlete's injury.

A facility manager must anticipate problems with a given activity and how those situations may be viewed from a legal perspective.

Although these cases are similar, their outcomes were distinctly different. The age of the participants was important in the outcome of each case. Therefore, determination of duty is many times situational. As a result, a facility manager must be cognizant of particular situations that could potentially arise in a given activity, how those situations may be viewed from a legal perspective, and whether that particular activity warrants a special relationship to the patron.

These standards of care outline what a *reasonably prudent professional* (RPP) would do. With this in mind, it is critical that sport managers be knowledgeable about the standards of care in their specific industry. Coaches, referees, and facility managers cannot eliminate all risks associated with the sport; some, such as the risk of collision, are inherent. Professionals in the sport industry can be expected to owe a duty to participants consistent with an accepted standard. For example, soccer fields should be maintained to a certain "acceptable" standard.

Although every particular situation is unique, standards of care are used to measure a particular professional's conduct in a given situation. In a sport or recreation setting, a professional should possess and use the degree of knowledge, ability, and skill "usually" possessed by competent professionals in the given field or industry. For example, if you are managing a summer high school football camp, it is important that steps be taken to ensure participant safety in the summer heat (e.g., provide adequate water breaks). Professional organizations such as the Texas High School Coaches Association (THSCA), the American Football Coaches Association (AFCA), the National Athletic Trainers Association (NATA), and the National Federation of State High School Associations (NFHS) all publish tips for safer two-a-day football workouts (National Federation of State High School Associations, 2002; Teaff & Max, 2000). Therefore, a reasonably prudent football coach would be expected to avail himself of this readily obtainable information and conduct practices in general compliance with the recommendations of these experts. Your conduct as a professional event/facility manager will be measured against the commonly accepted standards of the particular sports event. A professional sport manager must exercise the same degree of care that would be exercised by a reasonably prudent professional (RPP) in a similar situation when considering the current state of advancement of the profession (Coren, 1995).

The duty owed to participants is situational. For example, football coaches owe a duty to football players to provide water during practices.

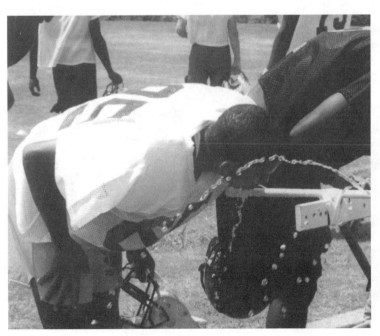

Breach of Duty

The next element a plaintiff must prove in a negligence case is breach of duty. Once a relationship or duty has been established, then a breach of that duty must be proven for a negligence case to continue. Breach of duty is "the failure to meet one's duties or obligations" (Carpenter, 2000, p. 59). Quite simply, breach of duty is when something the defendant (service provider) either did (*commission*) or did not do (*omission*) did not meet the obligation of the standard of care of a reasonably prudent professional (RPP). The professional's act breached the duty of care owed as a result of the relationship that existed.

Negligence, as a result of a breach of duty, can also be proven if the court decides, based on expert testimony, that the professional's conduct was negligent. Perhaps a football coach or professional athlete at a summer camp teaches a dangerous method of tackling that involves using the helmet as a weapon. This is contrary to accepted methods of teaching tackling. Organizations, such as the AFCA and the NFHS, publish standards for teaching tackling. Organization members are recognized experts in this specific professional field.

> Causation requires that the service provider/professional have done, or not done, something that could be reasonably expected to result in an unreasonable risk of harm.

Proximate Cause

Proximate cause is the connection or bridge between the breach of duty and the harm that occurred (Wong, 1994). In other words, there must be a connection between the negligent act and the injury. Although almost anything that a service provider/professional did or did not do could have contributed to a person's injury, cause in the sense discussed here must rise to a level required by society (the courts) to establish fault (Carpenter, 2000). In other words, "The RPP would have known better!" is the rule of thumb. The act need not be the sole cause of the injury, but should be a

There are often standards associated with teaching sport skills.

Sport and recreation participants often rely on the professional knowledge and judgment of service providers.

"substantial factor" (van der Smissen, 2001b, p. 41). To put it another way, for causation to occur, the service provider/professional must have done, or not done, something that could be reasonably expected to result in an unreasonable risk of harm. Although there may not be an absolute linkage of cause and effect between a service provider's actions and the injury, the court's judgment will be the benchmark. Furthermore, if the act was not an essential element of the harm, and the injury would have taken place regardless, a negligence claim would be negated.

Damage

Damage is the last part of the negligence equation, and it has a double meaning. First, damage refers to compensible harm suffered mentally or physically (van der Smissen, 2001b). Types of harm fall into four basic categories: (a) economic loss (medical expenses, lost wages), (b) physical pain and suffering, (c) emotional distress (fright, anxiety, humiliation), and (d) physical impairment (temporary or permanent; van der Smissen, 2001, p. 42). Second, "damage*s*" are what one receives in order for the injured person to be made whole again through financial means (Wong, 1994). In any event, the primary definition of damage, that is, harm, must be present for a negligent case to have merit. After all, without harm, there is no case.

Responsibility/ Liability

After establishing the elements necessary for negligence, it is important to determine who would be held responsible, or liable, if the negligence were to occur. In the past, suits primarily targeted those with the largest amount of resources, or those with "deep pockets." However, the trend has now become one in which not only are the wealthiest named in the suit, but also anyone remotely associated with the particular incident (Cotten, 2001c). For a facility or event, those potentially responsible in a negligence suit are the employees, the administrative or supervisory personnel, and the corporate entity (Cotten, 2001c).

Employee

In many situations, the employee is the person who commits a negligent act. The employees are the associates who are in direct contact with the patrons in the form of coaches, teachers, referees, fitness specialists, and lifeguards. If it can be shown that the employee had a duty and then breached that duty to a patron and that breach was a direct cause of the injury, then the employee will be considered negligent and thereby legally responsible (Cotten, 2001c).

Administrative or Supervisory Personnel

The administrative or supervisory role is one that is more complicated and convoluted than that of an employee. Ordinarily, the supervisor is not negligent for the actions of his or her employees. However, if a supervisor had knowledge of a particular employee's actions and failed to resolve the situation, if the administrator failed to enforce safety regulations, or if the administrator practiced inappropriate employment and hiring practices, the administrator might be liable.

Employing competent personnel and discharging unfit employees.

Providing proper supervision and having a supervision plan.

Directing certain services in the manner they should be done.

Establishing rules and regulations for safety and complying with policy and statutory requirements.

Remedying dangerous conditions and defective equipment or giving notice of this when there is knowledge of the conditions.

Table 9.1. Five Categories of Responsibilities for Administrators

(van der Smissen, 1990)

The Corporate Entity

The corporate entity determination of liability falls under the context of *respondeat superior* or vicarious liability. In each situation, the general rule of thumb is that if an employee is found to be negligent in the course and scope of his or her duties, then the employer is also negligent. If, however, the employee were negligent in a situation outside of a normal employment task, the employer would not be held liable. In general terms, an intern, volunteer, or trainee will be viewed by the courts as an actual employee, if at the time of the negligent act, the person was acting under the control of the corporation. However, athletes in a university setting, even though they may be under scholarship, are not considered employees of the institution. Therefore, the university would not be vicariously liable for their actions (Cotten, 2001c).

> If an employee is found negligent in the course and scope of his or her duties, then the employer is also negligent.

A weight room supervisor is responsible for establishing rules and regulations for the safety of patrons.

Facility Liability

Other methods of limiting corporate liability exist specifically with regard to facilities. If a facility is leased by an outside group, the determination of liability lies within the parameter "whether the injury was related to the premises or related to the particular activity" (van der Smissen, 1990). If the cause of the injury was directly related to the facility premises, the facility owner would probably be liable. If, however, the injury was activity related and the owner of the facility had no control over the activity, then the facility owner would most likely not be liable (van der Smissen, 1990). In the same manner, if an *independent contractor* (someone outside of the organization who is paid for a particular service) is negligent, this generally shifts liability away from the corporation and onto the independent contractor. Finally, waivers, or a release of liability, can be helpful in attempting to shift liability away from the facility (Cotten, 2001c).

Premise-Related Issues

As mentioned previously, if the cause of negligence was related to a facility premise issue, the facility manager would more than likely be held liable (van der Smissen, 1990). Therefore, the next section will explore a variety of premise-related situations and issues.

Premises Upkeep

In terms of a facility, the manager is responsible for upkeep of the facility so that it is reasonably safe for all who enter. This responsibility of "ordinary care" includes the duties to

1. Inspect regularly for hazards and dangers,

2. Maintain the premises and correct defects,

3. Warn users, participants, and spectators about hazards or dangers that are not readily apparent,

4. Warn users, participants, and spectators about participatory risks of the sport or activity; and

5. Keep users and spectators safe during their use of the premises by having a plan for reasonable supervision and security; using reasonable employee recruiting, selection, hiring, and training practices; and having an emergency medical plan (Maloy, 2001b, p. 108).

A facility manager is responsible for upkeep of the premises so that they are reasonably safe for all who enter.

Types of Patrons

For the facility manager, one must not only keep in mind a duty to the patron, but also the status of the patron. The four general types of patrons are *invitee, licensee, trespasser,* and *recreational user.* A "business" invitee is someone who has paid a usage fee, or can be expected to pay a fee in the future, for the use of the facility. A paying spectator at a game or a paid ticket holder at a ski resort would both be examples of business invitees. Furthermore, a guest at a health club or a person browsing in the pro shop would be considered a business invitee, because there is "expected economic benefit" arising from their visit (Maloy, 2001b, p.106). A facility manager is responsible to both types of invitee to provide a safe environment, inspect the premises, and reasonably foresee dangers that could arise.

> The facility manager does not afford a licensee the degree of care that's required for a business invitee.

In contrast, a licensee is someone who has been allowed, without expectation of monetary exchange, to use the premises. The facility manager does not afford a licensee the same degree of care as is required with a business invitee. Therefore, the premises operator has only the duty to warn of dangers that may not be readily apparent to the user. For example, the owner of a pond needs only warn swimmers of dangers that would not be readily apparent (Maloy, 2001b). In this situation, the facility owner need not inspect, foresee, or give warnings of obvious dangers. Patrons would be considered licensees at a church gathering, a public park, or on a city sidewalk where they were watching a parade.

Business invitees occupy seats during an MLB game at Coors Field.

Continuing down the continuum of duty to patrons, a trespasser, or someone who enters the premises without permission, is owed only the duty not to intentionally harm. In a related sense, a recreational user on particular premises who has not paid a fee is awarded the same general duty as that of a trespasser (Maloy, 2001b).

Activity-Related Issues

Almost every facility will have various activities with which it is associated. In order to protect patrons from harm, and the facility from legal action, it is important to note the proper conditions under which an activity should take place. Two primary responsibilities of facility managers with respect to emergency care consist of (a) ensuring appropriate personnel have first aid and CPR competence and (b) developing an emergency care plan (Hall & Kanoy, 2001).

Assessment of risk, training of personnel, regular review of emergency plan, and consent to give emergency care should take place prior to activity participation.

Emergency Care

Emergency care is defined as health care provided to those injured in a sport or recreation setting (Hall & Kanoy, 2001). Developing a plan to handle an emergency care situation may be a prime determinant in assessing liability in a negligence situation. Therefore, the facility manager must understand the duty to provide emergency care and who has the duty to do so. In the planning stage, the questions of who, what, when, and how should be addressed. In addition, assessment of risk, training of personnel, regular review of emergency plan, and consent to give emergency care should take place prior to activity participation. Finally, an understanding and rehearsal of the plan need to be implemented. (See chapter 11, "Medical Emergency and Evacuation Plans").

Supervision

In a sport activity negligence suit, inadequate supervision has been alleged in 80% of the cases (van der Smissen, 1990). Facility supervision includes inspection and preparation of the facility; proper instruction; provision of adequate warnings, match-up, monitoring, and rule enforcement; and furnishing of proper equipment and first aid (Gaskin, 2001; see chapter 6, "Hiring Personnel"; chapter 10, "Crowd Management"; and chapter 11, "Medical Emergency and Evacuation Plans").

Supervision falls into three categories:

1. General supervision, which consists of overseeing an activity, but not constantly remaining in one area;

2. Specific supervision, which is "constant and continuous"; and

3. Transitional supervision, whereby one transitions between general and specific depending on the nature of the activity (Gaskin, 2001).

The number of supervisors is not necessarily the factor in assessing liability for supervision; rather the *quality of supervision* is the key. Mismatching participants and having the supervisor become an active participant would be examples of poor quality supervision. To avoid poor quality su-

What steps would you take in developing a supervision plan for a field hockey venue?

pervision, a supervisory plan outlining supervisory ratios, locations, qualifications, and functions should be developed (Gaskin, 2001).

Conduct of the Activity

In the eyes of the law, a standard of conduct does not have to be perfect, but it should meet professional standards of care (see Duty, earlier in this chapter). In addition, the professional should have a good idea of the nature of the activity and participants' skill levels. For example, participants should be matched according to ability and physical compatibility. Finally, instruction is an important part of activity conduct, and instructors should ensure that participants are warned of an activity's inherent risks, not coerced into participating in an activity beyond their ability, and supervised very closely in a dangerous activity. In addition, supervisors must enforce the rules (which promote a safe environment), provide proper safety equipment, and inspect and properly maintain the facility (Trichka, 2001).

Defenses Against Liability

In order to decrease liability exposure, a facility manager should plan ahead by anticipating, identifying, and resolving potential risks (Cotten, 2001a). However, no facility and no facility manager can account for every imaginable risk. Therefore, it is important to identify various recourses available to a facility manager in the event a negligence liability case is brought forward. In this section, several possible defenses against liability are listed and briefly discussed. In addition, waivers and releases, and their use as a defense against liability, are covered in greater detail at the end of the chapter. Possible defenses against negligence include the following:

Negligence elements not met. In order for a negligence suit to have merit, all four elements (duty, breach, cause, and damage) must be present. If any one of these items is missing, there is no negligence (Cotten, 2001a).

Primary assumption of risk. Under this doctrine, the patron voluntarily put him- or herself in harm's way, the risk associated with their injury is inherent to the sport, and the participant is aware of the potential risks associated with the activity (Cotten, 2001a). For example, in the case of *Scaduto v. State* (1982), the college intramural softball player who voluntarily played, even though he knew the danger of the irrigation ditch, could be seen as assuming the risk associated within the game.

Contributory negligence. Contributory negligence can be used if the participant in some way contributed to his or her own injuries (Cotten, 2001a).

Ultra Vires *act.* If the act of negligence was by an employee and the act was beyond the normal duties of that employee, the employer would not be liable (Cotten, 2001a).

Facility lease agreements. In the scope of a facility lease-agreement negligent situation, the distinction must be made between injury related to an activity or to the premises (Cotten, 2001a).

Indemnification agreements. In this situation, one party will reimburse the other for injury (Cotten, 2001a).

Independent contractor. Generally, independent contractors, if they are primarily responsible for their duties and the facility manager exercises little control over them, will be liable for their own actions with little risk of vicarious liability for the facility (Cotten, 2001a).

Pure comparative fault. In this negligence defense, the amount of award is reduced by the amount of fault by the plaintiff (Cotten, 2001a).

Modified comparative fault. The plaintiff can recover up to the point at which he or she is 50% at fault (Cotten, 2001a).

Statute of Limitations. The time allotted for a negligence claim to remain viable varies by state. However, a minor's time clock does not start until the individual reaches the age of majority, despite when the action was committed (Cotten, 2001a).

Immunity

Recreational user immunity. This protects landowners who let others use their site for free (Cotten, 2001a). The rationale behind the law was to encourage landowners to open their land to the general public. For facility managers, this would not protect against injuries on the playing field, but it has been used successfully as a defense in the event that spectators were injured (Maloy, 2001a).

Volunteer immunity. A volunteer is classified as someone who donates time and services. Prior to passage of the Volunteer Protection Act of 1977, volunteers were treated like any other employee. However, after passage of this act, unless states mandate statutes against it, volunteers are protected from liability as long as they were acting within the scope of their duties. In addition, in order for this act to apply, volunteers must be licensed (when appropriate), the harm caused must not be due to the operation of a motor vehicle, and volunteers must undergo safety training (when appropriate; Maloy, 2001a).

> Volunteers are protected from liability as long as they are acting within the scope of their duties.

Good Samaritan. "Good Samaritan statutes have been enacted to provide immunity from liability for those who voluntarily and gratuitously come to the aid of injured persons" (Cotten, 2001a, p. 80). However, if a person is an employee of a facility, this defense would not apply, because as an employee, the person has a responsibility to help (Maloy, 2001a).

Human Resources Law

As a facility manager, negligence not only applies to incidents that occur on the field or court, but it may also apply to what happens in an office setting. There are many aspects of human resources law. One example is harassment. Every sport facility, event, or organization needs to have policies regarding harassment (van der Smissen, 2001a).

Negligence in the office or work setting can occur in many settings. A facility manager could be liable if an employee perceives a *hostile work environment*, and it is important to note that the litmus test for a hostile work environment rests solely with the person to whom the situation is occurring (van der Smissen, 2001a). A hostile work environment is present when interference with work performance occurs or an intimidating environment is created. In this scenario, five elements are necessary: (a) the employee is part of a protected class—based on sex, race, age, religion, disability, or ethnicity; (b) the harassment is unwelcome; (c) the harassment is based on gender, race, religion, age, etc.; (d) the harassment affects the employment situation; (e) the employer knows, or should know, of the harassment and fails to take corrective action (van der Smissen, 2001a).

Finally, facilities may be held liable for negligent hiring, negligent supervision of employees, negligent referral, and negligent retention of employees. For these reasons, it is important to conduct background checks on potential, and in some cases, current employees and if necessary, take corrective action (van der Smissen, 2001a). For a more in-depth discussion of this topic, see chapter 6, "Hiring Personnel."

Use of Waivers and Releases

If sport management students were to ask several lawyers or sport law scholars, "What are *waivers* and *releases*, and why should I use them?" they might receive several slightly different answers. Although both waivers and releases involve the intentional act of relinquishing a known right, Carpenter (2000) contends that the term *waiver* is often erroneously interchanged with release. She argues that a release is different from a waiver because a release is an agreement made after an injury has occurred. However, Cotten (2001a) described a waiver or *release of liability* as a contract in which a participant agrees to relinquish the right to pursue legal action against a service provider in the event that provider negligence results in participant injury (see chapter 7, "Contracts," for a discussion of the elements of a contract). In all of these definitions, individuals signing the waivers or releases are basically giving up their right to sue someone else for negligence.

Because the focus of this text is sport facility and event management, not sport law, and our discussion primarily involves transfer of risk prior to an accident, the term *waiver* will be primarily used, and it refers to any document that seeks to transfer liability from a service provider to a participant or spectator. Although various terms (waiver and/or release) may be used, the concept of transfer of liability is constant.

A waiver or "release of liability" is a contract in which one agrees not to pursue legal action for an injury occurring as a result of negligence (Cotten, 2001b). In contrast, an *agreement to participate* is similar to informed consent, but is not in the form of a contract and is signed by a minor (Cotten, 2001a). Any transfer of liability document (waiver) normally seeks to protect the service provider/professional from liability for ordinary negligence as defined above. In six states, a well-written waiver has protected against *gross negligence* as well. Through the use of a waiver, a service provider asks the patrons to whom the service is provided not to sue if they are injured. The waiver is a contract, so it is important that it be treated as such by both parties. In addition, waivers can indemnify the facility, if they are properly drafted and signed by the appropriate people as justified by that particular state's laws (Cotten, 2001a).

Each state has a different set of standards for how rigorous a waiver must be, but "in at least 45 states, a well-written, properly administered waiver, voluntarily signed by an adult, can be used to protect the recreation or sport business from liability for ordinary negligence by the business or its employees" (Cotten, 2001b, p. 87). A waiver is not a useless piece of paper. If properly written, presented, and completed, it can be a valuable tool in achieving transfer of liability.

Waivers, however, have certain limitations. For instance, a waiver cannot be contrary to public policy. If a waiver is not in the best interest of the general public, a court will not uphold it. In addition, if both parties to the waiver do not have equal bargaining power, the waiver or release will be void. Except in six states, waivers cannot attempt to waive liability for extreme negligence, gross negligence, reckless misconduct, or willful and wanton conduct.

Because minors cannot be bound by a contract signed only by the minor, they cannot waive their right to sue. However, courts in several states (CA, CO, FL, OH, MA) have recently upheld waivers signed by a parent on behalf of a minor child. Several other state courts (AZ, GA, ID, MS, HI) have submitted opinions that point out that waivers signed by parents on behalf of a minor child may be upheld in the future (Cotten, 2001b).

Evaluating a Waiver's Enforceability

The specific format of a waiver may vary from state to state or jurisdiction to jurisdiction. This discussion is not intended to tell the sport management student how to write a waiver. It is important for sport managers to remember that a licensed attorney should review any waiver or release document; however, experts suggest that there are minimum criteria that generally have to be met for a waiver to be enforceable.

It should be clearly labeled as a waiver.

It must be clearly written and understandable. (The font size should be large enough to be read.)

It must be filled out correctly, accurately, and completely. The person signing the release has to understand that it is a release from liability in the event of injury (Coren, 1995).

It can involve relinquishing only the right to sue for ordinary negligence (not gross negligence or intentional torts) (Carpenter, 2000).

There must be consideration or exchange of value involved in the contract.

The parties involved should be clearly specified. (Who is relinquishing their rights and who is the waiver protecting?)

The person signing the contract must have the capacity to contract. (Waivers signed by minors are unenforceable) (Cotten, 2001c).

Both parties must have equal bargaining positions. (A scuba instructor cannot ask a student to sign a waiver after the student has paid, the boat has left the dock, and there's no refund possible!)

Inherent risks should be mentioned because people can't give the right to sue for a risk that they were not aware of.

Mentioning the word *negligence* in the body of the waiver makes the waiver stronger in many states.

Table 9.2. Necessary Elements for a Waiver to Be Enforceable

Summary

1. The importance of a facility manager's having an understanding of negligence cannot be overstated. In fact, more lawsuits in this field are based in negligence liability than any other category.

2. Negligence, which falls under tort law, is an "unintentional act that injures".

3. To determine liability, the person accused of negligence will be compared to others of similar occupational status (Reasonable Prudent Professional – RPP) to determine prudence of action.

4. The elements used in a court of law to specifically determine one's negligence consist of "duty, breach of duty, causation, and damages". Furthermore, in order for a person to be held liable for negligent action, all four of the aforementioned items must be present.

5. A general defense to liability exists when any one of the elements of negligence has not been satisfied. Barring that situation, a variety of other defenses exist, which can help the facility manager in the event of a negligence suit.

6. Responsibility for facility negligence will generally rest with employees, administrative or supervisory personnel, and the corporate entity.

7. Responsibility for negligence may also be predicated upon whether the situation was "premise related or activity related". Premise-related situations are generally those that involve facility upkeep and patrons. Activity-related issues, on the other hand, pertain to the particular situation at hand.

8. From a facility manager's perspective, it is important to note that even if outside groups are directing an event, the staff should be prepared to deliver emergency care, including first aid and CPR, with appropriate direction derived from an established and written emergency plan.

9. Proper supervision should be emphasized, because inadequate supervision is alleged in 80% of the cases.

10. Insuring the proper conduct of a particular activity can ward off many problems before they become lawsuits.

11. One common defense for negligence is the use of waivers or releases. A waiver or release of liability is a contract. The participant agrees to relinquish the right to pursue legal action against the service provider in the event that the participant is injured as a result of provider negligence.

12. Although the enforceability of waivers may vary from state to state, certain minimum criteria can be used to evaluate the enforceability of

a waiver. A licensed attorney should review any waiver or release document before it is used.

13. Facility managers need to know what happens in an office setting just as much as what happens on the field. Developing harassment policies and effective hiring procedures will help prevent negligence lawsuits alleging harassment and help create a respectable working environment.

Questions

The Case of Alliah Jones Revisited

At the beginning of this chapter, the case of the young woman Alliah Jones was discussed. Based on the material presented in this chapter, please address the following questions to review the concepts presented as well as to check your understanding and develop critical thinking skills:

1. Did Alliah have a responsibility to supervise Jose?

2. If she had a responsibility to supervise, was Alliah negligent in doing so by stepping out of the fitness and weight room for a few minutes?

3. Would Alliah be responsible for the first aid applied to Jose's foot if not performed correctly? Could she perhaps defend herself via the Good Samaritan rule?

4. What role would the orientation program that Alliah gave to Jose play in this situation? In the same vein, how would Jose's competitive athletic background play into the scenario, and what impact would his potential lost winnings and sponsorship opportunities have in this case?

5. Would Alliah's boss, the BBHF manager, and that person's boss, the BBHF owner, be liable for Alliah's actions?

6. What can sport management professionals learn from this scenario and Alliah's situation?

Practical Application

Evaluating a Liability Release and Express Assumption of Risk Document

Using the principles discussed in this chapter, examine the *Liability Release and Express Assumption of Risk* document on page #140 and answer the following questions:

1. Is the document clearly labeled as a waiver/release?

2. Is it clearly written and understandable?

3. Is the font size large enough to be read?

4. What steps should be taken to fill it out correctly, accurately, and completely?

5. Do you think the person signing the release will understand that it is a release from liability in the event of injury?

6. Does the release involve relinquishing the right to sue only for ordinary negligence, not gross negligence or intentional torts?

7. Is there consideration or exchange of value involved in the contract?

8. Are the parties involved clearly specified? (In other words, is it clear who is relinquishing their rights and whom the waiver is protecting?)

LIABILITY RELEASE
AND EXPRESS ASSUMPTION OF RISK

Please read carefully and fill in all blanks before signing.

I, _____ , hereby affirm that I have been advised and thoroughly informed
Participant Name
of the inherent hazards of skin diving and scuba diving.

Further, I understand that diving with compressed air involves certain inherent risks; decompression sickness, embolism, or other hyperbaric injuries can occur that require treatment in a recompression chamber. I further understand that the open-water diving trips, which are necessary for training and for certification, may be conducted at a site that is remote, either by time or distance or both, from such a recompression chamber. I still choose to proceed with such instructional dives in spite of the possible absence of a recompression chamber in proximity to the dive site.

I understand and agree that neither my instructor(s), _____ the facility through which I received my instruction, _____ , nor International PADI, Inc., nor its affiliate and subsidiary corporations, nor any of their respective employees, officers, agents or assigns, (hereinafter referred to as "Released Parties") may be held liable or responsible in any way for any injury, death, or other damages to me or my family, heirs, or assigns that may occur as a result of my participation in this diving class or as a result of the negligence of any party, including the Released Parties, whether passive or active.

In consideration of being allowed to enroll in this course, I hereby personally assume all risks in connection with said course, for any harm, injury or damage that may befall me while I am enrolled as a student of this course, including all risks connected therewith, whether foreseen or unforeseen.

I further save and hold harmless said course and Released Parties from any claim or lawsuit by me, my family, estate, heirs, or assigns, arising out of my enrollment and participation in this course including both claims arising during the course or after I receive my certification.

I also understand that skin diving and scuba diving are physically strenuous activities and that I will be exerting myself during this diving course, and that if I am injured as a result of a heart attack, panic, hyperventilation, etc., that I expressly assume the risk of said injuries and that I will not hold the above listed individuals or companies responsible for the same.

I further state that I am of lawful age and legally competent to sign this liability release, or that I have acquired the written consent of my parent or guardian.

I understand that the terms herein are contractual and not a mere recital, and that I have signed this document of my own free act.

IT IS THE INTENTION OF _____ BY THIS INSTRUMENT TO EXEMPT AND RELEASE
Participant Name

MY INSTRUCTORS, _____ , THE FACILITY THROUGH WHICH I RECEIVED

MY INSTRUCTION, _____ , AND INTERNATIONAL PADI, INC., AND ALL RELATED ENTITIES AS DEFINED ABOVE, FROM ALL LIABILITY OR RESPONSIBILITY WHATSOEVER FOR PERSONAL INJURY, PROPERTY DAMAGE OR WRONGFUL DEATH HOWEVER CAUSED, INCLUDING, BUT NOT LIMITED TO, THE NEGLIGENCE OF THE RELEASED PARTIES, WHETHER PASSIVE OR ACTIVE.

I HAVE FULLY INFORMED MYSELF OF THE CONTENTS OF THIS LIABILITY RELEASE AND EXPRESS ASSUMPTION OF RISK BY READING IT BEFORE I SIGNED IT ON BEHALF OF MYSELF AND MY HEIRS.

_____   _____
ature   Date (Day/Month/Year)

_____   _____
applicable)   Date (Day/Month/Year)

139

Express Assumption of Risk Document. © International PADI, Inc.
on of International PADI, Inc.)

Chapter Ten

Crowd Management

Application Exercise

Mike and Kathy Tompkins attended a Miami Sharks football game at Shark Stadium in Miami on December 6, 1999. For approximately two years, Mr. and Mrs. Tompkins were season ticket holders whose seats were located in the Shark-pound, the pie-shaped end-zone section of the stadium behind the Shark's goalpost. During the last quarter of the December 6th game, the Shark's kicker attempted a field goal. The football was catapulted through the uprights of the goalpost, over the stadium net designed to catch it, and into the stands. Mr. Tompkins, who saw the ball coming his way, stood up in front of his assigned seat, extended his arms, and caught the football. When he attempted to sit down, Mr. Tompkins was pushed from his seat face first into the cement aisle by aggressive fans who stripped him of the souvenir ball. Mr. Tompkins suffered numerous injuries from this attack, including facial lacerations, a sprained shoulder and arm resulting in extensive physical therapy, and a broken nose that required surgery.

Prior to this incident, Mr. and Mrs. Tompkins and other patrons seated in the end-zone section of the stadium lodged complaints with Shark Stadium's Guest Relations Office and security personnel concerning the lack of security and crowd control in their seating area during field goal and extra point attempts. They often complained that the football regularly cleared the stadium net, landed in the stands, and caused a disturbance among the fans, resulting in a danger to the welfare of the patrons seated in their section. It was undisputed that the defendant, In Our Arms Security, was responsible for providing security services at Shark Stadium during home games.

Mr. and Mrs. Tompkins filed a complaint asserting negligence against In Our Arms Security as well as the Stadium Authority of the City of Miami, alleging that the defendants breached a duty of care owed to Mr. Tompkins by failing to supervise security guards at Shark Stadium and failing to regulate crowd control in the end-zone seating area. In Our Arms Security filed a motion for summary judgment, which was granted on October 11, 2000. Thereafter, the plaintiffs filed an appeal challenging the trial court's grant of summary judgment in favor of the defendants (see chapter 9, "Facility Negligence").

Some state Supreme Courts have held that facility managers are responsible for risks that are 'common, frequent and expected,' and in no way affect the duty of theatres, amusement parks, and sports facilities to protect patrons from forseeably dangerous conditions not inherent in the amusement activity. Although an operator of a sport facility for which admission is charged is not an insurer of his patron's safety he/she will be "liable for injuries to his/her patrons . . . where he/she fails to 'use reasonable care in the construction, maintenance, and management of the facility." Thus, it becomes clear that the main question was whether the injury to Ms. Tomkins resulted from a risk that was inherent in the activity (*Telega v. Security Bureau, Inc.,* 1998).

In this case, Mr. Tompkins stood up in front of his seat in the end-zone section of the stadium and caught a football that cleared the goalpost net during a field goal attempt by the Sharks. He was immediately attacked by a group of "displaced" fans who stripped the football and pushed him down into the aisle, crushing his face into the concrete and causing serious injury. The lower court had concluded that the risk of being trampled by a group of fans pursuing a souvenir was common to the football game and reasonably foreseeable based on Mr. Tompkins' experience. Although this type of unruly, improper fan conduct may have occurred in Mr. Tompkins' section of the stadium before, the State Supreme Court found that being trampled by displaced fans was not a risk inherent in or an ordinary part of the spectator sport of football. The lower court's reliance on Mr. Tompkins' prior knowledge of such "fan upheaval" and his report of this dangerous behavior to management and security personnel was an attempt to improperly shift the focus of the inquiry from the risks inherent in the game of football itself to an examination of other risks that were present in a particular football stadium. By creating the notion that "if it happened before, it must be customary," the trial court concluded that if a spectator was injured at a football game and had prior knowledge of the risk of injury, the risk was automatically an inherent part of the spectator sport and recovery was prohibited. This inappropriately forced Mr. Tompkins to ensure his own safety and protect himself from the behavior of aggressive fans despite the presence of the defendant whose primary obligation was to regulate crowd control.

The risk involved here is unlike the risk of being struck by an errant puck while a spectator at a hockey game, falling down or being bumped by other skaters at a roller skating rink, or being hit by a batted ball during baseball tryouts. Contrary to the current case, these other cases involved risks that were inherent to the activity itself and are specific to the activity at any type of appropriate venue. They are, therefore, as a matter of law, risks assumed by the spectators and participants who patronize the sport facilities. It is not a matter of common knowledge that an onslaught of displaced fans is a common, frequent, or expected occurrence to someone catching a souvenir football. Therefore, it cannot be said that the injuries suffered by Mr. Tompkins resulted from a risk that any spectator would be held to anticipate and against which a sport facility has no duty to protect. Certainly this matter would compel a different result had Mr. Tompkins been injured by the aerial football itself rather than the displaced fans intent on obtaining it.

1. Who won this case?

2. Do you agree with the court's decision? Why or why not?

3. What could In Our Arms Security have done to prevent this case from going to court?

4. What does "summary judgment" mean?

Adapted from Telega v. Security Bureau, Inc., 719 A.2d 372; 1998 Pa. Super. Lexis 2990

| Introduction to Crowd Management | As mentioned in previous chapters (chapter 8, "Risk Management," & chapter 9, "Facility Negligence"), an understanding of various event and risk management techniques and negligence would be advantageous for facility managers from a public relations as well as a legal standpoint. The importance of sport and entertainment events in our society has caused public and media attention to be focused on many diverse events around the world. This increased scrutiny has not only augmented public awareness of the various host facilities, but has also illuminated various issues pertaining to proper crowd management strategies used at sport facilities. Obvious concerns emanating from the 9/11 terrorist attack, the bombing at the 1996 Atlanta Olympics, the infamous Camp Randall Field crowd-rush case at the University of Wisconsin (1993), and injuries sustained from various championship "celebratory riots" emphasize the importance of proper crowd management plans. |

The litigious nature of our society also underscores the importance of proper crowd management training for facility managers regarding potentially contentious activities. Before September 11, 2001, the biggest concern for facility and event managers stemmed from alcohol problems. Now, facility managers must make their spectators feel safe while at sport facilities. The addition of metal detectors, security checks, and bomb-sniffing dogs as well as extra law enforcement officers helps to accomplish the current task (Tierney, 2001).

Preliminary research assessed game management practices at selected municipal football stadiums (Ammon, 1993). The data demonstrated that crowd management practices consisted of many elements including alcohol policies and crowd management strategies. A 1995 study investigated the impact of risk management practices (including crowd management strategies) on insurance premiums (Mulrooney & Ammon, 1995). The 1995 study's outcome included a preliminary risk management paradigm that identified criteria such as properly trained crowd management staff, appropriate alcohol policies, a consistent ejection policy, a well-written medical service plan, and the design and implementation of an emergency evacuation plan as important components for a comprehensive risk management plan.

Additional data from a 1998 study (Ammon & Fried, 1998) pertained to crowd management practices at stadiums with professional sport teams. This research indicated that the lack of consistent and approved alcohol policies and crowd management strategies could result in unnecessary injuries, countless lawsuits, decreased facility revenue, and a negative impact on a facility's public relations program.

> A pleasant environment free of non-inherent risks should be a primary goal for public assembly facility managers.

Beyond these previously mentioned studies, very little research exists relating to national crowd management practices in sport, community, and entertainment facilities. Legally, however, facility managers must provide various duties to their fans or guests (van der Smissen, 1990). As demonstrated in the few available research studies, providing a completely safe

An overcrowded event is one result of poor crowd management.

and secure environment for all patrons is impossible. Striving to achieve a pleasant environment free of noninherent risks should be a primary goal for public assembly facility managers in order to reduce the possibility of litigation. In addition, this mindset will assist the facility in providing positive public relations, which often leads to repeat customers and an increased revenue flow.

What Is Crowd Management?

Crowd management is an organizational tool to assist facility or event administrators in providing a safe and enjoyable environment for their guests by implementing the facility/event policies and procedures. The duties of a crowd manager include managing the movement and activities of crowds/guests, assisting in emergencies, and assisting guests with specific concerns related to their enjoyment and/or involvement with the event by communicating with the guests in a polite and professional manner (Ammon, 1997). A facility manager must recognize the importance of an effective crowd management plan in order to protect the event's image and reputation. This plan, however, should be created to assist facility management to *supervise* crowds, not to *control* them. Trying to control a crowd is a very difficult and potentially dangerous endeavor whereas supervising or managing a crowd is more achievable.

Why Is Crowd Management Necessary?

Many experts in the field of crowd management believe the most hazardous time at a sport or entertainment event is not during the event itself, but during fan ingress and egress from the facility. Thus, it becomes important for a facility manager to have an accurate count of the number of individuals in the facility. It is too late to worry about the number of spectators inside the facility after the event begins. Recent technology can provide not only easy access to the facility as well as a customer loyalty card, but also provide the facility management with an up-to-the-minute account of the numbers of spectators inside the facility (Nuttall, 2001b).

Significant liability issues exist at every event, and the inability of facility managers to provide a safe and secure environment due to poor crowd management strategies is an invitation for disaster. Unfortunately, many facility managers do not realize that crowd management strategies should affect many facility decisions from the facility design through the completion of the event. Additional tactics should include more standing room throughout the facility and creating space between sections to prevent overcrowding (Hiestand & Wood, 2001). Van der Smissen (1990) emphasized the importance of crowd management when she described it as part of the duty facility managers owe their patrons to protect them from unreasonable risk of harm from other individuals. However, even though facility management has the duty of care to provide a safe environment to the spectators, the duty of care to protect does not extend to unforeseeable acts committed by third parties (van der Smissen, 1990). Thus, some crowd activities do fall outside the responsibility of a facility manager.

The litigious nature of our society has demonstrated that lawsuits will be filed against sport facilities by a variety of groups. These plaintiffs include the athletes, spectators, and independent contractors, such as game officials, concessionaires, uniformed law enforcement officials, and members of peer group security companies. The litigation usually revolves around claims of some type of negligent behavior including negligent hiring of security personnel, negligent supervision, or negligent training (Ammon & Fried, 1998).

If the case goes to court, the jury will ask to see the crowd management plan. They will also ask about the special training that the crowd management staff received. Documentation specific to the crowd management plan will be scrutinized:

> The jury will consider the appropriateness of the crowd management plan contingent upon seven issues: 1) type of event; 2) surrounding facilities and environment; 3) known rivalries among schools; 4) threats of violence; 5) existence and adequacy of an emergency plan; 6) anticipation of crowd size and seating arrangements; 7) use of security personnel and ushers. (Miller, 1993 p. 32)

Foreseeable Duties

The concept of *foreseeability* is also a key element in the determination of negligence (Miller, 1993; van der Smissen, 1990). Facility managers are responsible for using a proactive or "anticipatory" type of philosophy when recognizing potential crowd management problems. If, in the past, an injury situation occurred at an event, then foreseeability dictates the circumstances may occur again, and "due care" needs to be implemented. Van der Smissen (1990) stated that "the reasonable and prudent professional must be able to foresee from the circumstances a danger to the participant, a danger which presents an 'unreasonable risk of harm' against which the participant must be protected" (p.45). However, a facility operator is not responsible for all injuries that occur at his or her stadium, although the courts will expect the operator to take reasonable precautions (Wong, 1994).

The duty of care owed to a group of spectators depends on their "status." As mentioned in chapter 9 ("Facility Negligence"), most fans and athletes are classified as *invitees*. An invitee usually provides the owner of the property with some monetary benefit (i.e., ticket and concession sales). These individuals are owed the greatest degree of care from any known defects or problems. An invitee enters onto the property of another with the owner's encouragement unlike a *trespasser*, who is owed the least degree of care.

Bearman v. University of Notre Dame (1983) was a seminal court decision that had far-reaching implications for facility managers regarding the issue of foreseeability and spectator status (Miller, 1993; van der Smissen, 1990). In October 1979, Ms. C. Bearman was walking across a University parking lot with her husband, after attending a Notre Dame football game. An intoxicated spectator fell on Bearman from behind, breaking her leg. No security or facility personnel were present at the time of the accident. Bearman sued Notre Dame, stating she was an invitee and the University had a duty to protect her from the negligent acts of a third party. The University maintained the incident was an unforeseeable accident. The Indiana Court of Appeals, however, disagreed and stated that Notre Dame allowed alcohol to be consumed during "tailgate" parties in the parking lots. With the presence of alcohol, it was foreseeable that some individuals could become intoxicated and pose a general danger to others. Therefore, the court found that the University had a duty to protect its "invitees" from negligent third-party acts.

> A connection has been observed between crowd safety and customer comfort; in other words, fans respond to the environment in which they find themselves.

Global Crowd Management Concerns

For many years, violence at British soccer matches was an almost foregone conclusion, prompting government officials to examine every possibility to curb this problem (J. Williams, Dunning, & Murphy, 1984). In England, violent crowd behavior was often termed *hooliganism*. In the early 1990s, legislation was introduced that required some soccer club fans to acquire identity cards. This was intended to restrict the "hooligans" who attended the soccer games to prey on opposing fans (Buford, 1991). Presently England has one of the most stringent pieces of legislation (Taylor Report) pertaining to crowd management in the world. These new policies have caused soccer violence to diminish tremendously. The Taylor Report was a comprehensive investigation of English football that emanated from the Hillsborough disaster, which claimed 96 lives in 1989. One of the themes that emerged from the report was a connection made between crowd safety and customer comfort; in other words, the fans will respond to the environment in which they find themselves (Nuttall, 2001b).

As previously mentioned, sport has become global. Unfortunately, so have the problems associated with sport. Thus, due to the prestige and significance of sport, crowd management plans need to be in place at every type of event throughout the world. The Monica Seles stabbing incident in May 1993 made stadium managers aware that violence can occur at any type of event, even tennis tournaments. In addition, at the 2000 Ericsson Open near Miami, officials were forced to deny entry to a fan who was identified as a stalker of Martina Hingis (Wilson, 2001).

The information discussed in this chapter is similar to that which you receive in other classes in many ways. However, unlike most other course information, failure to implement appropriate crowd management techniques can lead to disaster and tragedy. For soccer fans, the year 2001 was deadly: The tragedies began during April in South Africa when 43 people were killed and over 100 injured at a match between the Kaizer Chiefs and Orlando Pirates. Coincidentally, 42 people had died a decade earlier (1991) at a game between the *same* two teams. Eighteen days later, at a match in the Congo, fans began throwing bottles after the score was tied. The local law enforcement responded by firing tear gas, which caused a stampede as the crowd rushed to escape the gas, resulting in eight dead. One week later, during the first week of May, two spectators died at a soccer match in Iran, and one died at a soccer stadium in the Ivory Coast. Finally, on May 11 at a soccer stadium in Ghana, the supporters of one team began to throw objects on the field with 5 minutes left in the match. Police again fired tear gas, which sent the panicked crowd stampeding to the main stadium gates, which were locked. It was estimated that over 70,000 spectators were crammed into a stadium designed to hold 45,000. The ensuing riot resulted in the deaths of 126 fans (Selzer, 2001).

The Taylor Report led to the elimination of standing-room "terraces" at many English soccer matches.

Although North America, long believed by many to be immune from event violence, has not been forced to deal with the extreme bouts of violence witnessed in other parts of the world, it has had its share of difficulties. One of the first tragedies occurred in 1979, when 11 concertgoers were crushed to death before a Who concert at Cincinnati's Riverfront Stadium. In 1991, three teenagers died at an AC/DC concert in Salt Lake City after being crushed by the crowd. Later the same year, 5,000 patrons tried to cram into a 2,700-seat facility on the campus of New York's Harlem City College, resulting in nine deaths and 29 injuries (Newman & Dao, 1992). Crowd managers in the United States have also had to deal with "celebratory riots," which amounted to destructive celebrations after the 1993 Super Bowl in Dallas, 1993 Stanley Cup in Montreal, 1993 NBA Championship in Chicago, with the most damage occurring in Denver after the 1998 Super Bowl.

In the United States, some of the most violent actions have involved spectators at professional games. For example, an opposing equipment manager was knocked unconscious after being hit in the head with an iceball at a New York Giants game. Similarly in 2001, a Denver Broncos player was hit in the eye with a snowball (containing a battery) while walking off the field after a game. In addition, the 2001 NFL season witnessed two games being temporarily halted after irate fans protested referee calls by littering fields with plastic beer bottles in Cleveland and New Orleans (Hiestand & Wood, 2001). Crowd problems became so prevalent during Philadelphia Eagles games that officials put a courtroom in Veterans Stadium in 1997 to prosecute violators immediately. This unusual circumstance followed unruly incidents that occurred during a *Monday Night Football* game. The court was moved off site in 1998, but transgressors are still taken to the new location during the game (Hiestand & Wood).

Sometimes players have gone after these spectators as they did during the summer of 2001 at Wrigley Field, when a dozen Dodgers chased a fan that had pilfered a cap from one of the players. The NHL witnessed an odd incident when a Philadelphia fan leaped into the Toronto Maple Leafs penalty box. The fan was attempting to fight the Maple Leafs' Tie Domi, who had been squirting the Philly fans with his water bottle. Even the NBA has had its share of problems as evidenced by Jimmy Buffet's being ejected for foul language at a Miami Heat game (Zoltak, 2001b).

Crowd management pertaining to intercollegiate sport also came under investigation when 73 people were injured, 6 critically, when university students rushed the field at Camp Randall Stadium, after a October 1993 collegiate football game between Wisconsin and Michigan (Telander, 1993). More recently, crowd management came under additional scrutiny due to the two deaths attributed to the bombing at the 1996 Atlanta Olympics. Crowd management is equally needed at lesser known events such as the 1999 Phoenix Open Golf Tournament where a spectator was wrestled to the ground with a loaded semiautomatic weapon, within yards of Tiger Woods (Ferguson, 1999).

Because of the previously mentioned problems as well as the threat of terrorism, many changes have taken place at facilities across the United States. An obvious increase in the number of security personnel has occurred with more searches being conducted and many of those searchers using metal detectors. Some facility managers, such as those at Madison Square Gardens, have located large concrete barriers, often designed as flower beds, around the facility to prevent potential explosive-laden vehi-

Trained staff performs various types of searches to prevent prohibited items from being brought into the facility.

cles from coming near their outside walls. Major League Baseball now prohibits all vehicles from parking within 100 feet of any stadium (Miller, Stoldt, & Ayres, 2002). Implementing a strategy used at the 1991 Super Bowl in Tampa at the height of the Gulf War, the Federal Aviation Administration (FAA) has established certain no-fly zones over various sporting events. In addition, because of the possibility of biological hazards, security staff is being placed in front of fresh air intakes to keep people away from ventilation systems ("Venue Managers," 2001).

Obviously these changes are making attendance at sporting events more rigid and not quite as spontaneous. We live in an open society that enjoys a number of freedoms; however, these benefits may impact the safety of the individuals in your facility or event. As one crowd management expert recently stated, "Freedom becomes a little more restricted if you want to ensure a safe environment" (Tierney, 2001, p. 4).

Components of a Crowd Management Plan

A crowd management plan will help to ensure a safe and enjoyable environment for all spectators. As stated earlier, providing a safe and secure environment free from noninherent risks for all patrons should be the philosophy of sporting event facilities, and the crowd management policy should parallel this concept. A proper crowd management plan may be accomplished through the implementation of six fundamental concepts.

First, an effective crowd management plan must **be an integral element of a larger risk management plan**. As discussed in chapter 8, every facility should design, implement, and practice a risk management plan. The ability for a crowd management plan to provide a safe, enjoyable, and secure environment for all invitees may be accomplished through implementing various risk management components (Ammon & Fried, 1998). The facility's risk management plan needs to be constantly updated and modified, and those changes will affect the crowd management plan. Thus, evaluation of the risk management plan becomes a critical issue. A review after every event is paramount to identify the ingredients of the plan that were effective and those that need to be modified (Miller, 1993).

Second, an effective crowd management plan must **provide for trained and competent staff to carry out the crowd management plan.** Crowd management undertakes many responsibilities, and specific members of the crowd management staff must be trained to undertake each of the various duties.

• Coordinate the event and facilities

• Understand and comprehend facility risk management plans

• Assess crowd for potential problems

• Manage changing crowd behavior and demeanor

• Use good guest-service techniques

• Respond to guest concerns

• Implement facility/event policies and procedures

• Assess potential problem guests

• Emphasize appropriate reaction to problem guests

• Resolve credential/ticketing/seating problems

Table 10.1. Specific Duties of Crowd Managers

(Ammon, 1997)

Trained staff must be able to assist with emergency procedures as well as traditional crowd management.

Many courts recognize the amount of training necessary to secure a license; therefore, employing licensed crowd management personnel sometimes serves as partial protection against frivolous lawsuits (Ammon, 1993; Ammon & Fried, 1998). When a facility undertakes the responsibility to provide a service itself, it is known as doing it *in-house*. Thus, some facilities will conduct the crowd management duties in-house. Other facilities will *outsource*, or subcontract, the crowd management services to an independent company. One of the most recognized of these crowd management companies is Contemporary Services Corporation (CSC) based in Los Angeles, CA. CSC has been in business for over 30 years, uses more than 50,000 part-time employees, and averages nearly 5,000 events per year. Eighty percent of CSC's business pertains to sport, and they provide crowd management personnel to various NFL, NBA, MLB, and NCAA teams; the Super Bowl; major concert tours; and hundreds of sport facilities across the United States (Tierney, 2001).

Third, an effective crowd management plan must **address the specific procedures used to implement the emergency plan**. The emergency plan can "ensure that minor incidents don't become major incidents and that major incidents don't become fatal" (American College of Sports Medicine [ACSM], 1992, p. 29). To be effective, the emergency plan must have anticipatory and reactionary components (van der Smissen, 1990). The anticipatory area pertains to inspections, preventative maintenance, and potential crowd congestion as contained in the previously discussed SOPs (see chapter 8, "Risk Management"). For example, a good ingress through turnstiles should net around 660 people per hour, **but** that is for spectators who *already* have tickets. If the spectators were purchasing tickets as they came through the turnstiles, a facility manager would need to anticipate a *much* slower ingress (Nuttall, 2001a).

> Facility and event managers can help to defray some potential increases by reviewing their emergency and evacuation procedures.

The reactionary component of the emergency plan pertains to the procedures implemented after an emergency occurs. Emergencies take the form of many items such as medical problems (life-threatening and minor injuries), impending weather (lightning, tornadoes), natural disasters (earthquakes, floods), fire, bomb threats, power outages, and, in today's society, terrorist activities. The impact of the terrorist attacks continues to be felt in the facility and event management industry, and insurance premiums could still increase tremendously. Although there is no such thing as a 100% risk-free event, facility and event managers can help to defray some potential increases by reviewing their emergency and evacuation procedures (Glendinning, 2001).

A common thread throughout the plan must be to emphasize guest safety as a priority and prepare staff to assist guests with special needs. In the past, it was assumed that all customers were mobile, that they had perfect vision, normal hearing, and that they were otherwise free of any physical or mental differences. In recent years, however, facility and event managers have acknowledged the fact that variations exist in people's abilities, and we must make our facilities accessible and pleasant for everyone who wishes to enjoy them.

Fourth, an effective crowd management plan must **contain procedures necessary to eject disruptive, unruly, or intoxicated patrons**. The ejection duties should remain the responsibility of *trained* crowd management staff and, in some jurisdictions, uniformed law enforcement. These individuals must understand the concepts of *reasonable person theory* and *excessive force* and how they may be sued for negligence if an ejection is done incorrectly. It is important to mention that the facility ushers should not be used in this undertaking; their responsibilities should be to enhance communication and customer satisfaction (Miller, 1993). Because ushers are not trained to handle these disruptive behaviors, they may injure themselves or cause the problem to escalate if they attempt to become involved in an ejection (van der Smissen, 1990). Ejections should remain the primary responsibility of the crowd management staff.

Removing disruptive or intoxicated fans will provide a safer environment for the remaining spectators and help to protect the stadium director from potential litigation. Most spectators want to enjoy the event and will assist the crowd management staff with disruptive or intoxicated individuals. For example, in 1995 during a Knicks-Pacers NBA game at Market Square Arena, a spectator threw a crumpled cup towards the Knicks bench. Several fans "discreetly" pointed fingers at the guilty party identifying him to crowd management officials who promptly ejected the culprit (Vecsey, 1996). It has been the author's experience that many times upon the removal of an overly disruptive individual, the spectators in the immediate vicinity will actually applaud the ejection.

> Removing disruptive or intoxicated fans will provide a safer environment for the remaining spectators.

Every ejection must be properly documented. This is a crucial step in the ejection process, as it serves to produce possibly valuable defenses for the crowd management employee and facility administration if subsequent litigation ensues. Photographs should be used as an additional step in the ejection process. This measure accurately portrays the ejected fan's condition and further protects the employees from unnecessary legal harassment. With today's technology as a benefit, numerous facilities also use

Example of central command post at English soccer stadium

videotape to capture the arrest or ejection process (Ammon & Fried, 1998).

Fifth, an effective crowd management plan must **implement a competent communication network**. Communication has been found to be a critical aspect in providing spectator safety, enjoyment, and security. The use of a centralized area (command post) for representatives from each group involved in the management of an event (facility management, law enforcement, maintenance, medical, and security) will provide the opportunity to facilitate communication and improve decision making. Representatives from each agency involved in event management must have the ability to discuss immediate problems in an efficient and timely fashion. This command post should be located in a position to view the overall event and is critical for effective communications. Depending on the facility, the command post will normally be placed in, or on top of, the press box (Ammon, 1993).

Multichanneled radios are an integral element in the implementation of such a communication system. These types of radios allow simultaneous communication between various employees. In addition, by using binoculars, the command post operators can identify disruptive or intoxicated patrons. The patron's location can then be communicated over the radios to a responsible crowd management team. Also, medical emergencies and traffic congestion can be observed from the command post. Experience has shown that patrons will recognize the serious tone the crowd management plan conveys when these potentially dangerous situations are dealt in a swift and firm manner.

Sixth, an effective crowd management policy must **involve the use of proper signage**. Informational and directional signs build a support net-

Example of directional signage

work between fans and sport facility management staff. Spectators appreciate being treated fairly, and if previously informed, will normally abide by facility directives pertaining to no smoking sections, alcohol policies, and prohibited items.

Directional signs have a number of important uses. As spectators approach the facility, road signs are used to indicate the correct exits. In addition, these signs assist in providing parking information. Other signs serve to indicate the correct gate or portal, as well as direct the ticket-buying patrons to the box office. Signage will help to provide the answers to important questions asked by facility patrons regarding the location of concession stands, first aid rooms, telephones, and restrooms.

Informational signs regarding prohibited items in the facility assist patrons in making decisions upon entry. Cans, bottles, backpacks, weapons, food, recording devices, and sometimes cameras are not allowed in many facilities. The response of facility managers to the events on September 11, 2001, has dramatically impacted the types of items allowed into most facilities. Spectators appreciate being treated fairly and will normally abide by facility directives if previously informed.

Innovations in Crowd Management

Sport has become a passion for many individuals in our society. Sometimes the "fan" becomes more of a "fanatic," and measures must be implemented to ensure that these few individuals do not ruin the enjoyment of others. Crowd management has become an onerous and serious task for facility managers throughout the world. New methods and innovations are being undertaken to ensure that every spectator, employee, and athlete enjoys a safe and enjoyable environment.

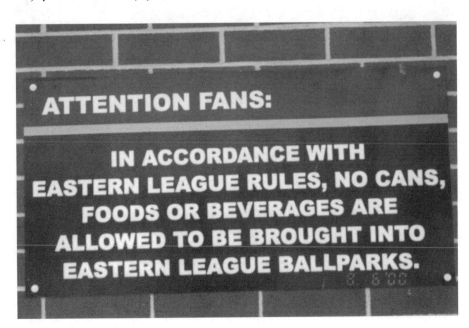

Informational signage decreases confusion

The celebration frenzy that occurs after championships recently has turned into destructive mob actions. Police are adopting new strategies to quell these occurrences. Extra police on patrol have orders to arrest anyone immediately before the looting or riots begin. New police techniques are being implemented to ensure that law enforcement doesn't overreact or resort to brutality during these "celebrations." Also, team members and coaches have begun to film public information commercials before actually winning the championship, asking fans to moderate their behavior (McIntyre, 1998).

In addition, video cameras with high-resolution zoom lenses have been mounted throughout many new stadiums, including Coors Field, Denver, and PNC Park, Pittsburgh. These cameras feed back to a central viewing room within the stadium, where facility officials monitor parking lots, ticket gates, concourses, and seating areas for indications of disruptive or criminal activity. Similar technology has proven successful at most British facilities, including Chelsea and Arsenal Stadiums, to diminish much of the crowd violence.

Most facilities use video cameras to monitor spectators throughout the venue.

The potentially high risks associated with large crowds have motivated security and crowd management operations to develop more sophisticated and high-tech security systems.

Various criminal acts have occurred at major sport events from minor pickpocketing and ticket scalping to the more serious extreme, such as the 1996 bombing at the Summer Olympic Games in Atlanta. These sporting events provide attractive targets for any terrorist or religious group wishing to draw attention to their cause. The potentially high risks associated with large crowds have motivated security and crowd management operations to develop more sophisticated and high-tech security systems.

At the Nagano Winter Games, over 50,000 spectators had to pass through metal detectors at the Minami Nagano Sports Park before they were allowed into the Olympic stadium ("Olympic Security," 1998). Spectators at the 1991 Super Bowl, held during the Gulf War, were also subjected to a search via metal detectors before being granted admission to Tampa Stadium.

The 2001 Super Bowl had received its share of criticism when the Tampa police at Raymond James Stadium employed a "face recognition system." The software created a "face print" based on various measurements of the human face. These types of programs have the ability to measure 40-80 various coordinates (distance between the eyes, shape of the mouth, width of the forehead) of hundreds of faces per minute and compare them against photos and databases of known terrorists. Although no arrests were made and only one ticket scalper was identified, law enforcement officials praised the potential of such technology (Miller et al., 2002).

The actions of September 11 have forever changed facility and event management. For the first time in history, the 2002 NFL Super Bowl was classified as a "National Special Security Event." This classification allowed the federal government to take over the control of the security of the event. The Secret Service was put in charge and, along with the Federal Emergency Management Agency (FEMA) and the FBI, a comprehensive security plan was devised.

Figure 10.1
Communications posted on 2002 Super Bowl website (courtesy of IAAM and facility manager)

> **Since the tragic events of September 11, 2001, special security measures have been implemented at the Louisiana Superdome:**
>
> - Coolers, bags, backpacks, fanny packs and large purses are banned.
> - Small receptacles such as small ladies' purses and diaper bags will be subject to visual searches at the gates.
> - Ladies' purses larger than 12' x 12' will not be permitted.
> - Prohibited items will not be stored or disposed at the gates, they must be returned to your vehicle r hotel.
> - All vehicles parking in the Superdome garages and anywhere on the grounds will be subject to inspection. Fans should make plans to arrive early.
>
> **THE BEST ADVICE IS TO ARRIVE EARLY AND COME EMPTY HANDED.**

Developments being tested at sport facilities have come from a variety of industries including the correctional facility, defense, and law enforcement sectors. New technology has been developed since 9/11 that provides high-powered capabilities to facility managers for spectator protection. One of these new marvels is a type of x-ray machine that examines a person's clothing layer by layer to detect weapons. "Bodysearch" scans both sides of an individual in less than 30 seconds, and only dense items such as weapons or explosives appear on the image. The amount of radiation received during the scan is less than what is experienced during a long plane flight (Nuttall, 2001b).

Surveillance is also being increased at sport facilities, and several groups are lobbying for a type of "smart" national ID card that may contain a digital photo or even a small sample of DNA. Obviously the development of this technology will antagonize some individuals who are concerned about privacy issues ("Into the Seats," 2002).

The question of privacy rights stems from the Fourth Amendment guarantee to be free from unreasonable searches. The courts will look at three issues if a suit is brought for illegal search: (a) if the conduct was considered to be state action, (b) if the conduct could be considered a search, and finally (c) if the search was reasonable. Most legal experts agree that all three criteria are met when photos are taken or a search is required to gain entrance to a sports facility. From a legal point of view, experts believe that members of our society are willing to give up certain legal rights in exchange for personal safety (Miller et al., 2002). Facilities that have never employed a search now are using a visual search to identify any prohibited items from entering the facility. However, Italian research has confirmed that some security techniques actually provoke hostility in spectators (Nuttall, 2001b). Thus, the ideal becomes to have properly trained customer-oriented staff that provides a more "humane" environment. After all, "a smile goes a long way." Searches may continue to become more intrusive, and some groups such as the American Civil Liberty Union (ACLU) will undoubtedly react. However, a Harris Poll illustrated that U.S. citizens are willing to provide law enforcement agencies more authority due to the attacks on September 11th.

> Events that used to employ visual searches at the doors and gates of the facilities are now using metal detectors.

Security and risk management measures at sport facilities and events have been implemented throughout the world since the tragic attacks on New York and the District of Columbia. Many of these measures have been used before at various facilities and events, but never to the degree that has occurred since September 11th. Coolers, backpacks, thermoses, and large purses are now prohibited in many facilities. Events that used to employ

A Harris Poll of 1,012 US citizens were asked if they were willing to allow law enforcement agencies to have more power as a result of the September 11 attacks	Favor	Oppose	Not sure/declined
Expanded under-cover activities to penetrate groups under suspicion	93%	5%	1%
Stronger document and physical security checks for travelers	93%	6%	1%
Stronger document and physical security checks for access to government and private office buildings	92%	7%	1%
Use of facial recognition technology to scan for terrorists at facilities & events	86%	11%	2%
Issuance of secure ID technique for persons accessing government computer systems to avid discrimination	84%	11%	4%
Closer monitoring of banking and credit card transactions, to trace funding sources	81%	17%	2%
Adoption of a national ID system for all US citizens	68%	28%	4%
Expanded camera surveillance on streets and in public places	63%	35%	2%
Law enforcement monitoring of Internet discussions in chat rooms and other forums	63%	32%	5%
Expanded government monitoring of cell phones and email to intercept communications	54%	41%	4%

Figure 10.2

Civil liberties vs. law enforcement (courtesy of IAAM and facility manager)

visual searches at the doors and gates of the facilities now are using magnetometers (metal detectors). The use of these detectors will probably increase in the future along with the use of explosive-sniffing dogs and a general increase in the number of uniformed law enforcement officials. After the Columbine High School tragedy, some crowd managers made the argument for the use of metal detectors at all professional sporting events. Others in the facility industry argued against the use of metal detectors stating they were "too intrusive" and would cause tremendous congestion during the ingress of spectators. This is an additional item that may become even more contentious in the coming years.

Summary

1. The litigious society in which we live underscores the need for proper crowd management training for facility managers involved in event management.

2. Few research studies have investigated crowd management, but those that do exist emphasize that the primary goal for public assembly facility managers should be a safe and secure environment for all patrons.

3. Crowd management is an organizational tool that assists facility or event administrators in providing a safe and enjoyable environment for their guests through the implementation of the facility/event policies and procedures.

4. Lawsuits filed against sport facilities usually revolve around claims of some type of negligent behavior including negligent hiring of security personnel, negligent supervision, or negligent training.

5. Facility managers are responsible for using foreseeability when recognizing potential crowd management problems. If an injury situation occurred in the past at an event, then a facility manager must be prepared as the circumstances may occur again and due care needs to be implemented.

6. A proper crowd management plan may be accomplished through the implementation of six fundamental concepts: It must be an integral element of a larger risk management plan; provide for trained and competent staff to carry out the crowd management plan; address the specific procedures used to implement the emergency plan; contain procedures necessary to eject disruptive, unruly, or intoxicated patrons; implement a competent communication network; and involve the use of proper signage.

Questions

1. Describe how *crowd* and *risk* management differ. Which is more important?

2. Discuss the seven issues that juries will examine to determine the appropriateness of the crowd management plan. Give an example of each.

3. How does a patron's "status" determine the duties a facility manager has to that person?

4. How would a new assistant facility manager know if the facility's crowd management plan is an integral element of a larger risk management plan?

5. List and discuss five of the responsibilities that members of the crowd management staff must be trained to undertake.

6. Describe a scenario in which a spectator would need to be ejected. Explain how the crowd management staff should proceed.

7. What components compose a competent communication network?

8. Explain the difference, through the use of examples, between directional and informational signage.

9. Describe three recent innovations in crowd management. How will they help to provide a safe and secure environment?

Chapter Eleven

Medical Emergency and Evacuation Plans

Application Exercise

You have been hired as the emergency services manager for an 8-day women's professional tennis (WTA) tournament to be held at the recently completed 5,000-seat Bowden, Georgia, Tennis Center. Your objective is to assemble an emergency management team, identify possible emergency/disaster threats, and develop a medical emergency and evacuation plan (MEEP) in response to these identifiable threats. You are responsible for developing the basic guidelines and response protocol for all identifiable threats and coordinating the responses of all identifiable disaster agencies in the area.

The development of the plan is your responsibility. Include all pertinent information required for a comprehensive emergency management plan. Information may be gleaned from a variety of sources, including your college or university department of public safety; local police or fire departments; or local, state, or federal emergency management agencies. Other pertinent sources may include the Internet, this text, class notes, and your professors.

What elements would you include in a tennis center emergency management plan?

The Federal Emergency Management Agency (FEMA; 2002) defines emergency management as "the process of preparing for, mitigating, responding to and recovering from an emergency" (www.fema.gov/). Emergency management is a dynamic process. Developing an emergency management plan is not the only element of emergency management. Training, conducting drills, testing equipment, and coordinating with other agencies are all critical emergency management components. However, planning is the first step in emergency management, and it will be the focus of this chapter.

Planning for emergencies that may arise in sport settings is similar to any other type of planning. It involves setting goals and specifying a program to achieve those goals (Chelladurai, 2001). A sport manager involved in emergency response planning will not, in all likelihood, be an expert in emergency management. In addition, although no emergency response or management plan will perfectly address the numerous and varied emergency situations that a sport manager might face, basic planning guidelines discussed throughout this text provide a solid foundation. In planning for any emergency, the adage "Plan for the worst, hope for the best" is a good maxim. However, as the events of September 11, 2001, have shown, the *worst* may be a disaster for which no plan is sufficient. The World Trade Center and Pentagon attacks have fundamentally changed any discussion of emergency response planning. The unimaginable is now imaginable.

In today's uncertain world the need for emergency response planning has taken on increased relevance. What can a sport manager charged with developing an emergency response or management plan hope to accomplish? Although sport managers cannot eliminate the possibility or minimize the losses of all emergencies, they can take steps to reduce staff uncertainty by educating employees about the existence of an emergency response plan and informing them of their responsibilities in case of an emergency.

Emergencies can occur in a variety of sport and recreational settings.

Emergency Management Components

Although there are numerous templates and guides for emergency management, the process involves answering some basic questions, such as "What's being planned for?" and "What needs to be done?" By finding answers to these questions, a sport organization can develop a viable emergency management plan. Developing an *emergency management plan* (EMP) is an ongoing process that must become part of the organization's risk management plan. This increases the likelihood of the plan's implementation.

Emergency Response Planning

As with most management processes, the first step in emergency response planning is asking, "What's being planned for?" An investigation of emergency response guidelines from various federal, state, and local agencies, including the Federal Emergency Management Agency (FEMA, www.fema.gov/emanagers), Occupational Safety and Health Administration (OSHA, www.osha.gov/), state emergency management agencies, and the National Safety Council (NSC, www.nsc.org/) provides evidence that the process of emergency response planning ultimately involves finding the best answers to this question. Although an effective emergency response plan may not provide all possible answers to this question, not seeking any answers guarantees that no planning will take place.

> The effectiveness of an emergency management plan may be compromised if its scope is too narrow or too broad.

Planning for emergencies that may arise in sport settings is similar to any other type of planning.

An emergency can be defined by its type and scope. The various types of emergency may be fire, natural disasters (tornado, hurricane), technical disasters (building or stadium collapse), or medical emergencies (slips and falls, heart attacks, or lacerations).

Types of Emergencies

Fire	Other Emergencies
Natural disasters	Bomb Threat
• Earthquakes	
• Severe Weather	Bomb Explosion
• Tornadoes	Criminal Activity
• Thunderstorm	Harassing and Disruptive Users
Technical disasters	Medical Emergency
• Structural Accidents	
• Transportation Accident	Security, Theft and Vandalism
• Power Failure	Terrorism
• Water	

Table 11.1. Types of Emergencies

The scope of an emergency may vary from a localized medical emergency (a spectator who suffers a heart attack) to a mass casualty situation (bleacher or stadium collapse) or an even larger catastrophic event (earthquake during a World Series game). Unless the type and scope of emergencies for which the plan is designed are clearly defined, the effectiveness of an emergency management plan may be compromised by its scope being too narrow or broad or by its not addressing various types of probable emergencies.

Scope and Types of Emergencies

In focusing the scope of an emergency management plan, a *local emergency* can be defined as a type of emergency that is confined to a single setting, such as a school gym, golf course, or sports event. Managing a local emergency may involve activating a local emergency medical service (EMS) component, such as a 911 system, and providing basic first aid. Local emergencies most often involve relatively few people. In addition to providing first aid and activating a 911 system, managing a local emergency requires a manager to ensure that calm is maintained among all persons directly or indirectly involved in the situation. A local emergency may be life threatening, but it is characterized as the lowest in scope of all emergencies. However, a local emergency such as a bomb threat may potentially escalate into a *major emergency*.

A major emergency requires the involvement of several groups outside the organization or event. The scope of a major emergency depends on the severity of the threat to people or property. Major emergencies may involve natural or technical disasters. An example of a major emergency might be a building fire, the collapse of bleachers, or a riot during a soccer match. An organization's ability to respond to a major emergency may vary, depending on the number of people involved in the emergency, the severity of injuries, and the extent of any property damage. Providing for protection of persons and property involved in the emergency, while minimizing additional injuries and damage through proper evacuation and security procedures, is a crucial component of a major emergency management plan. If a major emergency is a possibility at an event or location, based on the number of participants or the location of an event, a manager must ensure an increased level of communication and coordination with the EMS system. This may involve various agencies and will be discussed later in this chapter. Out of necessity, a major emergency management plan will be more detailed than a local emergency plan.

A *catastrophic emergency* may involve the entire community in which an event takes place. The local EMS system may not be equipped to handle such an emergency. A catastrophic emergency may, in fact, incapacitate the local EMS authorities. Planning for a catastrophic event may not, in some cases, even be possible for an individual organization or event planning staff. Catastrophic events, by their very nature, often task federal, state, and local agencies or systems. Examples of such emergencies are tornados, earthquakes, severe storms, and terrorist attacks.

> A catastrophic emergency may involve the entire community.

Defining and discussing emergencies often seem overwhelming, especially to a newly hired sport manager whose only previous emergency management experience may have been getting a bag of ice for a sprained ankle as a student-trainer. As you read this chapter, various questions may creep into your mind. "What if I forget to plan for a specific type of emergency? What if the plan isn't perfect? What if I only have a local plan and a catastrophic statewide emergency occurs?" Although these kinds of questions are natural, they aren't necessarily productive. These questions are examples of *paralysis by overanalysis*. A more productive step in this questioning process is to answer the basic question, "What needs to be done?" while maintaining a delicate balance between planning for emergencies that may

Building fire (major) and tornadoes (catastrophic) are examples of the differing scopes emergencies may encompass. (Photos courtesy of National Oceanic and Atmospheric Administration and the Federal Emergency Management Agency).

never happen and being adequately prepared to respond to the most likely emergencies. The Salt Lake Olympic Committee (SLOC) didn't have an emergency response plan for a hurricane, but they did have plans for a host of other possible emergencies, including a blizzard, an airplane crash, a terrorist attack, and even an avalanche at certain venues. This process of risk assessment and prioritization is a critical part of emergency planning (see chapter 8, "Risk Management").

The Georgia Dome's facility manager probably did not plan for an avalanche, but Atlanta's Super Bowl XXXVI was affected by a severe ice storm. (Photos courtesy of Federal Emergency Management Agency.)

Steps in the Emergency Planning Process

No plan can be *everything*. As has been discussed, before emergency planning can take place, an organization must answer the question "What are the scope and types of emergencies for which we are going to plan?" After this question has been at least partially addressed, the next step is answering the question "What needs to be done?" Dealing with this question involves a step-by-step process that includes building a preparedness culture, forming an emergency planning team (EPT), developing an emergency medical and evacuation plan (MEEP), and implementing the emergency management plan.

Building a Preparedness Culture

Instead of beginning with a predetermined group of people focusing on a specific plan for a specific emergency, a sport organization, like any organization, must involve everyone within the organization in developing a preparedness culture. Although everyone cannot be involved in all subsequent phases of emergency planning, everyone must be given the opportunity to become part of the organization's preparedness culture. An organization's culture is "the way we do things around here." Simply stated, planning for emergencies must not be seen as a negative, but must be looked upon as a proactive process that permeates everything the organization does.

Planning for emergencies must become a part of the organization's mission. Adoption of a formal, written mission statement can help foster this feeling within an organization. However, whether a sports organization is planning a local amateur 3-on-3 basketball tournament or hosting the NCAA national basketball championship event, preparedness must be seen by the organization as its moral obligation. Everyone in the organization must be committed to protecting staff, participants, clients, and community members through medical emergency and evacuation planning. As was discussed in chapter 2, an event manager must take into consideration the needs of the participants, spectators, and sponsors of an event. In the same way, emergency planning must address the safety of everyone associated with an event.

> Everyone in the organization must be committed to protecting staff, participants, clients, and community members through medical emergency and evacuation planning.

Not only does such planning allow for compliance with legal requirements, but when important stakeholders, such as sponsors, the media, and the general public, are aware of the existence of an emergency management plan, the organization's image and credibility also are improved. Participants, spectators, and sponsors expect an event management team to have a comprehensive emergency management plan in place. They expect an event's organizers to be prepared. The concept of "standards of care" or reasonable prudence (see chapter 9, "Facility Negligence") applies to emergency management planning. Your level of preparedness will be compared to that of other comparable events. If your preparedness is lacking, you may be found to be negligent. In short, preparedness is the right thing to do.

Forming an Emergency Planning Team (EPT)

From such a preparedness culture an *emergency planning team* must be created. There must be someone in charge of developing the plan, but the size and composition of the team must reflect the organization. The members of the team must be *active* members. Although there will always be a few who will do the bulk of the work, input must be obtained from all organizational levels. According to FEMA and other emergency management agencies, a team approach to emergency planning has numerous advantages.

If organization members have a sense of ownership (i.e., their views are considered and incorporated), then the EMP is more likely to be used in an emergency. In addition, in a team approach, more knowledge and expertise can be brought to bear on the planning effort. One person or group doesn't have all the answers. Insights, information, and creative solutions to challenges may come from varied resources. A team approach develops closer professional relationships among response organizations in the community. Because the EMS system is a team approach, it only makes sense that an EMP be developed from a team approach.

Although the development of an EPT can never follow a cookie-cutter approach, here are several suggestions to keep in mind. First, involve all functional levels of the organization. No matter the scope or type of emergency being planned for, involve all levels of your organization. Make sure that involvement is part of all members' job descriptions. Second, make sure the planning team has authority within the organization. Although it is important to involve members from all levels of the organization, the team must ultimately have the authority within the organization to move beyond the development of a team. Remember the ultimate goal is to implement the emergency plan, not just to form a team. Finally, don't reinvent the wheel. The team needs to realize that it doesn't have to develop a plan totally from scratch. Involve outside agency personnel as team members or consultants. Utilize existing plans and resources. FEMA, the American Red Cross (ARC), the Occupation Safety and Health Administration (OSHA), and state and local agencies have numerous plans that the team can use as models.

Developing an Emergency Management Plan

Move forward. **Complete tasks**. Although not an easy thing to accomplish, developing an emergency management plan can often be straightforward and uncomplicated. To develop a sound EMP, the planning team must achieve measurable objectives. The objectives are the result of answering the question about what needs to be done. Once it has been determined what scope and type of emergency planning are necessary, developing an emergency plan involves constructing a checklist of duties and responsibilities for team members to accomplish and then completing the tasks. Throughout the development phase, always think in terms of before, during, and after an emergency.

As has been stressed over and over, no single emergency-plan template applies to all emergencies. However, Figure 11-2 is an example of some fundamental components that might be addressed in a MEEP for the evacuation of a facility.

Sample Emergency Management Plan
Facility Evacuation

List all emergency phone numbers.
- Local EMS
- Hospital(s)
- Fire Department
- Local and state police, sheriff

Develop communication plan.
- Develop alternate methods of communication.
- Develop written responsibilities and duties.
- Develop emergency evacuation procedures.
  - Floor plan
  - Evacuation routes
  - Assembly areas - including disabled individuals

Assignment of critical duties prior to evacuation
- Specific duties
- Specific individuals
- Written procedures

Accounting procedures
- Safe area
- Roll call procedures
- Procedure for reporting missing persons to authorities

Medical or Rescue Duties
- Specific duties
- Specific individuals
- Written procedures
- Ensure training
- Ensure capabilities of individuals

Contact information
- Designate a specific person for questions.

Develop appropriate signage.
- Conspicuously post
- Update signage as appropriate.

Table 11.2. Sample Emergency Management Plan (EMP)—Facility Evacuation

Keep in mind that you must **analyze your organization's capabilities**. Determine what internal resources the organization has that can be utilized in planning for the determined emergencies. If the organization is not capable of dealing with a predetermined emergency, no amount of planning will eliminate that problem. If the internal resources don't exist, either the organization must acquire additional resources, or an alternative plan must be developed that relies on external resources. Be realistic and honest. Pretending you are prepared is not an option.

> Determine what internal resources can be used in planning for emergencies.

After you have completed an organizational capabilities analysis, you need to **identify codes and regulations**. Do your research to ensure that any plan complies with applicable federal, state, and local codes and regulations. Chapter 68 of Title 42 of the United States Code Service specifically outlines federal response plans. In addition, chapter 116 of Title 42 establishes state and local requirements pertaining to emergency planning, including emergency response commissions, emergency planning districts, and local emergency planning committees (United States Code Service [USCS], 2001). Because any individual emergency management plan is part of this established system of emergency preparedness, familiarity with these regulations and guidelines is a good idea.

The next step is to **write the plan**. Assign the task of writing different sections to various members of the planning team. Develop an aggressive timeline for completion. If the plan is not written down, you have no plan. Recognize that there can never be a *final* draft without a *first* draft. The process of revision and final distribution must start with a first draft.

The final step in developing an emergency management plan is to **seek final approval**. A MEEP does not exist unless it has been approved and instituted by the organization. The plan must not only be the *official* plan of the organization or event, but it must also be "the way we do things around here." There is no such thing as a covert emergency management plan.

Implementing an Emergency Management Plan

Once an emergency management plan has been developed, it must be implemented. The implementation process involves making the plan part of the ongoing operations of the organization or event. Insuring that the answers to the following questions are "yes" will lead to integration of an emergency management plan into the organizational culture of a sport organization:

Are all levels of the organization aware of the plan? The plan must be distributed to key members of the organization. In addition, the plan must be distributed to outside local agencies with which the plan is to be coordinated.

Are all personnel aware of and trained in their responsibilities? These two items are inseparable. Personnel must not only know their responsibilities, but they also must be trained and capable of carrying out their responsibilities. An ongoing training schedule must be developed. Critical parts of a training program must deal with the questions:

- Who will be trained?

- Who will do the training?

- What method of training will be used?

- Where and when will the training take place?

- How will the effectiveness of the training be evaluated?

- Have the emergency planning concepts been incorporated into all organization procedures?

- Have all opportunities for distributing the plan been effectively utilized?

All personnel must be trained in their responsibilities.

Medical Emergencies

In addition to developing an EMP for major or catastrophic emergencies that may involve the evacuation of a facility, an emergency medical response plan (EMRP) must be developed for medical emergencies such as heart attacks as well as "slips and falls" (the #1 facility accident). Slips and falls at a sporting event or facility often occur in conjunction with stairs, steps, and uneven surfaces. Other hazards include deposits of water, food, oil, or other debris—trash in aisles. At sporting events, fans may be inattentive or distracted. This may contribute to the likelihood of a slip or fall.

An EMRP must ensure the ability of event or facility management to rapidly respond to both life-threatening and non-life-threatening medical situations. Coordination of facility or event response is essential. To ensure a coordinated response, a facility or event should have a first aid station, base stations, roving medical personnel—stocked with advanced first aid supplies—and access to emergency support transportation (i.e., ambulances or rescue vehicles).

Slips and falls may occur even on well-maintained stadium steps or bleachers.

First aid stations. First aid stations should have the capability of providing the level of response deemed appropriate by the event or facility management. The level of medical care necessary will be affected by many factors including the time and/or distance to more advanced medical facilities, the standard of care normally associated with such an event, and the risks associated with the event or activity (see chapter 9, "Facility Negligence"). Local EMS agencies are an invaluable resource in helping event organizers determine the appropriate level of first aid care.

Base medical stations. The base medical stations are the focal point of the coordination of all emergency medical personnel. Base stations allow for command and control of emergency medical personnel and procedures in the event of large and/or complex emergency medical procedures. The location of base stations is critical to response effectiveness. In addition, specific base stations should be assigned specific responsibilities. For example, one base station may be responsible for coordination of minor first aid and on-site transportation (slips and falls). Another base station may be designated for special operations (heart attacks, more serious injuries), mass casualties, and roving medic coordination. Many times, each base station will have its own emergency transportation vehicles.

Roving medics. Roving medics provide a primary response mechanism to medical incidents until the patient can be cared for at the first aid location or base station or until transportation to another medical facility can be arranged. At many facilities or events, emergency medical technicians (EMTs) or paramedics provide backup for first responder or basic life support (BLS) medics. EMTs or paramedics act as advanced life support (ALS) personnel, and they are an important link in a coordinated emergency medical response team.

> It is sometimes best to have an ambulance on site for immediate patient transportation.

Emergency transportation. Coordination of transportation of injured or ill patients to an advanced medical facility is another element of a coordinated emergency medical plan. The most desirable situation is to have an ambulance on site for immediate patient transportation. However, in the event of mass casualties, activation of the local EMS system may be necessary. If an on-site ambulance is used for transportation, arrangements for a backup ambulance must be in place. If ground transportation is not practical, air ambulance evacuation procedures may be necessary.

Emergency transportation is a critical part of an EMRP.

Automatic external defibrillators. A specific medical emergency for which event and facility managers should be prepared is sudden cardiac arrest (SCA) or unexpected cardiac arrest. Sudden death from cardiac arrest occurs when the heart stops abruptly. The American Heart Association estimates that somewhere between 250,000 and 350,000 people die each year of coronary heart disease without being hospitalized (American Heart Association [AHA], n.d.; Cantwell, 1998). When a person experiences cardiac arrest, brain death and permanent death begin to occur within 4-6 minutes. According to medical experts, the single most important determinant to survival is the time from collapse to defibrillation: Each minute of delay decreases the chance of survival by 7% to 10%. Most patients will survive if defibrillation is achieved in less than three minutes; few will if the delay is 16 minutes or longer, despite CPR administration. (Cantwell, 1998, para. 3)

The AHA estimates that 100,000 deaths could be prevented each year with rapid defibrillation (AHA; Cantwell, 1998).

The recent technological development and availability of automatic external defibrillators (AEDs) allow sport event and facility managers another tool for responding to sudden cardiac arrest in participants or spectators. AEDs are self-contained devices similar in size to laptop computers. They are designed for use by laypersons with minimal training. "Non-physicians can learn to use an AED in about an hour. The user simply applies the two paddles to the left apex and right base of the chest" (Cantwell, 1998, para. 7). The AED reads the victim's heart rhythms, and a recorded

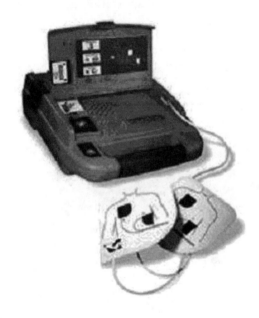

The availability and use of automatic external defibrillators (AEDs) is becoming more common at sports events and facilities.

voice tells the responder whether or not she should push the defibrillator button.

Fears over potential liability in the use of AEDs should not preclude the development of appropriate protocol and training for their use. In a lawsuit involving the use of an AED, the victim (plaintiff) would have to prove that whatever the defendant did or did not do was the proximate cause of the plaintiff's injuries (see chapter 9, "Facility Negligence"). Because a sudden cardiac arrest victim is already dead, if the defendant had not used the AED, the victim would have likely stayed dead (Hodes, 2002). Think of it this way: If a person is already *clinically dead* (not breathing and with no heartbeat), the use of an AED cannot be seen to have made the victim "deader."

AEDs are becoming common at sports events and facilities. Most professional and college football, basketball, and baseball teams have AEDs on their sidelines. The use of AEDs in high school sport settings is becoming more common. Airports and other public facilities often strategically place AEDs about one minute apart (AHA, n.d.). Such placement has led to dramatically increased survival rates for sudden cardiac victims in such locations. The use of AEDs is a medical development that has been seen to be immediately and obviously effective (AHA, n.d.; Cantwell, 1998; Hodes, 2002). The strategic placement of AEDs at sports events and facilities and the inclusion of AEDs in the response bags of trained medical personnel should be coupled with the training of all sport event and facility personnel. With these developments in mind, AEDs should become part of any sport manager's EMRP.

Model Protocol
Automatic External Defibrillator (AED)
Emergency Response Team Protocol for the U.S. Department of Energy
XYZ Office

1. *During Health Unit Duty Hours:* Monday through Friday.

In any potentially life-threatening cardiac emergency:

(a) The first person on the scene will:

(i) Call Security by dialing extension XXXX and inform them of the location and nature of the emergency.

(ii) Remain with the victim; send a co-worker to meet the emergency team at a visible location and escort to the site.

(b) Security Personnel immediately upon receiving the call will:

(i) Notify the AED/Emergency Response Team by dialing the group notification number for the AED team pagers and enter the code for the location of the emergency.

(ii) Notify local EMS (911).

(iii) Inform the EMS operator of location and nature of emergency and that an AED unit is on site.

(iv) Notify Security Officer(s) to meet the EMS personnel and escort them to the site of the emergency.

(v) Notify Security Officer(s) to respond to the site and offer any assistance needed if staffing allows.

(c) Health Unit Staff immediately upon receiving the notification will proceed directly to the scene with the Health Unit AED and other emergency equipment 2 nurses will respond if available.

(i) When the Health Unit Nurse is on the scene, he/she shall be in charge of directing the activities until the local EMS arrives and assumes care of the victim.

(d) Other AED responders immediately upon receiving the notification will:

(i) The team member previously designated to transport the AED unit will obtain the AED unit closest to them or to the site of the emergency and proceed with it to the emergency site.

(ii) Whichever AED responder arrives on the scene first will assess the victim. If AED use is indicated, the AED trained personnel will administer the AED and CPR according to established American Red Cross or American Heart Association Automated External Defibrillation Treatment Algorithm.

(iii) All other AED responders go directly to the site of the emergency.

(iv) Additional AED responders shall assist with CPR, recording of data and time, notifications, crowd control, escorting of EMS, as needed. Any additional AED units will remain on site as a back up.

(e) The building Occupant Emergency Coordinator, and the AED Medical Advisor, shall be notified within 24 hours after the response, by the person utilizing the AED, that emergency response was initiated and of any pertinent details or issues.

2. *During Non-Health Unit Hours*, and for DOE Buildings without a Health Unit, and all hours Saturday and Sunday and Federal holidays.

In any potentially life-threatening cardiac emergency:

(a) The first person on the scene will:

(i) Call Security dialing extension XXXX inform them of the location and nature of the emergency.

(ii) Remain with the victim; send a co-worker to meet the emergency team at a visible location and escort to the site.

(b) Security Personnel immediately upon receiving the call will:

(i) Notify the AED/Emergency Response Team by dialing the group notification number for the AED/Emergency Response Team; enter the code for the location of the emergency.

(ii) Notify local EMS (911).

(iii) Notify Security Officer(s) to meet the EMS personnel and escort them to the site of the emergency.

(iv) Notify Security Officer(s) to respond to the site and offer any assistance needed if staffing allows.

(c) AED/Emergency Response Team members immediately upon receiving the notification will:

(i) The team member previously designated to transport the AED unit obtain the AED unit closest to them or to the site of the emergency and proceed with it to the emergency site.

(ii) All other AED responders will go directly to the site of the emergency.

(iii) Whichever AED responder arrives on the scene first will assess the victim. If AED use is indicated, the AED trained personnel will administer the AED and CPR according to established American Red Cross or American Heart Association Automated External Defibrillation Treatment Algorithm until local EMS professionals arrive and assume care of the victim.

(iv) Additional AED responders shall assist with CPR, recording of data and time, notifications, crowd control, escorting of EMS, as needed. Any additional AED units will remain on site as a back up.

(d) The building Occupant Emergency Coordinator, and the AED Medical Advisor, shall be notified within 24 hours after the response, by the person utilizing the AED, that emergency response was initiated and of any pertinent details or issues.

I _____ M.D. licensed to practice Medicine in the State of _____, agree to serve as the AED/Emergency Response Teams Medical Advisor for the U.S. Department of Energy facilities located at _____. I endorse the above protocol for use by American Red Cross or American Heart Association AED Trained DOE Federal Employees at DOE facilities, and agree to provide medical oversight of the AED/First Aid program.

Signed:_____
Date: _____

Note: This protocol was adapted from the recommended protocol developed by the U.S. Public Health Service, *Guidelines for Public Access Defibrillation Programs in Federal Facilities* (Federal Register: May 23, 2001 [Volume 66, Number 100]), (Notices) (Pp. 28495-28511) from the *Federal Register Online* via GPO Access (wais.access.gpo.gov) (DOCID:fr23my01-89). This document may be found at http://www.foh.dhhs.gov/public/whatwedo/AED/HHSAED.asp

---

Figure 11.1. Sample Automatic External Defibrilator Protocol

1. Emergency management may be defined as the process of preparing for, mitigating, responding to, and recovering from an emergency.

2. Training, conducting drills, testing equipment, and coordinating with other agencies are all critical emergency management components.

3. Emergencies may range from localized medical emergencies (slips and falls) to mass casualty situations (bleacher collapse) and large catastrophic events (tornado).

4. Providing for protection of persons and property involved in the emergency and minimizing additional injuries and damage through proper evacuation and security procedures are crucial components of a major emergency management plan.

5. Risk assessment and prioritization are critical elements in emergency planning.

6. Planning for emergencies must be part of any sport organization's mission.

7. A team approach to emergency planning assists in developing a sense of ownership among organization members.

8. A sound EMP includes measurable performance objectives.

9. An effective EMP must be written, approved, and instituted throughout the organization.

10. Implementing a MEEP involves making the plan part of ongoing organization operations.

11. Slips and falls are the #1 facility accident.

12. An emergency medical response plan (EMRP) must ensure the ability of event or facility management to rapidly respond to both life-threatening and non-life-threatening medical situations.

13. Development of protocol for deployment, training, and use of automatic external defibrillators (AEDs) should be part of any event or facility EMRP.

14. Training in AED use is available from many sources, including the American Heart Association (AHA), the American Red Cross (ARC), and Divers Alert Network (DAN).

Summary

1. Identify and discuss critical emergency management elements.

2. What are some steps that you would take to reduce your staff's uncertainty about your MEEP and their responsibilities in the event of various types of emergencies?

Questions

3. What is the first step in emergency response planning, and why is it so important?

4. What are some important considerations in the development of a major emergency management plan?

5. Identify and discuss the steps in the emergency planning process.

6. Why is it important to analyze your organization's capabilities when developing an emergency management plan?

7. What are the critical parts of a MEEP or an EMRP training program?

8. What is an AED?

9. Why should AEDs be part of an event or facility EMRP?

Chapter Twelve

Alcohol Management

While leaving a T. J. University football game, Ryan Anderson and his brother Harry were returning to their truck. An intoxicated fan knocked Ryan down, causing him to sustain a broken leg. Anderson sued the University for damages resulting from that injury. The trial court ruled in favor of T. J. University. Anderson filed an appeal stating that T. J. University had a duty to protect him from injury caused by the acts of third persons.

The evidence showed that on October 27, 1999, the Andersons attended a football game on the campus of The University. The two men left the game shortly before it ended. As they were walking through a parking lot toward their truck, they observed two men who appeared to be drunk. The men were fighting. One of them fell down, and then the combatants walked away from each other. One of the men walked past the Andersons. A few moments later, the man fell into Mr. Anderson from behind, knocking him to the ground. Mr. Anderson suffered a broken leg from the fall. There were no ushers or security people in the parking lot when the incident occurred.

Anderson argued that he was a business invitee of T. J. University; therefore, T. J. University owed him a duty to protect him from injury caused by the acts of other persons on the premises. On the other hand, the University argued that absent notice or knowledge of any particular danger to a patron, the University cannot be held liable for the acts of third persons. Generally, the operator of a place of public entertainment owes a duty to keep the premises safe for its invitees. This duty includes a duty to provide a safe and suitable means of ingress and egress and a duty to exercise ordinary and reasonable care to protect a patron from injury caused by third persons. However, the inviter is not the insurer of the invitee's safety. Before liability may be imposed on the inviters, they must have actual or constructive knowledge of the danger.

Because the landowner is not an insurer of the visitor's safety, the owner is ordinarily under no duty to exercise any care until he or she knows or has reason to know that the acts of the third person are occurring or are about to occur. The owner may, however, know or have reason to know, from past experience, that there is a likelihood of conduct on the part of third persons in general that is likely to endanger the safety of the visitor, even though the owner has no reason to expect it on the part of any particular individual. If the place or character of the owner's business or past experience is such that the owner should reasonably anticipate careless or criminal conduct on the part of third persons, either generally or at some particular time, the owner may be under a duty to take precautions against such conduct and to provide a reasonably sufficient number of staff to afford a reasonable protection.

T.J. University was aware that alcoholic beverages were consumed on the premises before and during football games. The University was also aware that "tailgate" parties were held in the parking areas around the stadium. Thus, even though there was no evidence that the University had reason to know of the particular danger posed by the drunk who injured Mr. Anderson, it had reason to know that some people had become intoxicated and posed a general threat to the safety of other patrons. Therefore, T. J. University was under a duty to take reasonable precautions to protect those who attended its football games from injury caused by the acts of third persons.

1. The sale of alcohol at the T. J. University Fighting Pelicans' football games is a vital source of revenue for the athletic department.

2. Do you agree with court's decision? Why or why not?

3. Should T. J. University continue to sell alcohol?

4. What can the athletic department do to ensure that similar litigation does not occur in the future?

5. How could this court decision affect other universities?

(Adapted from Bearman v. Notre Dame, 1983)

Introduction

Sporting events are friendly outings that many times involve drinking for many spectators all over the world. It is an opportunity to get out of the house, cheer for the local team, and socialize with good friends. Most of these "social" drinkers are responsible sport fans; however, a small minority is irresponsible, and their "friendly outings" become troublesome burdens for facility managers. Although alcohol sales may become a litigious undertaking when managed improperly, in many facilities around the world alcohol is sold and managed effectively. An effective alcohol policy will make the difference.

Some facilities, especially those at smaller universities with low attendance figures, would find it difficult to generate a profit if it were not for home-game beer sales. "'In many cases on the revenue side, food and beverage sales drive whether a facility will carry its own weight'," according to Reggie Williams, director of the Augusta (Georgia) Civic Center (qtd. in Waddell, 1999, p. 2). Thus, one contingent in the sports industry argues that revenue generated from beer sales at sport and entertainment events is substantial and worth the risks. Other facilities determined that alcohol sales are not worth the liabilities associated with this increased revenue.

> In many facilities around the world, alcohol is sold and managed effectively.

Although some facility managers weigh the pros and cons of beer sales, others have different decisions to contemplate. Stadiums and arenas with private restaurants and clubs usually allow hard liquor and wine to be purchased by their members. In addition, a few facilities allow luxury suite owners to serve hard liquor. However, these VIP guests are not allowed to take their drinks into other areas of the facility. Some facilities have experienced a backlash from annoyed VIP guests. It became a large enough issue that the State of Washington considered a proposal that would have allowed any fan to drink hard liquor in the main stands. Public opposition to the proposal, however, caused lawmakers to withdraw support (Mapes, 1998).

As discussed in chapter 8 ("Risk Management"), sport and entertainment facility managers must attempt to provide a safe and secure environment for all patrons in order to reduce the possibility of litigation. Undoubtedly, a potential liability exists if a facility allows the sale of alcohol; therefore, a comprehensive alcohol policy, in addition to an effective crowd management strategy, should be an integral part of any facility's risk management plan. However, intoxicated patrons may not only create safety concerns for themselves, but their disruptive actions may also endanger others around them. Eliminating the dangers posed to innocent spectators from intoxicated third parties, therefore, must be an important component of any alcohol plan.

One such danger occurred in December of the 2001 NFL season when games in Cleveland and New Orleans were interrupted due to fans' throwing plastic beer bottles on the field. Concessionaires had been bottling beer in the plastic bottles for two years because fans liked the fresh taste the plastic bottles provided. In fact, one stadium, Texas Stadium, had gone so far as to sell only plastic bottles and nothing else. Irate fans at Cleveland

Stadium and the New Orleans Superdome expressed their frustration about perceived poor officiating by bombarding the fields with the plastic bottles. This caused facility managers and concessionaires to rethink the policy. Some facilities continued to vend the plastic bottles (Lambeau Field and Pro Player Field), whereas others (Giants Stadium) felt the risks were too great and eliminated all plastic bottles (Muret, 2002). Ironically, an NFL spokesman ruled out a ban on beer sales themselves by stating, "'Beer has been sold at our games for many years and these incidents are few and far in between'" (qtd. in Wood, 2001, p. C1).

Some venues rely upon alcohol sales to generate a profit.

Foreseeable Risks

The consumption of alcohol at athletic events is often blamed for injuries that produce litigation. Intoxicated patrons may injure themselves or innocent third parties, and this concern has prompted some sports facility administrators to eliminate alcohol sales. However, if a facility could anticipate likely alcohol risks and then introduce countermeasures, the resulting liability could possibly be alleviated (Miller, 1993). Some facility managers are lacking in their ability to foresee these potential dangers. Therefore, they either eliminate a potential revenue source by refusing to sell alcohol, they outsource alcohol sales to an outside vendor, or they gamble that any litigation pertaining to alcohol sales will be manageable or covered by insurance (Ammon & Fried, 1998).

> If a facility could anticipate likely alcohol risks and then introduce countermeasures, a potential liability could possibly be alleviated.

Foreseeability is a key determinant in most court decisions involving alcohol-related incidents. Administrators and managers are expected to take reasonable care to avoid acts they can reasonably foresee causing injuries (Ammon, 1995). If an injurious situation has occurred in the past, then foreseeability dictates the circumstances may occur again, and due care needs to be implemented. A facility manager's ability to foresee harmful alcohol risks is an important way to potentially reduce liability (Miller, 1993). Documenting incidents and reviewing records to determine the problems that occur more often than by random chance is a means of measuring foreseeability. Preventive measures that guarantee these incidents do not recur must then be undertaken.

Bearman vs. University of Notre Dame (1983). The *Bearman* case described in chapter 10, "Crowd Management" (and used as the example for this chapter's Application Exercise), was the seminal case pertaining to foreseeability and its relation to alcohol policies. The Indiana State Supreme Court determined that Notre Dame had a "duty" to its paid fans. In addition, the facts of the case demonstrated that the University was aware of the "tailgating" activities taking place on University property. During ensuing litigation, the facts of the *Bearman* case demonstrated that intoxicated individuals might pose a general danger to University patrons. Previous court decisions have determined that a *duty of care* is considered the responsibility of an individual or group to conform to the standards that have been established as the minimum allowable conduct for a profession (Ammon, 1995). Berry & Wong (1993) further state that a facility manager's duty "is subject to liability for known dangers or dangers that could be identified based on inspection" (p. 413). Pertinent to the *Bearman* case, a New Jersey case (*Cassanello v. Luddy*, 1997) concluded that "foreseeability does not depend on whether the exact incident or occurrence was foreseeable. The question is whether an incident of that general nature was reasonably foreseeable" (Mazier, 1997, para. 22). Thus, foreseeability dictated that Notre Dame had a duty to protect its fans from the potential dangerous actions of intoxicated third parties.

Alcohol Legislation

Believing that the legal problems compound an uncontrollable situation, some facilities have gone so far as to eliminate beer vendors from the stands (Stooksbury, 1994). Two statutes make it essential that facility managers implement alcohol management strategies to prevent their patrons from drinking too much. *Dram shop* statutes in many states allow injured plaintiffs to bring suit against the defendant, in addition to the owner of the establishment that allowed the defendant to become drunk. Some states allow plaintiffs to sue restaurants, bars, and other establishments under these statutes; others allow recovery by common negligence theory and some states allow both (Miller, 1993). In *Chalaco v. Munoz* (2002), after two males were out drinking at several bars, they were involved in an accident with a truck parked along the side of the road. The plaintiff passenger, who sustained serious injuries, successfully sued the defendant driver and one of the taverns for $1.1 million dollars. The plaintiff stated that the two men were served alcohol even though they were visibly intoxicated and thus did not have the capacity to realize the risks of driving or riding in an automobile ("Jury Awards," 2002).

A second ordinance for sport facility managers to monitor is *social host liability*. This type of statute provides injured plaintiffs the opportunity to prefer charges "upon a social host who knowingly serves alcohol to a minor in the event that the minor causes injury or damages as a result of his or her intoxication" (Hoffman, 2002, p. 4). Significantly, however, not all jurisdictions follow this line of thinking.

In one case, a drunk at a sports pavilion knocked down a 16-year-old girl. She sustained a catastrophic injury from the incident and sued the facility. The court found that because the facility did not serve alcohol, neither the injury nor the intoxicated patron was foreseeable (Miller, 1993). In a similar case, a superior court in New Jersey ruled that an intoxicated fraternity student at a Rutgers football game was responsible for his own injuries because Rutgers did not serve or sell alcohol at its football games (*Allen vs. Rutgers The State University of New Jersey*, 1987).

Placing restrictions on alcohol sales will limit concessionaire liability.

Alcohol Training Programs

Training individuals who serve alcohol or handle intoxicated patrons is an extremely important facet of a successful alcohol-management strategy and a crowd management plan. Within the past ten years, two national programs have received national recognition for their effective impact on alcohol-related situations. Training for Intervention Procedures by Servers of Alcohol (TIPS) and Techniques for Effective Alcohol Management (TEAM) provide successful training to individuals in effective alcohol management. Major League Baseball uses TEAM at their facilities whereas Aramark, a concession corporation, uses both TIPS and TEAM, depending on the facility where the corporation is employed.

> Training individuals who serve alcohol or handle intoxicated patrons is extremely important.

Anheuser-Busch provides a similar type of program, the Good Sport Program, which also includes a fan communication program, and the Safe Ride Program (Waddell, 1999). The California Department of Alcoholic Beverage Control sponsors a program called LEAD (Licensee Education on Alcohol and Drugs). Finally, Volume Services, another large concession company, provides training to staff through its Responsible Vendor Program, which is licensed by the state of Florida (Stooksbury, 1994).

Components of an Effective Alcohol Plan

Successful alcohol management plans usually have a strong connection between policy setting, policy adherence, and the training programs (Stooksbury, 1994). When discussing the importance for the staff to understand management's commitment to implementing the policies, the manager of one arena stated, "It is important for employees to know it (the commitment for implementing the policies) comes from the top of the organization" (Stooksbury, 1994, p. 6). Therefore, in order to provide the framework for a successfully managed sport facility, a facility manager should employ a comprehensive risk management plan containing equally extensive crowd management strategies and alcohol management policies.

To administer an effective crowd management plan as previously discussed, the plan and its associated alcohol strategies must treat spectators in a humane fashion and assist in providing a safe environment. Industry practices have identified several necessary elements for such a plan. First, every individual attempting to purchase alcohol should have his or her identification checked. If patrons meet the 21-year age restriction, a plastic "wristband" is placed around their wrist. If applied properly, this band is extremely difficult to remove without breaking it and thus negating its validity. The wristband will eliminate having to recheck the person's ID upon succeeding trips.

Second, a restriction on the number of beers served should be instituted, and the quantity sold should also be limited. Industry standards usually enforce a two-beer limit to any fan at one time, and the size of each serving is normally no larger than 12 ounces.

Third, beer sales must be eliminated at a specific point during the event. Normally, for basketball this is the end of the third period; hockey, the end of the second intermission; football, the beginning of the third quarter; and baseball, the end of the seventh inning.

Fourth, two crowd management techniques will ensure that the alcohol plan is properly implemented. The deployment of trained crowd management personnel at the facility entrances will prohibit intoxicated individuals from entering the facility. This will decrease the potential for injury to these individuals. In addition, the trained crowd management employees can prevent patrons from entering the facility with alcoholic beverages. This step will allow the TIPS- or TEAM-trained servers of alcohol to use their training to determine when someone has had too much to drink. These two procedures assist in controlling alcohol consumption, thus protecting the facility from the previously discussed dram shop liability suits.

Finally, the incorporation of a designated-driver program will provide a popular service by building rapport with event patrons and increasing individual awareness of the need to drink responsibly. Free carbonated drinks are often provided to the designated driver, and some facilities provide free taxi service for those who have had too much to drink (Stooksbury, 1994). The Miller Brewing Company (1992) provides brochures and other written information about designated-driver programs for interested facilities. These tips remind fans of their own alcohol limitations and describe how to make patrons recognize the problems with alcohol abuse, thus reducing alcohol-related accidents.

Key Strategies for Alcohol Sales

In addition to the previously mentioned components, various management strategies, when implemented, will assist the facility manager in curtailing irresponsible alcohol-related actions. The Miller Brewing Company (1992), in combination with previous research, has provided several suggestions regarding an effective alcohol-management plan.

1. Depending upon the philosophy of the facility, the facility manager should decide if alcoholic beverages should be sold during the event. Recent studies demonstrated that many facilities allow the sale of alcohol, but use security personnel and signage to prohibit outside alcohol and other prohibited items from being brought into the facility (Ammon & Fried, 1998).

2. The time of the event will affect the crowd; night events are more susceptible to problems than are those held in the daylight (Ammon, 1993). In addition, the weather will often affect the crowd's mood and attitude.

3. The appropriate use of signage will enlighten the spectators that responsible drinking will be allowed and irresponsible drinkers will be ejected. A strong ejection policy will help.

4. During the event, keep the emphasis on the sport, not on the drinking. Do not have any promotions that encourage patrons to drink.

5. Be aware of the demographics of the crowd attending the event; a younger blue-collar crowd will handle alcohol differently from an older

white-collar group. Contacting other venues about the age of the patrons is necessary because some events may cater to an under-21 crowd where alcohol sales should be curtailed. In addition, before the event, determine if the composition of the crowd consists more of one gender than the other, because males tend to become more violent when drinking than do females.

6. If alcohol is sold, policies regarding the consumption and sale of alcoholic beverages should be created including limitations on the size and number of beverages permitted per sale. These sales should be ceased at some common point before the end of the event.

7. The facility management should provide alcohol management training such as TIPS or TEAM to employees involved in alcohol sales.

8. Alcoholic beverages should be prohibited from being brought into the facility; anyone judged to be under the influence of alcohol should be denied entry to the facility.

9. Tailgating should be permitted only in parking lots under supervision from law enforcement officials.

10. Nonalcohol sections, or "family" sections, should be made available to those patrons not wishing to drink. David Bolger, the executive secretary for TEAM stated, "The trend is to become more customer service oriented and more family oriented." (qtd. in Stooksbury, 1994, p. 5)

Restricting the location of alcohol consumption will limit potential problems.

Summary

1. Some facilities would find it difficult to generate a profit if it were not for home-game beer sales. Other facilities believe that the liabilities associated with alcohol sales are not worth the increased revenue.

2. Obviously, if a facility allows the sale of alcohol, a potential liability exists. Thus, it should become paramount for a facility risk management plan to include a comprehensive alcohol policy, in addition to an effective crowd management strategy.

3. Because foreseeability is a key determinant in most court decisions involving alcohol-related incidents, a facility manager's ability to foresee harmful alcohol risks is an important way to potentially reduce liability.

4. *Bearman vs. University of Notre Dame* (1983) was the seminal case pertaining to foreseeability and its relation to alcohol policies. Due to the concept of foreseeability, Notre Dame had a duty to protect its fans from the potentially dangerous actions of intoxicated third parties.

5. Dram shop laws and social host liability are two state statutes that make it essential for facility managers to implement alcohol management strategies in order to prevent their patrons from drinking too much.

6. Training for Intervention Procedures by Servers of Alcohol (TIPS) and Techniques for Effective Alcohol Management (TEAM) are the two main alcohol training programs implemented in most sport facilities. Others include Anheuser-Busch's Good Sport Program, the California Department of Alcoholic Beverage Control's Licensee Education on Alcohol and Drugs (LEAD), and Volume Services' Responsible Vendor Program.

7. An effective alcohol policy should include the following elements: plastic "wristband" placed around the wrists of every legal drinker over 21; a two-beer limit to any fan and no serving larger than 12 ounces; beer sales eliminated at a specific point during the event; deployment of trained crowd management personnel at the facility entrances to prohibit intoxicated individuals from entering the facility; trained crowd management employees preventing patrons from entering the facility with alcoholic beverages; and the incorporation of a designated-driver program.

Questions

1. Should facilities serve alcohol at athletic events? Support your argument with specific examples.

2. Foreseeability is a key determinant in cases regarding alcohol. Discuss the concept of foreseeability, and explain why it is important in crowd and alcohol management.

3. What is the difference between dram shop laws and social host liability? As a student, which will impact you the most before graduation? How?

4. Using the Internet, conduct some basic research into the TIPS and TEAM alcohol training programs. What seems to be the main differences between the two?

5. Review the Miller Brewing Company and research suggestions regarding an effective alcohol plan. Pick out what you believe to be the three most important elements and explain your reasoning.

Chapter Thirteen

Concession Management

Application Exercise

Donna Starke worked for the athletic department at Normal University, a large Division I institution in the Southeast. She was the concession manager and provided food and beverage for all events taking place on the university campus. Before the school year, Donna conducted various preliminary planning meetings with other athletic department staff, campus police, and university community members who staffed the concession stands as a fundraiser. She was confident that most of the logistics were in place and that the various events occurring during the next two months would have the appropriate concessions available.

The school year was to begin with a concert by one of the most popular college bands out on tour. The 14,000-seat convocation center sold out 2 weeks before the event. On Wednesday, 3 days before the concert, Donna received a disturbing phone call. One of the local senior citizen communities had provided individuals who managed the main concession stand for the past 6 years. Apparently a contagious viral infection had incapacitated the individuals who had assisted in the past, and the home was unable to provide staff for the concert. After several frantic calls, Donna was able to convince the intramural department of the local community college to work one of the concession stands during the concert as a fundraiser. To simplify their training and to reduce potential problems, Donna placed the new group at the "Beers of the World" stand that only served draft beer.

Monday, after the concert, Donna was calculating the "cost of goods" (COG) for the event. Donna had estimated a COG of 22% for the draft beer stand and was shocked to find out that the *actual* COG was ***much*** higher. After checking her records she determined the following. The stand had supposedly sold five kegs of beer. Each keg cost the university $80.00. Donna knew from past experience that each keg held 15.5 gallons, which translated to 1,984 ounces per keg. The stand sold beer only in 16-ounce cups. The records of the intramural club showed that they had sold a total of 450 cups of beer at $3.00 per cup, grossing $1,350.00.

1. How many cups should they have sold per keg?

2. How many total cups should they have sold?

3. What should their total revenue have been?

4. What was the COG percentage for the beer that the intramural club sold?

5. As the president of the intramural club what explanation could you provide for Donna?

"Buy me some peanuts and crackerjacks" are familiar lyrics from "Take Me Out to the Ballgame." They symbolize the relationship between concessions and athletic events for over a hundred years. In the past, the term concessions usually connoted only food or beverage sales. However, gone are the days when only hot dogs, popcorn, candy, and beer constituted the concession fare. Recently, technology and customer service have drastically changed the concession industry. These changes, along with a dramatic increase in the number of new facilities and their accompanying amenities, have created a two-tier business among the concession industry that now includes merchandise sales as well.

Introduction

Organizing a concession stand may even include the condiments!

Concessions

An efficiently managed concession operation plays a vital role in the financial success of any facility. Estimates are that concession revenue generates almost 60% of operating revenue for some facilities (Mulrooney & Farmer, 1995). Concession revenue is not only specific to professional sport. Game-day revenue at major college football games can amount to as much as $350,000. In addition, college basketball and hockey games may produce $40,000-$55,000 per game (Spanberg, 1999). Generally, colleges pay around 25% to outsource their concession operation, and approximately 30% of all colleges choose this option. Major colleges with large football programs and professional teams usually pay in the neighborhood of 40% commission to outsource their concessions (Lee, 2001). If a facility's concession operation is to increase its productivity and profitability, management must be concerned with more than just serving good-quality food at reasonable prices. An individual interested in becoming a successful concessionaire needs to possess extensive knowledge about marketing, financial management, purchasing, inventory management, legal aspects, insurance, and personnel issues.

> According to estimates, concession revenue generates almost 60% of operating revenue for some facilities.

Obviously long lines, cold food, warm beer, or dirty conditions will cause customers to refrain from making purchases, but other issues such as customer service and employee appearance also affect overall sales. Concession stands should be brightly lit, conveniently located, and ergonomically designed. Using trained staff members who employ effective sales techniques will speed up the process, ensuring a satisfied customer while increasing the facility's bottom line. Pricing the products in twenty-five-cent increments will also assist in a speedy checkout (Farmer et al., 1996).

The lines to purchase products need to be clearly delineated to promote efficient yet effective service. Most fans do not want to miss any of the game while standing in line; thus, TV monitors should be conveniently located, so the customers may view the action that continues to take place. The organization of the stands is not only important to promote fast service but it also will help to eliminate most crowd management problems (chapter 10, "Crowd Management"). Menu boards should have attractive and appealing pictures of the food being served. Signage should be colorful and neon lit rather than hand painted.

1. Beer and alcohol account for the highest percentage of concession profits.

2. Popcorn is a large revenue producer, with the cost of a box of popcorn around $.05 whereas patrons pay $2.00 to $2.50 per serving.

3. Concession sales are usually constant one hour before the game with 80% of sales taking place at halftime. The remaining 20% take place after halftime.

Table 13.1. Facts Concerning Facility Food Service Operations
(Farmer et al., 1996, p. 191)

Concession Operations

Concession operations may be *outsourced* (contracted to an outside organization) or provided by the facility, which is known as doing it *in-house*.

Outsourcing

This option involves negotiating with an outside organization to provide the entire food service operation for a specific number of years. This arrangement usually nets the facility anywhere from 25 to 50% profit, depending upon variables such as the facility size, type of facility, and length of contract (Farmer et al., 1996). A major reason to subcontract (another word for outsourcing) the concessions is the liability for the food service operations is transferred from the facility to the concessionaire. Obviously, this would help to reduce potential litigation. However, this type of operation will result in a lower profit potential for the facility and may prove disastrous if the outsourced company drives away spectators because of poor product or dirty conditions.

Because these subcontracted companies are usually large in scope, they often have a regional or national network of expertise that they can rely upon. This often translates into cheaper costs.

Advantages of this arrangement are that volume purchasing enables the vendor to provide quality products at reduced prices, as well as provide the facility operation with efficiency, expertise, and capital equipment. Operational management, staffing, purchasing, maintenance, inventory, and storage become the contractor's responsibility. In addition, facility management is able to reduce the number of problems pertaining to employees and their associated problems, such as worker's compensation, equal opportunity, and hiring or firing. Additionally, there is less political interference when compared with an in-house operation (Farmer et al., 1996).

In-House

This option leaves the responsibility of the concession operation to the facility manager. Facility management does not have to share the revenues with anyone else, but it also does not have anyone else to share a loss with either. An in-house operation gives facility management control regarding the types of employees hired, the product offered, the price charged for the product, and the way the product will be marketed. Unfortunately, this option also means that facility managers are responsible for all employee and administrative problems. If the facility is a public operation, the political and bureaucratic red tape will be substantial (Farmer et al., 1996).

Facility Design and Concessions

The design of the food service operation is extremely important, and since the late 1990s, architects of many of the newer facilities have included representatives from the food industry to assist in the design. Concession design and construction have accounted for as much as 10-15% of the budgets for these newer facilities (P. Williams, 2001).

Good food is not the only requirement for a facility's concession operations to be successful. Concessions will not prove to be an effective source of revenue if the locations (stands) are not conveniently placed. If the facility design does not allow for this convenience, vendors or "hawkers" (vendors who walk among the crowds) should be utilized to bring the product to the fans. In most facilities there should be sufficient numbers of concession stands to serve the total number of seats, with each patron being able to reach the nearest the point of sale (concession stand) from his or her seat within 60 to 90 seconds (Farmer et al., 1996). Ideally, there should be a ratio of one point of purchase per 75 spectators (P. Williams, 2001). However, some industry experts believe that the number of stands will depend on their location in the facility. For example, there should be a ratio of one stand per 200 spectators (1:200) on the upper levels, 1:175 on the lower levels, and 1:150 on the club level (Cameron, 2001d).

In order to be effective, concessions must be conveniently placed.

Installing wide concourses will assist with concession stand accessibility and will help prevent congested concession lines. Not only would this congestion reduce the volume of customers, but it could also incite a crowd management problem. A general rule of thumb mandates one foot of concourse for every row in the stadium bowl. For example, Invesco Field at Mile High Stadium has 38 rows of seats in the stadium bowl, but the concourse is 44 feet wide, more than 8 feet wider than necessary (Cameron, 2001d).

Examples of wide concourses at Invesco Field and Mile High in Denver.

Projecting Operational Costs

Sales projections are a crucial and difficult task because the amount of revenue generated from event to event is often difficult to estimate. Variables such as weather, temperature, crowd size, and demographics will influence spectators' buying habits. For this reason some individuals in the facility industry term food and beverage sales as "necessary evils" (Holtzman, 2001). However, relatively accurate projections can be determined provided the proper documentation is kept for each event (Farmer et al., 1996).

The operational costs need to be recorded for any facility concession operation. Generally, these costs will decrease as the food service operations become more streamlined. Rent and insurance are usually fixed operating costs. The rent is usually a fixed monthly figure. Insurance costs associated with insurance premium amounts and worker's compensation will vary depending on the numbers of claims, but these costs must also be documented. Concession labor costs are also an important item, and in most cases, management salaries are a fixed monthly cost, whereas employee salary expenses will be a variable cost that fluctuates with total sales. Concession managers must understand that employee labor costs should be covered by profit from sales (Farmer et al., 1996).

Facility managers can estimate some food service operating costs such as labor, repairs of equipment and/or buildings, advertising, promotional expenses, equipment rental, licenses, and travel. The costs of scheduled maintenance and emergency repairs, all business licenses (i.e., operating licenses, health permit, liquor license, etc.), and business travel must also be determined. Social security, federal and state unemployment tax, local taxes, and sales taxes must be anticipated as well (Farmer et al., 1996).

One of the problems with the costs incurred with food and beverage is the perception of many in the facility management industry. Normally, depending on the type, beverages are viewed as a profit maker, whereas food services are perceived to operate at a loss. However, not all beverages are the same when it comes to profit margins. For example, alcoholic drinks have one profit margin, fountain drinks a second, and bottled soft drinks and juices a third. Within each category exists a variety of profits as well. Liquor has a lower cost of goods (COG) than does beer whereas wine has the highest COG in the alcohol category. The soft drink industry provides an additional example. The expense of a 20 oz. drink, including ice, cup, straw, and lid, runs around 25 cents. If a concession stand sells the 20 oz. drink for $1.50, the facility nets $1.25 in profit with a 17% pour cost (.25/1.50). A *pour cost* is what the product costs the facility for the product container and any associated labor. Beverage distributors, however, charge concession providers 50 cents per 20 oz. *bottle* of soft drink. Everything else being equal, the facility captures $1.00 in gross profit while assuming a 30% (.50/1.50) pour cost. For *specialty* drinks and some juices, beverage distributors charge concessionaires up to $2.00 per bottle, which obviously negates any profit margin for the concession operator. Beer is similar when comparing draft beer vs. bottles (glass or plastic) and cans (Holtzman, 2001).

A trend that carried over from the 1990s is consumer belief in brand names and the popularity of regional foods at entertainment events.

Concession Industry Trends

Three major trends have permeated the food and beverage industry so far in the 21st century. The first pertains to the number of companies involved in the industry. Similar to many other industries, consolidation and merger have become buzzwords in the concession industry. Second, as the price of tickets to athletic and concert events has increased, so have the expectations of the ticket purchaser. Hamburgers, beer, and cotton candy no longer satisfy the palate of many consumers. Finally, a trend that carried over from the 1990s is consumer belief in brand names and the popularity of regional foods at entertainment events.

Consolidation

The concession industry has changed dramatically through consolidation. Not only have a variety of companies merged, but the resulting competitors have also begun to enter the venue management industry (Deckard,

2001a). The antithesis of this phenomenon is that some venue owners have kept concession management in-house.

During the first half of the 1990s, the concession industry comprised between 6 and 8 main companies and 12-15 smaller companies. In 1998, Volume Services and Service America merged to form Volume Services America VSA. In 2000, the largest corporation, Aramark, bought out Harry M Stevens and the Ogden venue concession businesses (Cameron, 2001b). Then, in February 2003, VSA changed its name to Centerplate, and in April they filed with the SEC to become a publicallly traded stock. Global Spectrum, a newly formed venue management company, bought Ovations Food Service, a concession company that served several minor league baseball teams. Two European concession giants became involved in the United States when Sodexho bought out Marriott Management Services and Compass, the largest concession company in the world, bought 49% of Levy (Cameron, 2001b,c). Thus by 2002, the number of small companies had shrunk to around 8-10, but the overwhelming majority of concession contracts are controlled by four or five large companies. Aramark, though smaller than Compass, is the largest food and beverage company in North America, and in 2001 Aramark served 25 amphitheaters, 30 convention centers, and 45 professional sport facilities (Deckard, 2001a).

Premium food services are provided at a variety of locations, including glassed-in restaurants at Jacobs Field and Toronto's Sky Dome.

Premium Food Services

Specialized food provided to club seats and luxury suites has spawned a new area of the concession industry. Although "Joe Fan" still consumes the traditional fare of hamburgers and hot dogs, items such as lobster bisque and smoked salmon have become staples to those sitting in premium seats (Spanberg, 1999). Levy Brothers were in the restaurant business in Chicago, and during the 1980s, they recognized a need to provide premium restaurant-style quality food to premium seat holders at sporting events. Although these premium seat holders were willing to pay top dollar for seats in many of the new sport facilities, they wanted quality food and beverages to complement their upscale seats. Levy Brothers began catering their restaurant expertise, excellent chefs, and formidable menus to luxury-box and club-seat owners. The Levys found that unlike the restaurant business a sports event offered stable numbers. The unpredictability of the restaurant business often leads to costly waste (Deckard, 2001a). Amazingly, Levy Brothers suddenly found a high demand for their catering services. They expanded from one facility in 1982 (Comiskey Park) to 55 sport facilities across the United States and Canada ("About Levy," 2002). Levy established a niche market and became the envy of the other concession companies.

Brand Names and Regional Favorites

The previous section mentioned that ticket consumers have been willing to pay higher prices for better quality seats, but they also want better quality food and service, as well as a variety of brands (Cookson, 2001). The president of Levy commented, "For a long time spectators at sports events were treated more or less like captives, and fed that way. We approached the market from a restaurant perspective, which is where Levy's background was rooted in the first place" (Cameron, 2001c, p.25). However, what started as an increase in quality of food for club and suite owners now permeates all areas of the concession business.

Providing recognizable brand-name products (e.g., Ballpark Franks, McDonald's, Taco Bell, Coors beer, and TCBY yogurt) will ensure the customer's confidence about the quality of food being served. Some facilities actually cross-promote with brand-name products. For example, Volume Services America has begun selling Krispy Kreme donuts in three of their MLB venues. In addition, Miller Park has a TGI Friday's, and PNC Park has an Outback Steakhouse in their parks. These restaurants not only draw fans during the baseball games, but also draw customers to the facilities on nongame days (Cameron, 2001b). Although more facility managers are incorporating similar trends, they are by no means the first to do so. SkyDome in Toronto has had a Hard Rock Cafe located on site since the stadium opened in 1989.

> What started as an increase in quality of food for club and suite owners now permeates all areas of the concession business.

In addition to brand names, serving local gastronomical favorites has become the rage for concession companies all across North America. Fish tacos in San Diego, Rocky Mountain oysters in Denver, and cheese-steaks in Philadelphia are but a few examples of the regional favorites offered in various stadiums. Although sushi has found a niche in many sport venues, some stadiums still offer specific localized favorites. At Cleveland Brown Stadium, chocolate chip cookies are sold in the shape of dog bones and nachos are served in plastic dog dishes (Cameron, 2001b).

Brand-name recognition helps customers choose quality products they can trust.

Merchandise

Merchandise includes a variety of products such as hats, shirts, CD screensavers, sweatshirts, posters, and authentic jerseys. The distribution and organization of merchandise stands are similar to those of concession operations, and operators use many of the same techniques. Interestingly enough, many of the larger concession companies, such as Aramark, manage and staff the various merchandise operations.

Virtually every new sport facility has a team store located on site. These stores have a variety of catchy names such as CAVS Town in Cleveland and The Dugout in Colorado. These stores have the potential to be major sources of revenue if managed properly. Whoever manages the store needs to decide if they want to operate the shop as a customer service or as a profit center. If the shop is to be operated as a profit center, four key ingredients must be followed to control costs. First, qualified staff must be hired. Facility managers don't know retail, and experienced sales people must be hired to ensure the necessary customer service. Second, partnerships should be solicited. If the sport facility has excess space available, rent it out to a retail operation whose product complements the events that take place at the facility. Third, overhead must be kept low to ensure a profit margin; however, never let cost-cutting measures affect customer service. Last, good customer interaction must be a priority. The customer must feel that the small merchandise store offers benefits not offered by a large sporting goods store (Bynum, 2001).

The sale of unlicensed merchandise is known as *bootlegging*. It is common practice for most major events, with merchandise for sale, to obtain a federal injunction dealing with copyright law infringement. This provides police with the authority to arrest and/or confiscate unauthorized merchandise. Local city ordinances governing the sale of items on the street

Merchandise sales occur
in a variety of settings.

can be most beneficial in dealing with and eliminating bootleggers
(Farmer et al., 1996).

Summary

1. Concessions include food service management (food and beverage sales) as well as the sale of merchandise.

2. Concessions may be outsourced to an outside company or they may be conducted in-house where the facility controls everything. When concessions are outsourced, the facility management must maintain a certain degree of control to ensure product quality.

3. Customers want warm food and cold drinks sold from attractive locations, by highly trained, energetic, and customer service-oriented staff.

4. Recent trends in concession management include (a) consolidation, (b) premium food service, and (c) brand names and regional food.

5. Merchandise stores are often operated by concession companies and may be oriented as a profit center or for customer service.

1. Explain the following terms: outsource, hawkers, cost of goods, pour cost, consolidation, premium service foods, cross-promote, and bootlegging.

2. Describe the circumstances that would require you to outsource the concession operations at your facility.

3. Describe how pouring costs can be estimated.

4. Why would a sport facility use the same company to manage both the concessions and merchandise operations?

Chapter Fourteen

Box Office Management

You are the box office manager for a 12,000-seat arena at Hoops University, the home of the Screaming Wombats, a very large Division I university. The athletic department oversees a program made up of 17 varsity sports (nine male and eight female). Your men's basketball coach Tom Terrific has been at Hoops University for 8 years, and he has built the program from scratch. Before Coach Terrific arrived, fan attendance was horrible. Since his sixth year, *every* home game has been sold out. It has been estimated that the basketball program generates between $1,000,000 and $3,000,000 in profit during the season, depending on the year. It is the *only* sport that has ever been a revenue producer in the athletic department. Attendance has been escalating to where the average attendance at the 12,000-seat Wombat Arena for the past season was over 12,500. Hoops University does *not* field a football team.

The Hoops Basketball program has over 10,000 season ticket holders. In addition, at the beginning of each season 1,500 individual game tickets are put on sale for every game and are usually sold in a matter of hours. Finally, as a service to the Screaming Wombat fans five hundred (upper level) $10.00 seats are put on sale at 9:00 am each game-day morning. The athletic department has placed a five-ticket maximum for each purchaser to eliminate scalpers. Fans are allowed to line up beginning at 6:00 AM for the 9:00 sale.

As the box office manager, you have begun to a notice a disturbing trend during these game-day sales. Individuals you perceive to be scalpers have begun hiring people, mostly students, to stand in line. You believe that these unscrupulous individuals are trying to corner the market for the 500 day-of-game tickets. You have received reports that some of these game-day tickets are being resold for as high as $150-$200 each.

1. What can you do to prevent these scalpers from taking over?

2. What type of policies can you try to implement to ensure that as many "fans" as possible have the opportunity to see the Wombats play?

3. Your city does not have a local ordinance against selling tickets for more than face value. What could local legislators do to help your situation?

4. What procedures should the campus police implement?

Introduction

The Daytona 500, Lollapalooza, the Rolling Stones, the Super Bowl, the WNBA Finals, and the World Cup all have at least one thing in common. In order to gain admittance to these events most spectators must purchase a "ticket." In a majority of sport/entertainment facilities, ticket sales are the responsibility of the *box office*. Recently the number of spectators attending professional games and concerts has declined. Although some experts believe this to be a result of the current recession, others believe the trend to be a residual effect of the terrorist attacks on September 11. 2001, and still others believe fans are becoming turned off by the obnoxious, selfish attitudes of some pro players and rock stars. Regardless of the reason, spectators at sporting events spend an average of $20 for tickets, parking, and programs. Playing to half-empty stadiums and arenas represents a major source of lost revenue for the sports and entertainment industry (Cohen, 2001).

Until recently, the traditional way to secure tickets was to travel to the facility and buy them at the box office. During the 1980s, large ticket companies such as Ticketmaster began to provide point of sales in malls and other more convenient locations away from the sport/entertainment facilities. Within the last decade, fans have been able to use their credit cards and order tickets via mail and later over the phone. Recently, however,

The Internet may be used to purchase tickets from your office.

technology and the Internet have changed the box office industry. For example, Ticketmaster reported that 61% of the tickets sold in Las Vegas were sold via the Internet (Collins, 2002). The Internet has become a very effective way to sell tickets. World Wrestling Entertainment (WWE) had an "Internet only pre-sale" for an event in Australia and sold 20,000 tickets on line. This was before one single ticket had been sold at the box office (Collins).

Thus, regardless if the numbers of spectators are down or not, the ticketing industry is advancing very quickly. Fan-loyalty programs, bar-coded ticket entry cards and other electronic advances are spurring the growth of the industry. Some individuals in the business believe a new label is required since ticketing has changed so dramatically; they believe it should be called the "admission service industry" (Cohen, 2001, p. 61).

Tickets

Types of Tickets

Tickets are normally classified as either **reserved** or **general admission**. *General admission* (GA) tickets allow individuals to sit virtually anywhere they want on a first-come, first-served basis. The ticket is not for a specific seat, but for a seat somewhere in the facility.

> Facility managers must determine if the extra revenue from festival seating is worth the increased risks and liability due to fainting and other bodily injuries.

During the past decade a controversy has erupted over the sale of *festival-seating* tickets at concerts. This general-admission designation is somewhat misleading because the concertgoer does not have an actual seat. The floor in front of the stage is void of seats, and the fans stand on the floor, packed tightly together and as close to the stage as possible. Although the bands enjoy the "closeness" of the audience, the promoter enjoys the revenue from the extra tickets not available with regular GA or reserved seating. Facility managers must determine if the extra revenue is worth the increased risks and liability due to fainting and other bodily injuries.

When ticket buyers purchase a specific seat for an event, they have bought a *reserved ticket*. This ensures that the ticket buyer has a specific section, row, and seat for the event. The majority of sporting events in North America use reserved seats. In fact, after a series of deadly "crowd crushes," many of the stadiums in England have resorted to using reserved seats. These stadiums are termed *all seaters* by the British.

Most facilities prohibit refunds and all sales are considered final. This is because the owner of the event in many situations is a promoter and not the facility. Therefore, the facility becomes an agent for the promoter and should not make exceptions for property that is not their own. In addition, a ticket is recognized by the courts as a license; thus, it can be revoked at any time. If a spectator or concertgoer refuses to comply with facility procedures, the facility manager may ask the offending party to leave, and the ejected party need not be reimbursed (Farmer et al., 1996).

Lost Tickets

For most events the promoter and facility manager will establish a policy regarding ticket refunds or exchanges. A lost ticket, however, is a different situation, and most ticket managers have the authority to issue a seat-replacement pass for any lost season ticket. These passes void the original ticket (Farmer et al., 1996). In most cases, these seat-replacement tickets are **sold** to the season-ticket holder to preclude the chance of two individuals' gaining access to the facility with only one paid ticket. If the ticket is later discovered, it might be returned to the ticket office for a refund. This precludes the ticket holder from having to pay twice for the same ticket. Nonseason tickets are not covered by this arrangement unless the ticket holder has documentation (i.e., a credit card receipt) that he or she actually purchased the ticket.

Box Office Design and Administration

The box office is often the first contact a patron has with a sport or entertainment facility. Access, therefore, is important to ensure positive public relations. All box offices should be in an accessible location, and they must be compliant with the Americans With Disabilities Act.

The size of the box office area should accommodate the sale, pickup, and distribution of tickets. An adequate number of windows should be available to handle an unexpected number of "walk-up" sales. It is suggested that sales windows be located on all sides of the facility rather than just at the main entrance to the facility (Mulrooney & Farmer, 1995).

The main box office may be the only location available to purchase tickets on nongame days. The availability of multiple windows generates repeat business and will help to promote sales of future events. In addition, a specific location for "will-call" tickets needs to be easily identifiable. The ticket windows should be covered to a depth of 15-20 feet to protect the ticket buyers from the elements. Windows should be located both inside as well as outside the facility to help keep ticket-buying patrons from interfering with those who already possess tickets and are entering the facility. Having outside windows is also useful for the presale of future events without having to open the entire facility on nongame days (Farmer et al., 1996). Box offices have normal business hours from 9:00am –5:00pm on nonevent days. However, on the day of an event, the box office should remain open at least until halftime or intermission, depending upon demand (Farmer et al.).

> The box office area should be large enough to accommodate the sale, pickup, and distribution of tickets.

Advanced ticket sales may also occur at the venue box office.

Because the box office is the primary source of information for spectators, its personnel should be trained to provide information on the facility, personnel, and specific policies. In addition, a recorded message should be available during nonbusiness hours to inform the public of upcoming events. Box-office policies should remain relatively simple and uncomplicated, with the ultimate goal being to provide an efficient, secure, and service-oriented operation with employees trained to provide a pleasant attitude and effective customer service (Mulrooney & Farmer, 1995).

Although the box office is very important for an efficiently managed facility, it normally employs a minimal number of full-time staff. Usually a manager and two to three assistants constitute the full-time employees. On game day, additional ticket sellers are scheduled to assist with the increased demand. Other individuals will be used for ancillary ticket activities such as season-ticket sales, group sales, and suite sales.

The box office manager will be responsible for the operation and supervision of all box office personnel. This person ensures that the ordering, distribution, and sale of tickets are conducted in a professional manner. The director or manager is also responsible for the final box office statement.

Depending on the specific facility, additional responsibilities include policy development, personnel selection, safety, employee discipline, and operational support (Mulrooney & Farmer, 1995).

Price Strategies

Sport and entertainment facilities are highly complex and technologically advanced business enterprises. However, the strategies used to establish the price of a ticket are relatively simple. If the main tenant or the facility itself establishes the price, the strategy is known as house scale. This often occurs with professional sport teams that establish the pricing strategy each year if they play multiple games at the facility. If an outside promoter or event establishes the price for a one-time or once-a-year event, a performance scale is used (Farmer et al., 1996)..

Most sporting events will also have different prices for their various seating locations. Recently built outdoor stadiums such as Miller Park, Safeco Field, Minute Maid Park, and Bank One Ballpark have an area, usually in the outfield, where the lowest-price tickets may be found. A few teams charge as little as $1.00 for some of these tickets. The closer a spectator sits to the center of the activity, the higher the price of the ticket. Most sport facilities will have four to six differently priced locations spaced throughout the stadium or arena.

> Many intercollegiate and most professional teams have recognized that club seats have become an important source of non-shared revenue.

One of the highest-priced locations in a majority of facilities is the **club seat**. These seats are in prime locations to view the athletic contest and offer various amenities. Normal seats in most facilities are approximately 19 inches wide; however, a club seat is usually 23-24 inches wide and is more thickly padded. Depending on the facility, some club seats are provided with wait staff that take the fans' order and deliver it to their seat. Other facilities will provide separate concession stands for their club-seat guests. Additionally, the selection of food is usually of a higher quality for patrons sitting in these seats. Many intercollegiate and most professional teams have recognized that club seats have become an important source of nonshared revenue. Thus, the need for club seats has become a driving force behind many of the requests for new stadiums and arenas.

Methods of Purchasing Tickets

Tickets to sport and entertainment events may be sold or distributed in a variety of ways. Although the marketing department and box office must agree on the methods to be used, the box office has the final responsibility to implement the agreed-upon procedures. As previously mentioned, fans may purchase tickets in person at the box office, via mail or phone, or over the Internet. Ordering by phone requires the use of a credit card and usually will incur various service charges. Outside agencies such as Ticketmaster also allow fans the opportunity to buy tickets at various locations away from the stadium or arena. In addition, members of the organization, team, or band may leave tickets for fans. These tickets are often free of charge and are termed *comps*. Finally, new technology such as the Internet allow fans the luxury of purchasing and even printing tickets from the comfort of their own homes.

Some pro teams have begun to sell their tickets through the team's web page.

Primary Third-Party Sales

Ticketmaster, through mergers and acquisitions, has become the giant in the ticket sales industry. They make a profit from attaching a "transaction fee" to every ticket that they sell. Team owners are beginning to question, however, why, after spending millions of dollars establishing a brand loyalty with their consumers, they are willing to pass their customers on to a third party to purchase the tickets (Cohen, 2001). As an alternative, some pro teams have begun to sell their tickets through the team's web page. This procedure cuts out companies such as Ticketmaster (and their attached fees) and places the fan in direct contact with the specific team. Controlling the sale of their tickets while eliminating the middle company will help many cash-starved teams realize an additional source of revenue. Teams are beginning to implement this type of system in many sports, and presently three organizations (University of Colorado, Ohio State University, and the Colorado Rockies) are implementing this type of system, which uses electronic commerce via IBM (K. Fenton, personal communication, July 8, 1999). Teams could also sell merchandise and tickets via their web page as long as no preexisting merchandise contracts exist. In the not too distant future, pro teams will also be selling tickets to non-team-related events such as concerts, ice shows, and religious gatherings. This trend will be interesting to watch because it will bring the teams in direct competition with existing ticket companies such as Ticketmaster.

Secondary Season Ticket Sales

Several professional organizations are beginning to offer their season-ticket holders the opportunity to sell back any tickets not used for a specific game. The San Francisco Giants MLB team began such a program called "Double Play Ticket Window." The exchanges can only take place online, which requires the marketplace to be technologically knowledgeable. Each season-ticket owner is provided with a password that allows access to the system to post his or her ticket information. Potential buyers access the web site and, if interested, contact the Giants box office by email with a credit card number. The box office deactivates the barcode on the ticket, and a new barcode is issued. The buyer picks up the ticket at the Giant will-call window and enters the stadium. The facility managers at Pac Bell Park have installed new automated turnstiles that read the barcode on the tickets. The Giants realize profit from each transaction by receiving 10% of the resale value from the ticket seller as well as 10% from the ticket buyer. The season-ticket holder is able to recapture revenue from tickets that may have gone completely unused, and the ticket buyer has access to seats that would normally not have been available for purchase (Deckard, 2001b).

UsherPro has taken the concept one step further. They purchased software that enables organizations to resell their own premium tickets. In 1999, UsherPro signed the Staples Center in Los Angeles, the SkyDome in Toronto, and the Gaylord Entertainment Center in Nashville as clients. UsherPro felt that a lot of organizations have a difficult time in managing their ticket inventory. Some organizations may have blocks of tickets to NBA, NHL, AFL, and minor league events as well as concerts and other entertainment events. Oftentimes because of the sheer number of events, some of the tickets go unused. The software will allow the organization to manage their tickets and allow individuals to exchange the tickets if they are unable to attend the sport or entertainment event (Cameron, 2001a).

Kiosk-Based Ticket Sales and Service

Due to the large number of Internet sales, many facility managers have had to increase the number of will-call windows. Tickets ordered via phone (paid for with a credit card) and those left as comps are distributed at the

Several windows will be designated for will-call tickets.

facility box office will-call window. This location provides patrons with the opportunity to pick up prepaid or comp tickets before or on the day of the event. When the fan arrives to pick up the tickets, a photo ID is normally required before the tickets may be released, in order to ensure proper security (Farmer et al., 1996). Although prepaid tickets have previously been paid for, they remain the property of the team or event. If the tickets are not picked up by a specific time during the event, some facilities may release the remaining tickets for sale, depending on facility policy. Other facilities will retain the ticket until it is claimed, even if this means storing the unclaimed tickets after the completion of the event.

Fan loyalty programs have been in existence for several years and were originally associated with "fan cards." AIM Technologies, Inc., based in Austin, Texas, claims to be the first company to create and implement the fan-card program (Schaffer, 1999). Interested fans signed up for the program by completing a short questionnaire upon entering the ballpark. On each subsequent visit the fan answered a question or two at an interactive kiosk. In return, the fan received "credits" towards concessions or merchandise similar to airline mileage bonuses. The responses were placed in a database where club officials might glean ticketing or marketing information whenever necessary. The program began with two minor league baseball teams and has progressed to include teams in the MLB, NHL, NBA, and one MLS team. The cards are free to the fans, and the team pays AIM Technologies, Inc. Teams could provide sponsors, who could ask a question or two on the survey, to place their logos on the kiosks and accompanying literature (Schaffer). A program such as this has obvious marketing implications, and futuristic box office managers could gain valuable information about the needs of their ticket buyers (Dial, 1999).

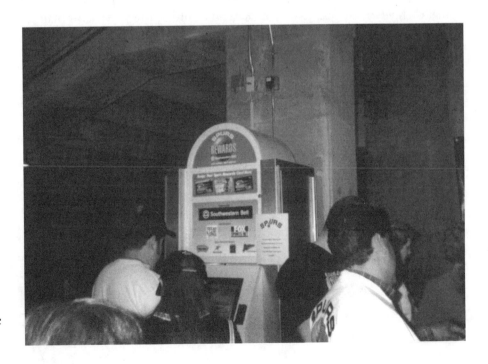

Example of an interactive fan-card kiosk.

Customer Relationship Management (CRM)

CRM provides facility management with a number of benefits such as allowing organizations the ability to track their ticket distribution. This provides the opportunity to see who is using the ticket and who is accompanying the ticket holder as a guest (Cohen, 2001). This "smart-card" technology has been available at Scotland's Ranger Football Club Ibrox Stadium since the 2000-2001 season. The system was the very first to be used in the United Kingdom and one of the first used anywhere. All 39,000 season-ticket holders use a "credit card" in place of traditional tickets to gain access to Ibrox Stadium. The card uses a proximity antennae for entry into the stadium, taking less than three seconds for each entry. In addition, a computer chip stores information on the card pertaining to seat details such as section, row, and seat number. The card also allows "e-loyalty" points to be accumulated. For every match attended or item of merchandise purchased, "loyalty points" are accumulated similar to those from the fan cards in the United States. Also, the cards contain an "e-purse" service where fans can credit cash to their cards exactly like a credit card (McGlynn, 2001).

Future Trends

A couple of potential trends pertain to methods implemented in order to increase ticket prices. The elasticity of tickets and the accompanying price has shown that fans for the most part will continue to purchase tickets even as the price rises. However, fan complaints due to the increasing prices may cause public relations problems. A potential solution could be to sell multiyear season tickets with a built-in price escalator. The fans would see the increase several years in advance, when they contracted for the season ticket. This program would provide a consistent source of revenue, with yearly increases, whereas it would diffuse the yearly complaints, because the increases were pre-announced (Friedman, 1999).

During the 2002-2003 hockey season, the Boston Bruins tried offering "demand pricing" to their fans. To ensure a full house, facility and team owners used a variable ticketing-pricing technique. For example, if the upcoming game had traditionally been a less attractive matchup, the Bruins decreased their ticket prices. For those "high-demand" games the box office increased the ticket price significantly. The philosophy is similar to that of the airline industry and assumes that demand will increase the elasticity of the tickets (Cameron, 2002b).

> The elasticity of tickets and the accompanying price has shown that fans for the most part will continue to purchase tickets even as the price rises.

Industry Concerns

Obviously, many new technological advances are challenging the ticketing industry. However, a recent sports-ticketing survey of box office managers and directors of ticket operations said their biggest problem currently was interfacing with their customers to maximize sales.

They found it difficult to move high volume sales in a short period of time (basic supply and demand problems).

Because of the technological advances available for the common purchaser, the industry as a whole is finding it more and more difficult to detect fraudulent tickets.

Due to the huge influx of Internet sales, they were finding it difficult to distribute the tickets to their customers in a timely fashion.

They found it more difficult to capture information about their consumers (this capturing of data is often called *data mining*).

A common problem for most ticket managers was that after ordering the tickets many people failed to pick them up (known as "no-shows").

Table 14.1. Challenges for Box-Office Managers and Directors of Ticket Operations. (Nutall, 2001)

Summary

1. The Internet has become a very effective method of selling tickets. Although estimates vary, many people use the web to purchase their tickets.

2. General admission (GA) tickets are not for a specific seat, but for a seat somewhere in the facility. A reserved ticket ensures that the ticket buyer has a specific section, row, and seat for the event.

3. Festival seating provides the promoter with additional revenue but constitutes a potential problem due to lawsuits stemming from injuries caused by overcrowding.

4. For many patrons, the box office is the first contact they have with the facility. It also provides a central location for individuals with questions, problems, or concerns.

5. Although one main central location should exist, ticket windows should be provided for the public in various locations around the facility.

6. *House scale* occurs when the main tenant, or the facility itself, establishes the price. An outside promoter or event uses a *performance*

scale when they establish a ticket price for a one-time or once-a-year event uses.

7. Club seats have become an important source of nonshared revenue for intercollegiate and professional sport facilities. They are located in prime sites and offer various amenities such as wider seats and higher quality food.

8. Tickets to sport and entertainment events may be sold or distributed in person at the box office, via mail, by phone, or through the Internet. Free tickets left for friends or relatives by members of the organization, team, or band are termed *comps*.

9. Primary third-party sales, secondary season ticket sales, kiosk-based ticket sales and service and customer relationship management are all currently being used as programs and opportunities to increase ticket sales and box office management strategies.

10. Fan cards, multiyear season tickets with built-in price escalators, and teams selling tickets on their web pages are just several of the many future trends in store for box office managers.

Questions

1. What are the major differences between general admission and reserved seats? Name a sporting event, and explain which type of ticketing classification would best suit the event.

2. If professional organizations begin to sell tickets to nonsporting events through their web page, what do you think will be the reaction of ticket companies such as Ticketmaster?

3. Describe why the box office plays an important role in the facility operation process.

4. As a newly hired box office manager for a minor league baseball team, what do you think would be the first major problem that you would encounter?

5. List two additional trends that you feel box office managers may encounter in the next five years.

References

Allen v. Rutgers, The State University of New Jersey, 523 A. 2d 262 (NJ. Sup. Ct. 1987).

American College of Sports Medicine. (1992). *ACSM's health/fitness facility standards and guidelines.* Champaign, IL: Human Kinetics.

American Heart Association. (n.d.). About sudden death and cardiac arrest. Retrieved June 28, 2002, from www.americanheart.org/presenter.jhtml?identifier=604

Ammon, R., Jr. (1993). Risk and game management practices in selected municipal football facilities. (Doctoral dissertation, University of Northern Colorado, 1993). *Dissertation Abstracts International, 54,* 3366A-3367A.

Ammon, R., Jr. (1997, August). *An executive's guide to crowd management issues.* Paper presented at the International Association of Assembly Managers 72nd Annual Conference and Trade Show, Dallas, TX.

Ammon, R., Jr. (1995, April-June). Alcohol and event management: Two sides of the same coin. *Crowd management, 1*(4), 16-19.

Ammon, R., Jr. (2000). The globalization of sport: Preparing sport managers for the 21st century. *International Journal of Sport Management, 1*(3), 151-153.

Ammon, R., Jr. (2001). Risk management process. In D. J. Cotten, J. Wolohan, & T. J. Wilde (Eds.), *Law for recreation and sport managers* (pp. 265-277). Dubuque, IA: Kendall/Hunt Publishing Company.

Ammon, R., Jr., & Fried, G. (1998). Assessing stadium crowd management practices and liability issues. *Journal of Convention & Exhibition Management, 1*(2-3), 119-150.

Barbieri, K. (2001, November 12). Aftershocks of terrorist attack still being felt in touring industry. *Amusement Business, 113*(45), 6.

Bearman v. University of Notre Dame, 453 N.E.2d 1196; 1983 Ind. App. LEXIS 3387

Belize Divers, Inc. (1992, March). *Dive Briefing Checklist.* Belize City, Belize, C.A.: Author.

Berman v. Philadelphia Board of Education, 456 A.2d 545 (Pa. Super. Ct. 1983).

Berry, R. C., & Wong, G. M. (1993). *Law and business of the sports industries.* (Vol. II, 2nd ed.). Westport, CT: Praeger.

Billing, J. (2000). Staff recruitment, selection, retention, and termination. In H. Appenzeller & G. Lewis (Eds.), *Successful sport management* (2nd ed., pp. 5-21). Durham, NC: Carolina Academic Press.

Bolman, L. G., & Deal, T. E. (1997). *Reframing organizations: Artistry, choice, and leadership* (2nd ed.). San Francisco: Jossey-Bass Publishers.

Buford, B. (1991, February). Among the thugs. *Esquire, 126*(2), 77-84.

Bynum, M. (2001, December). One-stop shopping. *Athletic Business, 25*(12), 91-96.

Cameron, S. (2001a, April 30-May 6). UsherPro tackles secondary tickets. *Street & Smiths SportsBusiness Journal, 4*(2), 5.

Cameron, S. (2001b, May 28-June 3). Premium service marks sole shift in industry. *Street & Smith's SportsBusiness Journal, 4*(6), 23, 28.

Cameron, S. (2001c, May 28-June 3). Levy goes global, while keeping eye on quality. *Street & Smith's SportsBusiness Journal, 4*(6), 25.

Cameron, S. (2001d, July 30-August 5). Traffic flow inside venue as important as outside. *Street & Smith's SportsBusiness Journal, 4*(15), 22.

Cameron, S. (2002e, March 4-10). Facilities projects total $7.8 billion. *Street & Smith's SportsBusiness Journal, 4*(46), 1, 37.

Cameron, S. (2002f, May 27-June 2). Bruins to set prices hourly. *Street & Smith's SportsBusiness Journal, 5*(5), 1, 50.

Cantwell, J. D. (1998). Automatic external defibrillators in the sports arena: The right place, the right time. *The Physician and Sportsmedicine, 26*(12), 33. Retrieved June 28, 2002, from www.physsportsmed.com/issues/1998/12dec/cantwell.htm

Carpenter, L. J. (2000). *Legal concepts in sport: A primer* (2nd ed.). Champaign, IL: Sagamore Publishers.

Catherwood, D. W., & Van Kirk, R. L. (1992). *The complete guide to special event management: Business insights, financial advice, and successful strategies from Ernst & Young, advisors to the Olympics, the Academy Awards, and the PGA tour.* New York: John Wiley & Sons.

Chelladurai, P. (2001). *Managing organizations for sport and physical activity: A systems perspective.* Scottsdale, AZ: Holcomb Hathaway Publishers.

Cialdini, R. B. (1993). *Influence: Science and practice* (3rd ed.). New York: Harper Collins College Publishers.

Cohen, A. (2001, September). Ticket for the future. *Athletic Business 25*(9), 55-61.

Collins, B. (2002, May 31). Hear and there. *Show and tell: A newsletter for event venues and touring attractions, 1*(1), 2.

Cookson, B. (2001, May 28-June 3). Bigelow specializes in what stadiums, teams need. *Street & Smith's SportsBusiness Journal, 4*(6), 29.

Coren, E. S. (1995). *The law and the diving professional.* Santa Ana, CA: International PADI, Inc.

Cotten, D. J. (2001a). Defenses against liability. In D. J. Cotten, J. T. Wolohan, & T. J. Wilde (Eds.), *Law for recreation and sport managers* (2nd ed., pp. 59-74). Dubuque, IA: Kendall/Hunt.

Cotten, D. J. (2001b). Waivers and releases. In D. J. Cotten, J. T. Wolohan, & T. J. Wilde (Eds.), *Law for recreation and sport managers* (2nd ed., pp. 87-96). Dubuque, IA: Kendall/Hunt.

Cotten, D. J. (2001c). Which parties are liable? In D. J. Cotten, J. T. Wolohan, & T. J. Wilde (Eds.), *Law for recreation and sport managers* (2nd ed., pp. 47-58). Dubuque, IA: Kendall/Hunt.

Cotten, D. J. (2001d, June). Another state okays waivers for minors. *The Sports, Parks, and Recreation Law Reporter, 15*(1), 9-11.

Crossett, T. W., Bromage, S., & Hums, M. A. (1998). History of sport management. In L. P. Masteralexis, C. A. Barr, & M. A. Hums (Eds.), *Principles and practice of sport management* (pp. 1-19). Gaithersburg, MD: Aspen Publishers.

Deckard, L. (2001a, May 7). Professional teams are sinking their teeth into food and drink. *Amusement Business, 113*(18), 22.

Deckard, L. (2001b, May 28). MLB Giants score with double play program. *Amusement Business, 113*(21), 20-21.

Dial, M. (1999, June 14-20). Loyalty-card firm gets a boost. *Street & Smith's SportsBusiness Journal, 2*(8), 45.

Facilities adapt to change. (2001, October 1). *IAAM News,* 1.

Farmer, P., Mulrooney, A., & Ammon, R., Jr., (1996). *Sport facility planning and management.* Morgantown, WV: Fitness Information Technology, Inc.

Federal Emergency Management Agency (FEMA) 2002. Retrieved 12/26/02 from www.fema.gov/.

Ferguson, D. (1999, February 4). Security again becomes an issue after Phoenix arrest. Retrieved April 21, 1999 from http://web.lexisnexis.com/universe/document?_m=3f61aba53b4f6766beecaecb1661e1d7&_docnum=2&wchp=dGLbVtb-lSlAl&_md5=18eee9fc9da598954bfa8d503acb51a9.

Fried, G. (1997, Spring). Risk management for recreation programs in the 1990's. *Texas Entertainment and Sports Law Journal, 6*(1), 6-12.

Fried, G. (2001, December 24-30). Blood sport: The boom turns into a glut. *Street & Smith's SportsBusiness Journal, 4*(36), 29.

Fried, G., & Miller, L. (1998a). The master servant relationship. In H. Appenzeller (Ed.), *Employment law: A guide for sport, recreation, and fitness industries* (pp. 3-32). Durham, NC: Carolina Academic Press.

Fried, G., & Miller, L. (1998b). Creating the job. In H. Appenzeller (Ed.), *Employment law: A guide for sport, recreation, and fitness industries,* (pp. 33-54). Durham, NC: Carolina Academic Press.

Fried, G., & Miller, L. (1998c). Employee information gathering. In H. Appenzeller (Ed.), *Employment law: A guide for sport, recreation, and fitness industries* (pp. 55-114). Durham, NC: Carolina Academic Press.

Fried, G., & Miller, L. (1998d). Discrimination in hiring. In H. Appenzeller (Ed.), *Employment law: A guide for sport, recreation, and fitness industries* (pp. 115-154). Durham, NC: Carolina Academic Press.

Fried, G., & Miller, L. (1998e). Negligence in the employment setting. In H. Appenzeller (Ed.), *Employment law: A guide for sport, recreation, and fitness industries* (pp. 155-170). Durham, NC: Carolina Academic Press.

Fried, G., & Miller, L. (1998f). Terms and conditions of employment. In H. Appenzeller (Ed.), *Employment law: A guide for sport, recreation, and fitness industries* (pp. 171-232). Durham, NC: Carolina Academic Press.

Fried, G. B. (2000). The Americans with Disabilities Act and sport facilities. In H. Appenzeller & G. Lewis (Eds.), *Successful sport management* (pp. 363-375). Durham, NC: Academic Press.

Friedman, A. (1999, June 7-13). In ticket-pricing announcement, timing is everything and early is better. *Street & Smith's SportsBusiness Journal, 2*(7), 15.

Garner, B. (Ed.). (1999). *Black's Law Dictionary* (7th ed.). St. Paul, MN: West Group.

Gaskin, L.P. (2001). Supervision. In D. J. Cotten, J. T. Wolohan, & T. J. Wilde (Eds.), *Law for recreation and sport managers,* (2nd ed., pp. 141-152). Dubuque, IA: Kendall/Hunt.

Glendinning, M. (2001, December). Sport surveys security risk. *SportBusiness International,* (64), 25.

Glover, T. D. (1999). Propositions addressing the privatization of public leisure services: Implications for efficiency, effectiveness, and equity. *Journal of Park and Recreation Administration, 17*(2), 1-27.

Graham, S., Goldblatt, J. J., & Delpy, L. (1995). *The ultimate guide to sport event management and marketing.* Chicago, IL: Irwin.

Graham, S., Neirotti, L. D., & Goldblatt, J. J. (2001). *The ultimate guide to sports marketing* (2nd ed.). New York: McGraw-Hill.

Graney, M. J., & Barrett, K. (1998). Facility management. In L.P. Masteralexis, C.A. Barr, M.A. Hums (Eds.), *Principles and practice of sport management* (pp. 307-327). Gaithersburg, MD: Aspen Publishers.

Hall, R., & Kanoy, R. (2001). Emergency care. In D. J. Cotten, J. T. Wolohan, & T. J. Wilde (Eds.), *Law for recreation and sport managers* (2nd ed., pp. 131-140). Dubuque, IA: Kendall/Hunt.

Hallman, G., & Rosenbloom, J. (1985). *Personal financial planning.* New York: McGraw-Hill.

Heilman, J. G., & Johnson, G.W. (1992). *The politics and economics of privatization: The case of wastewater treatment.* Tuscaloosa, AL: University of Alabama Press.

Hiestand, M., & Wood, S. (2001, December 19). Fan conduct rises on NFL agenda: Some see violence at recent games as precursor to soccer-style hooliganism. *USA TODAY,* p. 3C.

Hodes, J. (2002, March 29). Buying automatic defibrillator may save financial, legal headaches. *The Business Review.* Retrieved June 28, 2002, from Albany.bizjournals.com/Albany/stories/2002/04/01/focus3.html

Hoffman, C. M. (2002, May 17). Prom season: Reviewing the Social Host Liability Act. *New York Law Journal 227,* 4.

Holtzman, M. (2001, December). Liquid cash. *Athletic Business, 25*(12), 99-103.

Into the seats: How technology has changed going to games. (2002, April 8-14). *Street & Smith's SportsBusiness Journal, 4*(51), 22.

Jury awards $1.1 million to victim of car crash. (2002, March 11). *National Law Journal, 24*(27), B2.

Kaiser, R., & Robinson, K. (1999). Risk management. In B. van der Smissen, M. Moiseichik, V. Hartenburg, & L. Twardzik (Eds.), *Management of park and recreation agencies* (pp. 713-741). Ashburn, VA: NRPA.

King, B. (2002, March 11-17). Passion that can't be counted puts billions of dollars in play. *Street & Smith's SportsBusiness Journal, 4*(47), 25-26.

Lee, J. (2001, May 28-June 3). Colleges work up appetite for pro service. *Street & Smith's SportsBusiness Journal, 4*(6), 24.

Leger v. Stockton, 202 Cal. App. 3d 1448; 1988 Cal. App. LEXIS 673.

Levy Restaurants. (n.d.). About Levy Restaurants. Retrieved June 20, 2002, from www.cafebrauer.com/aboutlevy/alr_sports_factsheet.cfm

Li, M., Ammon, R., Jr., & Kanters, M. (2002, Summer). Internationalization of sport management curricula in the United States: A national survey. *International Sports Journal, 6*(2), 178-194.

Linnehan, F. (2001). Human resource management in sport. In B. L. Parkhouse, (Ed.), *The management of sport: Its foundation and application* (3rd ed., pp. 111-122). New York: McGraw-Hill.

MacPherson v. Buick Motor Co 217 N.Y. 382; 111 N.E. 1050; 1916 N.Y. LEXIS 1324.

Maloy, B. P. (2001a). Immunity. In D. J. Cotten, J. T. Wolohan, & T. J. Wilde (Eds.), *Law for recreation and sport managers* (2nd ed., pp. 75-86). Dubuque, IA: Kendall/Hunt.

Maloy, B. P. (2001b). Safe environment. In D. J. Cotten, J. T. Wolohan, & T. J. Wilde (Eds.), *Law for recreation and sport managers* (2nd ed., pp. 105-118). Dubuque, IA: Kendall/Hunt.

Mapes, L. (1998, January 29). Plans for hard liquor in stadiums seem dead. *Seattle Times*, B3.

Mason, J. G., Higgins, C. R., & Wilkinson, O. J. (1981). Sports administration education 15 years later. *Athletic Purchasing and Facilities 5*(1), 44-45.

Mazier, E. E. (1997, June 30). Tavern had duty to protect its patron from attack by other drunken patrons in tavern parking lot and on the street. *New Jersey Lawyer*. Retrieved June 9, 2002 from http://web.lexis-nexis.com/universe/document?_m=f0dd835fa8ab20692bfdc47a4e53cf67&_docnum=19&wchp=dGLStS-lSlzV&_md5=9683c24847e3cd9f3408a8ef63a91ba5

McGlynn, J. (2001, November). Good relations. *Stadia, 12*, 166-169.

McIntyre, K. (1998, February 2). Managing riot risk is a winning idea. *Business Insurance, 32*(5), 37.

McMillen, J.D. (2001). Game, event, and sponsorship contracts. In D. J. Cotten, J. T. Wolohan, & T. J. Wilde (Eds.), *Law for recreation and sport managers* (2nd ed., pp. 397-406). Dubuque, IA: Kendall/Hunt.

Miller Brewing Company. (1992). *Good times: A guide to responsible event planning.* Milwaukee, WI: The Miller Brewing Company.

Miller, L. (1993). Crowd control. *Journal of Physical Education, Recreation and Dance, 64*(2), 31-32, 64-65.

Miller, L. (1997). *Sport business management.* Gaithersburg, MD: Aspen Publishers.

Miller, L. (1998). Employment law issues. In H. Appenzeller (Ed.), *Risk management in sport; Issues and strategies* (pp. 403-415). Durham, NC: Carolina Academic Press.

Miller, L., Stoldt, G, & Ayres, T. (2002, January). Search me: Recent events make surveillance efforts even more likely to pass judicial muster. *Athletic Business, 26*(1), 18, 20-21.

Montalvo v. Radcliffe, 167 F.3d 873 (4th Cir. 1999).

Mooradian, D. (2001, May 28). Regardless of the league, the real name of the game is putting butts in seats. *Amusement Business, 113*(21), 11-18.

Mulrooney, A., & Ammon, R., Jr. (1995, Fall). Risk management practices and their impact on insurance premiums and loss reserves. *Journal of Legal Aspects of Sport 7*(3), 57-67.

Mulrooney, A., & Farmer, P (1995). Managing the facility. In B. Parkhouse (Ed.), *The management of sport: Its foundation and application* (2nd ed., pp. 223-248) St. Louis, MO: Mosby-Year Book.

Mulrooney, A., & Farmer, P. (1998). Risk management in public assembly facilities. In H. Appenzeller (Ed.), *Risk management in sport: Issues and strategies* (pp. 267-281). Durham, NC: Carolina Academic Press.

Muret, D. (2002, January 7). Incidents lead some to take a hard look at plastic bottles. *Amusement Business, 114*(2), 8.

National Federation of State High School Associations. (2002). *Heat stress and athletic participation.* Retrieved June 21, 2002, from www.nfhs.org/sportsmed/heat%20stress.htm

National Safety Council 2002. Retrieved from www.nsc.org/

New Boston Garden Corporation v. Baker 97-1433A, Superior Court of Massachusetts, at Suffolk, 1999 Mass. Super. LEXIS 46.

New England Patriots Football Club, Inc. v. University of Colorado et al, 592 F. 2d 1196 (1979).

Newman, M., & Dao, J. (1992, December 27). A year after nine deaths, the scars endure at City College. *The New York Times*, 14.

Nutall, I. (2001a, March). A question of choice. *Stadia 8*, 77-84.

Nutall, I. (2001b, July). Secure all areas. *Stadia, 10*, 83-84.

Occupational Safety and Health Administration, Department of Labor 2002. Retrieved from www.osha-slc.gov/index.html on 12/26/03.

Olympic security in full operation. (1998, February 7). *Kyodo News.* Retrieved February 5, 2001 from .http://www.shinmai.co.jp/olay-eng/19980207/98020705.htm.

Reason Public Policy Institute. (n.d.). *Privatization.org.* Retrieved April 4, 2002, from www.privatization.org

Regan, T. H. (1997). Financing facilities. In M. L. Walker & D. K. Stotlar (Eds.), *Sport facility management* (pp. 43-50). Sudbury, MA: Jones and Bartlett Publishers.

Regan, T. H. (2001). Financing sport. In B. L. Parkhouse (Ed.), *The management of sport: its foundation and application* (3rd ed., pp. 396-407). Boston, MA: McGraw Hill.

Roberts, K. (2001, December). Is there a future for major events? *SportsBusiness International*, (64), 24-25.

Sawyer, T., & Smith, O. (1999). *The management of clubs, recreation, and sport: Concepts and applications.* Champaign, IL: Sagamore Publishers.

Scaduto v. State, 446 N.Y.S. 2d 529 (N.Y. App. Div. 1982).

Schaffer, A. (1999, June 14). Tracking fans goes hi-tech. *Amusement Business, 111*(24), 23-24.

Seidler, T. (1997). Facilities for impaired persons. In M. L. Walker & D. K. Stotlar (Eds.), *Sport facility management* (pp. 196-201). Sudbury, MA: Jones and Bartlett Publishers.

Selzer, T. (2001, July-August). Safety at events: Disaster strikes again and again at football stadiums around the world, when will we learn? *Facility Manager, 17*(4), 36-44.

Sharp, L. (1996). Contract law and sport applications. In B. L. Parkhouse (Ed.), *The management of sport: Its foundation and application* (2nd ed., pp. 185-198). St. Louis, MO: Mosby.

Slack, T. (1997). *Understanding sport organizations: The application of organization theory.* Champaign, IL: Human Kinetics.

SMG's homepage. (n.d.) Retrieved December 30, 2002 from www.smgworld.com.

Spanberg, E. (June 21-27, 1999). Buy me some peanuts and chardonnay. *Street & Smith's SportsBusiness Journal, 2*(9), 26.

Starr, P. (1988). The meaning of privatization. *Yale Law and Policy Review, 6*, 6-41.

Stein, J. U. (1998). Accommodating individuals with disabilities in regular sport programs. In H. Appenzeller (Ed.), *Risk management in sport: Issues and strategies* (pp. 321-331). Durham, NC: Carolina Academic Press.

Stocker, S., & Fitzgerald, S. (1998, January 29). DPL working hard to change its image. *Denver Rocky Mountain News.* 2P.

Stooksbury, C. (1994, May 23). From TEAM to TIPS, industry wages battle on alcohol abuse. *Amusement Business, 106*(21), 3-6.

Telega v. Security Bureau, Inc., 719 A.2d 372; 1998 Pa. Super. Lexis 2990

Teaff, G., & Max, J. (2000). *Tips for a safer two-a-day workouts [sic].* Retrieved June 21, 2002, from thsca.com/heat.htm

Telander, R. (1993, November 8). Violent victory. *Sports Illustrated, 87,* 60-62.

Tierney, R. (2001, September 24). Zumwalt examines the new threat. *Amusement Business, 113*(38), 1, 4.

Trichka, R.E. (2001). Conduct of the activity. In D. J. Cotten, J. T. Wolohan, & T. J. Wilde (Eds.), *Law for recreation and sport managers* (2nd ed., pp. 153-164). Dubuque, IA: Kendall/Hunt.

Uniform Commercial Code. (1972).

United States Code Service. (2001). *Title 42. The public health and welfare Chapter 68. Disaster relief emergency preparedness power and duties* (42 USCS §5196, 2001). Retrieved December 27, 2001, from Lexis-Nexis Academic Universe: web.lexis-nexis.com/universe

van der Smissen, B. (1990). *Legal liability and risk management for public and private entities.* Cincinnati: Anderson Publishing Co.

van der Smissen, B. (2001a). Human resource law. In D. J. Cotten, J. T. Wolohan, & T. J. Wilde (Eds.), *Law for recreation and sport managers* (2nd ed., pp. 189-200). Dubuque, IA: Kendall/Hunt.

van der Smissen, B. (2001b). Negligence theory: Elements of negligence. In D. J. Cotten, J. T. Wolohan, & T. J. Wilde (Eds.), *Law for recreation and sport managers* (2nd ed., pp. 37-46). Dubuque, IA: Kendall/Hunt.

VanderZwaag, H. L. (1998). Facility funding. In H. L. VanderZwaag, *Policy development in sport management* (2nd ed., pp. 177-200). Westport, CT: Praeger Publishers.

Vecsey, G. (1996, June, 16). Like players, fans should be held accountable for their actions. *The Dallas Morning News,* 4B.

Venue managers address new security measures. (2001, October 29). *Amusement Business, 113*(43), 9.

Waddell, R. (1999, March 15). Williams: Use effective alcohol management; Reggie Williams at the IAAM District VI Mid-winter Conference. *Amusement Business, 111*(11), 2.

Walker, M. (1994). Educational and financial considerations in planning sport facilities. In P. J. Graham (Ed.), *Sport Business: Operational and theoretical aspects* (pp. 179-185). Madison, WI: WCB Brown & Benchmark Publishers.

West's Encyclopedia of American Law, (vol. 10). (1998). St. Paul, MN: West Group

Wheeler, B. C. (1998). The state of business education: Preparation for the past. *Selections, 14*(2), 19-21.

Wilde, T. J. (2001). Defenses against liability. In D. J. Cotten, J. T. Wolohan, & T .J. Wilde (Eds.), *Law for recreation and sport managers* (2nd ed., pp. 363-372). Dubuque, IA: Kendall/Hunt.

Williams, J., Dunning, E., & Murphy, P. (1984). *Hooligans abroad.* Boston, MA: Routledge & Kegan Paul.

Williams, P. (2001, July 30-August 5). Being part of the design, key for concessionaires. *Street & Smith's SportsBusiness Journal, 4*(15), 24.

Wilson, C. (2001, April 3). Hingis to stalker: "Get out of my life." *The Detroit News.* Retrieved June 20, 2002, from http://detnews.com/2001/moresports/0104/03/sports-207604.htm.

Wolohan, J. T (2001a). Athletes with disabilities. In D. J. Cotten, J. T. Wolohan, & T. J. Wilde (Eds.), *Law for recreation and sport managers* (2nd ed., pp. 509-520). Dubuque, IA: Kendall/Hunt.

Wolohan, J. T. (2001b, December). Sports law report; Watch your step; Quinton won its case, but the effects of product-liability law are wide-ranging. *Athletic Business 25*(12), 18-22.

Wong, G. M. (1994). *Essentials of amateur sports law.* (2nd ed.). Westport, CT: Praeger.

Wong, G. M., & Masteralexis, L. P. (1998). Legal principles applied to sport management. In L. P. Masteralexis, C. A. Barr & M. A. Hums (Eds.), *Principles and practice of sport management* (pp. 87-116). Gaithersburg, MD: Aspen Publishers.

Wong, G. M. (2000, January). Sit-down strike: The validity of an arena's club-seat license agreement is upheld. *Athletic Business 24*(1), 22, 24.

Wood, S. (2001, December 19). Debris barrages bring NFL crackdown. *USA TODAY,* C1.

Zoltak, J. (2001a, May 28). Buildings now designed to maximize revenue. *Amusement Business, 113*(21), 24-25.

Zoltak, J. (2001b, May 28). Crowd control: When fans step over the line. *Amusement Business, 113*(21), 22-23.

About the Authors

Dr. Robin Ammon, Jr., is the Sport Management Program Coordinator for the Physical Education and Sport Management Department at Slippery Rock University in Slippery Rock, Pennsylvania. He graduated with an EdD in sport administration from the University of Northern Colorado and his areas of research include legal liabilities in sport, risk management in sport and athletics, and management and marketing components for special events. Dr. Ammon has written extensively with over a dozen articles in refereed journals, eight chapters in sport management books, and two textbooks. He has presented over 40 times at local, regional, national, and international conferences on a variety of topics including facility legal, security, and crowd management issues. In 2002, Dr. Ammon was elected as the 17th President of the North American Society for Sport Management (NASSM).

Dr. Richard M. Southall, received a BA (Summa cum Laude) in English from Western State College of Colorado in 1980. After teaching and coaching in high school for eight years, he worked in the scuba diving industry for twelve years. A Professional Association of Diving Instructors (PADI) Course Director, Dr. Southall has worked in the United States, the Caribbean, and Central America in retail management, dive charter operations, diving research, and scuba training in both private and collegiate settings. In 1997 he received an MA in Pedagogy—Physical Education at the University of Northern Colorado and completed his EdD at Northern Colorado (2001). Presently employed at the State University of West Georgia, he teaches undergraduate and graduate courses in sport facility and event management, sport law, social and economic influences in sport, sport ethics, sport promotion and marketing, and organizational theory. Dr. Southall's areas of research include risk management in sport and recreational settings, organizational culture, college sport, and sport marketing. In addition, he serves as a consultant to the scuba industry, as well as for collegiate and professional sports organizations. His interests include scuba diving, skiing, mountain biking, weight training, and traveling. In 2003, Dr. Southall was elected President of the Sport and Recreation Law Association.

Dr. David A. Blair earned his B.S. in history with a minor in French from Montana State University. He holds an M.A. in sport administration from the University of Northern Colorado. His Ph.D. (earned with distinction) in education with emphasis on leadership is from the University of Kansas. Dr. Blair's teaching experience includes the University of Kansas, Colby-Sawyer College, and Southern New Hampshire University. In addition, Dr. Blair has been a consultant for International Management Group (IMG), a visiting scholar at Harvard Law School, as well as a member of the Sport Management Program Review Council (SMPRC). Dr. Blair's research interests include Title IX, sport law, and student engagement. Dr. Blair is currently the Director of Institutional Research at Southwestern University in Georgetown, Texas. Dr. Blair is married and has one son. He is an avid outdoor enthusiast who enjoys skiing, biking, mountain climbing, and golf.

Index